The Bern Book

Vincent O. Carter

THE BERN BOOK

A Record of a Voyage of the Mind

DALKEY ARCHIVE PRESS
Dallas / Dublin

Originally published by The John Day Company, 1970, 1973

First Dalkey Archive edition, 2022

ISBN 978-1-628973-16-7 (paperback)
CIP Data available upon request

Dalkey Archive Press
Dallas, TX / Dublin

There are peculiarities of the style in this book, which we decided to
keep from the original edition.

Printed on permanent/durable acid-free paper.

www.dalkeyarchive.com

To My Mother and Father
To Whom I Have Not Written
As Often As I Should.

Preface

THE REPRINTING OF Vincent Carter's *The Bern Book* for the first time since 1973 returns to us a text that has survived for half a century principally as rumor, a dusty hardback known to certain bibliophiles or, in rare instances, as a scholarly footnote. It is one of the "shadow books" of African American literature, a phrase the poet Kevin Young has given to those missing works, both real and imagined, which haunt the tradition like a phantom limb.

The reception afforded to uncompromising or eccentric literary works in their own time is rarely a seat at the welcome table. The genius of Zora Neale Hurston and Nella Larsen had to wait for Alice Walker, Mary Helen Washington, and Toni Morrison to create a landscape in which they could be more widely read. There is also no doubt that Black writers who experiment with form have always steeply increased the odds of their work disappearing from view. The alleged difficulty in such cases is typically compounded by the suggestion that they are belated (and possibly inauthentic) because of their debt to European modernism. The Joycean encryption of language in William Melvin Kelley's *Dunfords Travels Everywheres* was held to be too derivative when it appeared in 1970. Yet Kelley was writing in a very different wake: not Finnegans', but his own attempt to sound the linguistic depths produced by the Middle Passage (something quite alien to Joyce's otherwise omnivorous sensibility). Despite a profusion of powerful and ambitious undertakings—one thinks of Leon Forrest, Gayl Jones, and Fran Ross, to name just a few

writers at work in the 1970s—the afro-modernist novel continues to dwell at the margins of postwar literary history.

In the case of Vincent Carter, however, it must be con-
ceded that one of the principal reasons for his eclipse is simply
biographical. In 1953 he decided to go into a self-imposed exile
from the United States, but not in the standard fashion. He
relocated—not to one of the hubs of literary culture like Paris
or London—but to Bern, capital of the Swiss Confederation, a
city that to this day the average Helvetic citizen is likely to find
terribly provincial. Why Carter decided to stay as the only Black
resident in that city was the question he would grapple with in
his writing and the quandary that would come to define his life.

Vincent O. Carter was born in Kansas City, Missouri, in 1924.
His boyhood in the early years of the Depression was full of the
hardships of poverty but also the wonders of a Black cultural
Renaissance. The Negro League's Kansas City Monarchs and
their star pitcher Satchel Paige filled the front pages of local
Black newspapers like Chester A. Franklin's *The Call*; nightclubs
in the Black neighborhood of Eighteenth and Vine stayed open
all night, and a still-legendary jazz scene including the likes of
Count Basie, Bennie Moten, Mary Lou Williams, and a young
Charlie Parker, made Kansas City the "Paris of the Plains."

The section of Eighteenth and Vine where Carter grew up
no longer exists. Between 1956 and 1958, it was replaced by
the cloverleaf intersection of I-29 and I-70 as Eisenhower's
Interstate Highway System transformed the American landscape, accelerating white flight to the suburbs and causing inner
cities to decline. One of the buildings razed was the William
Lloyd Garrison School, a segregated grade school, which Carter
mentions attending in *The Bern Book*. His parents, Joe and Eola
Carter, were working poor. Carter's father was a building maintenance man and later a bellhop in a hotel; his mother did hair
and also worked as a laundress. The sounds, colors, and voices
of this lost world animate Carter's magnificent novel *Such Sweet
Thunder*, published posthumously in 2003. From his perch in

the Alps, Carter recreated in swinging vernacular prose the cry of the crawdaddy vendor, the slang of pool-hall hustlers, the sermons and song of the Black church, the clang of streetcars, the gossip of the society clubs, but also the normalized violence of lynching and police brutality. It is a novel of communal love, written for the people Toni Morrison writes for—liberated, in a way *The Bern Book* is not, from the white gaze.

Carter served in the US Army during World War II, and in 1945, while waiting to be demobilized, he went to England in a failed attempt to enroll at Oriel College, Oxford. Upon his return to the United States, he enrolled at Lincoln University in Pennsylvania, the country's oldest historically Black university, at the time led by Horace Mann Bond. After graduating in 1950, he moved to Detroit where he worked in an automobile factory, saved his money, and dreamed of returning to Europe to become a writer. He finally arrived in Paris in the spring of 1953, joining the vogue of famous Black writers like James Baldwin, Richard Wright, and Chester Himes who had decamped to the City of Light, a scene the literary historian Michel Fabre dubbed the "rive noire." Carter didn't care for Paris, though, and kept heading deeper into Europe. His odyssey would have its terminus in the high Alps, where he began writing down an account of his unusual trajectory.

Published by the John Day Company, *The Bern Book* was steered into a contract and got to press through the support of Herbert R. Lottman (1927–2014), a noted biographer and cultural historian of twentieth-century France, who was then working at the Paris offices of Farrar, Straus & Giroux. In effect, he became Carter's sole conduit to the literary world. Lottman was able to get *The Bern Book* to press, but the sales were abysmal. Carter insisted that his next project, a novel about Kansas City, would be the breakthrough. When it was ready in late 1963, Lottman took it to Ellen Wright, Richard Wright's widow, who was still living in Paris. She was thrilled. With her support the manuscript made its way into the offices of American publishers, but none took it up. By the late seventies, Carter had given up on writing altogether and become a strict Buddhist. He occasionally worked for Radio Bern and taught English, and, also began a relationship with one of his students, Liselotte Haas, who remained his partner until his death in Bern in 1983.

Darryl Pinckney reminded the world of the existence of Vincent O. Carter on the occasion of the inaugural Alain LeRoy Locke Lecture at the W. E. B. Du Bois Institute at Harvard University in 2001. Pinckney recalled being given *The Bern Book* as a gift by Susan Sontag and Robert Boyers, who had come across it, apparently randomly, in a second-hand bookstore in upstate New York. Almost at the same time, Chip Fleischer, the publisher and founder of Steerforth Press, learned of the novel through a friend who had noticed the author was a fellow Kansas Citian. Intrigued by Herbert Lottman's description of the unpublished manuscript in the preface, Fleischer decided to see if he could track it down. He contacted Lottman in the summer of 2001. Lottman informed him that his files of correspondence with Carter had been lost while he was moving between apartments in Paris. He recommended trying to find and contact relatives in Kansas City, a search that Fleischer undertook without success. Through several friends, however, Lottman was able to retrieve the name of Carter's Swiss girlfriend, Liselotte Haas, who it turned out was still living in Bern. She had the 805-page yellowing manuscript in a box under her bed. She sent it to Fleischer, and Steerforth Press published a hardcover of the novel in 2003 under the title *Such Sweet Thunder*.

Vincent Carter's known autograph manuscript materials are now in the hands of Chip Fleischer at Steerforth Press, and Oliver Franklin, OBE, of Philadelphia, an amateur bibliophile and devoted graduate of Lincoln University and Balliol College, Oxford, whose independent research into Carter's connections to Lincoln, including interviews with fellow alumni, provide the precious few firsthand sources we have. Without their heroic efforts, and those of Liselotte Haas, Carter's writings and much of what we know about his life would have been lost.

Written in the city of Bern between 1953 and 1957, Vincent Carter subtitled *The Bern Book* "A Record of a Voyage of the Mind," an enigmatic phrase that immediately highlights the text's ambiguous relation to genre, one situated at the intersection of travelogue, memoir, and personal essay. Carter himself suggests it is best conceived as a philosophical or literary experiment and calls it, "essentially a travel book, a *Reisebuch*." His use of the German alerts us to one of the text's signal strategies: inverting the racial authority of the ethnographic gaze. Carter poaches from both literary and scientific registers, signifying, to use Henry Louis Gates Jr.'s term, on the fields of ethnography and structural anthropology then commanding the heights of postwar humanist discourse, particularly the French school pioneered by figures like Michel Leiris in *Phantom Africa* (1934) and Claude Lévi-Strauss in *Tristes Tropiques* (1955).

The Bern Book was part of a wave of Black writings that responded in various ways to this allegedly universalist turn, as writers used their sense of alienation and isolation to self-fashion new kinds of literary and cultural authority. When James Baldwin declared in his 1953 essay "Stranger in the Village" that, "this world is white no longer, and it will never be white again," he was in the Swiss town of Leukerbad (not very far from Bern); the Martiniquan Édouard Glissant's *Soleil de la conscience* (1956) records the solitude and anomie of his student years in Paris but also his awakening to the world-historic implications of the Bandung Conference; the Ivorian Bernard Binlin Dadié's *Un Nègre à Paris* (1959) is a French colonial subject's wry survey of Parisians in their natural habitat; Frantz Fanon's *Black Skin, White Masks* (1952) presents a now classic phenomenological account of racial antagonism and the alienation of a Black intellectual. These were, among other things, the forerunners of the "afropolitan" flâneur to come in Caryl Phillips's *The European Tribe* (1987); Paul Beatty and Darryl Pinckney's Black Berliners; the transnational fictions of Teju Cole, Taiye Selasi, and Chimamanda Ngozi Adichie.

Can a Black writer who wishes to be a flâneur melt into

the urban crowds of modernity? What distinguishes *The Bern Book*, but also makes it challenging, is the troubling oscillation between sly humor and genuine melancholy that Carter brings to this question, as he toys with the inversion of relations between provincial and cosmopolitan, primitive and civilized, racial Blackness and cultural whiteness. This is reflected in *The Bern Book*'s parodic relation to the stylistics of classic European travel writing, exemplified by its mock-Victorian chapter headings and its casual dispensation of the sort of digressive generalizations on national character and habits typically associated with the literature of the "Grand Tour." Few writers have gotten so much signifying mileage out of judiciously timed italics.

Carter is tongue-in-cheek when he says that he is in Switzerland to study a "primitive" culture, and yet his ethnographic readings of the inhabitants of Bern, inevitably do end up constituting something like a study of their "whiteness." The suitability of trams as a method of public transit, the precarious social status of girls who work in tearooms, the tendency of the Bernese to overdress, aspects of Swiss politics both domestic and international, and, naturally, the many difficulties in trying to secure lodgings in Bern as a Black man are all fodder for his Shandyesque ramblings. He is particularly concerned about the Swiss tendency to stifle any creative impulse, forcing artists to leave and go into exile. Carter implicitly makes a rapprochement between Swiss and American cultural "whiteness" as worldviews obsessed with order, regulation, and commerce, a program well-suited to the interests of property and capital but inimical to artistic values such as experimentation and creativity.

The urban passageways of Bern effectively become a test site for a Black desire for writerly freedom, which Carter's narrative repeatedly reenacts as a series of disappointments and disruptions, undone by the reassertion of racialization. Subtle moments of repression, of training oneself to ignore and elide slights as one navigates shifting forms of passive-aggressive surveillance, amount to a pointed racial farce that anticipates Claudia Rankine's vignettes in *Citizen* (2014) and the strategies of Jordan

Peele's satirical film *Get Out* (2017). In the end we are left in a situation that has become utterly claustrophobic, teetering on solipsistic madness and apocalyptic visions of Cold War annihilation, a Conradian voyage into the heart of whiteness.

What is Bern? It is a negative landscape—or a landscape in negative—where the high-contrast figure of a lone Black writer is fixed against a social background unable or unwilling to acknowledge his existence, let alone hear what he has to say. The happy occasion of this reprinting offers us an opportunity to lend Vincent Carter an ear and, in so doing, to challenge anew our assumptions about the history of Black writing, what it has been, and what it may yet become.

Jesse McCarthy
Harvard University

Introduction

I HAVE NO intention of making a book of this, of altering the facts and impressions which have cost me so much pain and effort to acquire, in order to poach upon the sacred domains of art. I merely intend to give utterance to certain strong feelings which have changed my life to such a great degree that I can say— neither in despair nor optimism, but with utter realism— that I shall never be the same. The changes of which I shall speak began, of course, with life itself. The tensions which necessitated them bespoke the "time" and the "place" in which I was born. Had that event occurred in China or, say, Sweden, my predicament would not be the same. Were my hair blond instead of black, I would be writing an entirely different story. Even if I were African-proper, having just arrived from Nigeria, where my ancestors were born, I think (I have seen wood carvings and ivory statuettes of the folk who came from there and they very much resemble me), my song would be pitched in another key or most certainly sung in another tempo. One hundred years ago I might not have written this "book" at all.

On the other hand, that little aspect of truth which I have gleaned from my experiences with other folk in other lands is probably very similar—if not identical—to that which I might have found (if Truth is really Truth) had I *derived* it from any of the circumstances suggested above. For it has become clear to me that the possible actions of my life—my problems and illusions—are framed, as it were, within the limitations of my time, and that my time differs from other periods of human history only in degree, since human beings in every age and clime are fundamentally the same.

However, I have not always thought this, though I have almost always professed it. As a result of a "purely intellectual" calculation of sorts I have tried to convince myself of the validity of the observation I have just stated, knowing, however, that my so-called "understanding" was nothing more than an expression of faith in the abstract hope that there prevailed in the world that species of justice which we euphemistically call "poetic."

The changes of attitude with which I am primarily concerned in this "book," then, are the following: the transition from that state of mind in which I considered myself innately different from other people (by which I meant "white" people) to one in which that difference disappeared only to embarrassingly reappear in the form of a new and more subtle illusion, that of myself as a distinct entity as differentiated from all other entities; and more, the further transition to that state of mind in which my newly discovered distinctness (which I doted upon) proved to be the greatest illusion of all, and I was finally revealed to myself to be (but only in rare visionary moments) merely a state of mind, a mere thought of myself; which condition I shared with all other entities in the universe!

This realization, I say, was inspired by my travels. The scene of my partial metamorphosis (which is still going on) is the city of Bern—the object upon which I focused my attention, giving and taking from it those fragmentary impressions which cast some light upon my own identity. So this is essentially a "travel book," a *Reisebuch*. But as I have asserted the relativity of the "time" and of the "place," and have reduced the experiencing "self" to a state of consciousness, this must be considered, above all, a record of a voyage of the mind. Nor would I have it thought that I intend these pages to represent a social scientific study of the city of Bern or of the Swiss nation, that formidable task having already been accomplished by others whose interest lay in that direction.

VOC

Contents

The Bern Book

Since I Have Lived in the City of Bern:

WHETHER I HAVE idled over a glass of wine in the Mövenpick or in the Casino, or dined with friends, a week seldom goes by in which some new acquaintance does not approach me with a host of questions, most of which I can handle rather easily. *He* asks, "Aren't you cold!" if it is winter, and, "Aren't you happy now that the sun is shining!" if the sun is shining. In the first case I reply, "Yes," and in the second case, which is unfortunately very rare, "Yes indeed!" *She* asks, "How long have you been in Switzerland?"

"Oh, about three and a half years now . . ." I reply.

"So long!" she exclaims, while I try to smile as surprisedly as her exclamation seems to warrant.

On a less auspicious occasion *It* asks me rather suspiciously and with a somewhat anxious twist of the lips, or with perhaps a smile which might be a sort of half-timid apology, "How do you like it?" Its smile (I pause a little at this point in order to heighten the effect) deepening before my answer, "Oh . . . I like it well enough . . ." issues from my mouth, as though He, She or It would dismiss the expected derisive remark before I intoned it.

The conversation rambles on a bit after that but I see that my interlocutor is not satisfied. He has never or seldom met a real black man before. He has, however, heard much and wondered much. He knows or has heard one or three Negro spirituals and he is an ardent jazz fan. He studies me as inconspicuously as he can, comparing the strong definite impression before his eyes with all the images he has seen and heard of during a lifetime. Finally he hazards another question:

"Are you a musician?"

"No," I reply—coldly.

"Student?" he persists, noticing now my ancient briefcase, remembering that he has seldom seen me without it.

"No, I'm not a student," I reply, a little irritated but not altogether unsympathetic. This has happened to me many times. I am only irritated because my invention is running out and because I fear that I might not tell my tale interestingly. His curiosity is so great, he *apparently* expects so much, much more, in fact, than I can ever hope to give him. It makes me sad.

"I just thought you might be a student. There are so many medical students in town."

"Oh no! . . . no : . ." I reply with an uneasy smile, feeling that I have been a little mean, seeing that I will have to go through it once more, racking my brain for a new way to tell it and, finding none, suffering myself now because he does not come right out and ask me.

The conversation dawdles on. He hopes that he will find out indirectly, I think, really moved by his discretion, and yet not wishing to be indiscreet myself by volunteering information which is not directly asked for.

"How do you like Bern?" he asks during a lull. And I reply, "Oh, I like it all right," a little grateful that we are at last getting down to specifics. In the meanwhile he has heard me make an appointment with one of the young men sitting at our table for two o'clock the next day. The departing friend had at first suggested ten in the morning, but then changed to two o'clock in the afternoon because he had forgotten that he had a class at ten in the morning. At two o'clock in the afternoon almost everybody works in Bern.

"I see you have plenty of free time," he remarks with a nervous laugh. "You're lucky not to have to go to the *Büro*," by which he means office.

"I can't write *all* the time!" I reply at last.

His face lights up.

Write? Write what? I hear him thinking a split second before he inquires: "You're a journalist?"

"No," I reply.

"He writes stories!" the friend who introduced him to me exclaims a little impatiently. At this point I light my pipe and try to think of an opening line, for now will come, I know, the question which I do not like because it is so difficult to answer. Even so, I am grateful for the little time which answering this question will give me because the one which comes after that will shake me to my very foundations!

The Preliminary Question:

"WHAT KIND OF stories do you write?" His tone is that of a Customs Inspector, scrutinizing a suspicious-looking piece of luggage. He has never or seldom met or heard of, though he suspects there probably must be, Negroes who write. "What kind of stories do you write?"

I breathe deeply.

"Oh . . . I—I don't really know. That is, it's hard to say."

He smiles sardonically. I take a deep breath and prepare to be more specific, shifting my weight from the right to the left hip.

"Love stories?"

"Oh, no—not exactly . . . But, of course, there's love in them sometimes. After all, love is . . . People, I mean, have—"

"Psychological?"

"Of course! People do have psychological aspects, don't they? Still, I can't really say—"

"Philosophy?"

"There's always *some* philosophical implication in every story. *Naturally!* But—"

"What kind of stories do you write?"

"Well, look, I try to write a story that shows how a character has some particular problem. And I try to relate it to some of my own—general moral conviction—"

"Universal."

"What!"

"Timeless."

6

I breathe deeply.

"The problem, you mean—"

"Do you write for a newspaper?"

"No."

"Magazines?"

"I don't write for anybody . . . For myself. That is, I try to write them first and then sell them wherever I can."

"Do you have any books already printed? I'd like to *write* something you've *read*—"

"You mean *read*—"

"I'd like to—"

"You mean *read* something I've . . . But I don't have anything. Nothing much. One story. Once I published a little story—not very good—in—in *Annabelle* . . ."

"Where?"

"In *Annabelle*. Last year . . ."

"Detective story?"

"No. It was a love story—"

"Oh . . ."

"Not exactly a love story. It had love in it."

"What—"

"It was about a white girl and a Negro boy. They were in college together."

"American democracy!"

I breathe deeply.

"I've done a few radio programs."

"Where?"

"Radio Bern."

"When!"

"Since I've been here. The last one was Christmas before last."

"I've never heard of them."

"Do you listen to Radio Bern much?"

"Sottens. They have better programs . . . That's too bad. I'd like to *write* something you've *read* . . ."

I wipe my forehead with the back of my hand while he studies me more closely. I don't look like a writer, he thinks: I feel it. And then he thinks, How should a writer look? His eyes grow narrow, as though he is on the verge of asking me for my passport. I stare back at him, feeling like a prostitute in a Dutch bordel.

And now I perceive a new change in his appearance. The large vein which divides his forehead into two unequal parts swells and throbs violently, as though it will burst the skin. I can literally see him straining his imagination to accommodate the new idea of me with which I have confronted him. I can feel him lifting me out of the frame of his previous conception of the universe and fitting me first this way and that, like a piece of a puzzle, into the picture of the writer his mind is conjuring up. He is struggling with Goethe and Rilke and Gotthelf and Harriet Beecher Stowe and me. Suddenly a wild look of ecstasy comes into his face. He points at me with an extended forefinger, as though a liberated part of his mind would reveal to an enslaved part the upsetting contradiction of all his actual experience. But then, as though overpowered by the effort of changing his viewpoint, his finger falls limply and his eyes grow dull and lifeless. But only for a second, for now I perceive, as though he has pushed the old problem aside, that his expression is reanimated by a new problem. My bosom heaves with dread. He is going to ask me the hated question—*I know!*—the question which kills me once, twice and sometimes four times each and every week twice a month all of these past three and a half years.

The Foundation-Shattering Question:

"BUT WHY—"

"I have to go," I say, trying to divert the conversation. I wiggle in my chair, and look desperately this way and that.

"But why—"

"Waiter!"

"But why—"

"Why what!"

"Why did you come to *Bern*?"

I sink down into my chair with a weary groan and look at my man carefully. I try to evaluate the intensity of the glint in the pupils of his eyes. I try to penetrate with my own analytical glance his hidden motives. Maybe he doesn't even realize the import of his question. Maybe he is like "this" instead of like "that," one of "these" types instead of one of "those"; in which latter case I can get out of it and rush to Marzili Bath and lie in the sun with my eyes shut tight and try not think of such things. The desire to escape is so pressing that I can feel it, the coolness of the wet breeze washing over the river, bathing my face. I can hear the voices of children running on the grass and see the men and women stretched out under the sun. In the din of the Mövenpick I can hear the egg-white ping-pong balls cracking on the cool cement tables:

He waits!

Now what is so special about a little question like that? I hear you asking.

Personal Problems Involved in
Answering the Question

IT ALL DEPENDS upon who is asking it, the tone of voice in which it is asked and in the aura of what light gleaming in his eyes. It depends upon whether or not there is a smile upon my inquisitor's face, and what kind of a smile. It depends upon my peculiar feeling of security or insecurity, which is very much influenced by the weather and by my metabolic rate on that particular day. And finally, it depends upon whether or not I will have to spend my last centime for the wine.

He may be one of those inferior-feeling Swiss who has lived in Bern all his life, who hates himself and the society in which he lives and can't understand why anyone who is in his right mind would come to Bern (as a tourist, for a day or two, sure, but for three and a half years!). Flattering myself that I understand his feelings thoroughly, comparing him to people whom I know back home in Kansas, Texas and Missouri, I say the following:

"Oh—I like it well enough in Bern. It is a very beautiful town. Very clean . . . Well taken care of. Comfortable—if you have enough money to really enjoy it . . ."

His eyes darken with a suspicious gleam. He suspects satire. But I convince him: "Oh, yes, I know. Many people are surprised that I have come to such a small town in the center of Europe. Well, I find it interesting enough. The life here is in many ways different from the life I have known in Kansas City. There I lived not as I chose to live, but as a dwarf among apparently normal-sized people. Accordingly, I had dwarf-sized loyalties, aggressions and fears—both real and imaginary. For life was both real and fantastic at the same time. It was also earnest and, above all, dangerous.

"But here in your ancient city my stature has increased. Here I am like a dwarf, but with three-league boots. I can move around a little more freely, and I am exposed more or less to the society at large. My loyalties, aggressions and fears have become modified in proportion to my new social status. And yet, I find life here to be both as real and as fantastic as I found it in Kansas City. Furthermore, I have found it to be just as earnest and just as dangerous. Most of all I find life in your city, as well as the life in my city, to be interesting. There can be no doubt that the Bernese are among the most interesting people on earth . . ."

Now I Philosophize a Little

"LOOK AT THAT tree," I say, pointing to an imaginary tree in the middle of the room. "Over there—between those two tables which the waitress is setting for supper." He looks at the tree. "Now look at the other one. There—sprouting out of the cash register by the counter, near the frozen lobster flying through the air." He looks excitedly at the second tree and follows the flight of the frozen lobster in a sweeping circle, which I indicate with my fingertip. "They look the same, don't they? From here it would appear that all the leaves are of the same shape and color. Are they of the same shape and color?"

"No," he answers, feeling a little uncomfortable. And I answer that he is right, "They are certainly not all of the same shape and color," adding:

"The longer you look at those two trees the more you realize what fascinating things they are. Watch!—watch the light fall upon them. Notice—the shading of the leaves, the patterns they make upon the ground. Pluck them. Hold them up to the light. No two are exactly the same, especially the cluster upon the branch hovering over the fishpond with the little blue fishes. He stares at the cluster of imaginary leaves upon the branch hovering over the imaginary fishpond with the imaginary blue fishes in amazement. "But wait!" I cry. "You see that pattern only now. It's changing. It changes every minute, every instant. How does it look in the morning? in the evening? at noon when all the people are going home to lunch? And how does it look at two and three o'clock when all of the people are returning to the offices? Is it the same at four o'clock on a sunny afternoon in August? when its leaves have flown in October? when it is covered with ice in January? It is not! And we have only considered the most superficial, the most banal aspects of those two trees. However— however, I say, perceive fully only that much about a tree and you may be able to enter Heaven without even showing your pass!"

But what has that got to do with Bern or the Bernese people? his expression says, and I stop him before he can get it out:

"Are not people more complex, more intricate, more vital than trees?" Before he can answer, "Yes," I add:

"Even Bernese people?"

And while he frowns:

"How much more interesting are people, even Bernese people, than trees?—Infinitely!" I reply to my own question. "Now, if I want to write, and I am interested in people, can I not write about the Bernese people if I have the ability to do so?"

"But there are much more interesting places for a writer," he protests. "Paris, Rome, London!"

"Wait!" I interrupt. "I cannot speak of Rome or London, but I will tell you why I did not stay in Paris, Amsterdam and Munich." I tell him this:

Why I Did Not Go to Paris

"Oh, I THOUGHT of Paris, all right. When I was in America, in Detroit, working in the automobile factories in order to save enough money for the trip, I thought, I must go to Paris! And I had good reason, for I had visited Paris as a soldier and had therefore, many intimate feelings about the place. Why, I had had beautiful experiences with the French people even before I got to Paris, in Normandy and in Rouen. I promised myself then that one day I would return. So you see, I was highly in favor of the idea. But upon my arrival in '53 many unfortunate things happened.

Firstly, I had made the mistake of coming in April—the weather was bad. And then, although I had a very pleasant crossing on the *Île de France*, when I got off the boat at Le Havre I received a shock. The city was much changed since I first drove through its bombed-out ruins on a cold rainy night ten years ago. The port was new, the town was new, there were many strangers ordering me around: 'Go here! Go there!' I guessed they said, because they spoke a language which I didn't understand—was that French!

"Before I could finish being disappointed about Le Havre and summoning up old memories of this and that experience (Cherbourg was close, and Barfleur, the little port at which we landed during the invasion, was only twenty-five miles from there) I was on the train, puffing and sweating, with my luggage crowded all around me, sitting among strangers who spoke in

foreign tongues while my beloved Normandy receded in the falling darkness. Names came to mind, faces to mind, sounds and
smells. Somewhere—in Barfleur!—there was an old cathedral
standing in the rain, and a pretty-legged fisherman's daughter
who wore rubber boots and whose breast heaved nervously when
I pulled the rusty fishhook from the palm of her father's hand,
and a girl named Françoise and a schoolteacher named Simone
. . . The pain, oh the bitter-sweet pain of a few precious moments
ten years ago were swallowed up, drowned in the darkness . . .

". . . I should remember that tree I thought, as we sped
through the twilight. . . 'That house! . . . There was a little house
over there by that ruin, which . . . But it was gone. The train
sped indifferently by.

"Well—anyway, I thought, anyway, I am in France. Soon
will be in Paris.

"When I was a soldier my outfit, the 509th Port Battalion,
ran the train guard for supply trains headed for various supply depots throughout France. We were stationed in Barfleur,
where many beautiful things happened to me for the first time.
We were stationed in Rouen after Barfleur, and from there we
branched out all over France. That is why I knew the roads pretty
well, and why I knew Paris a little. We used to stop there for a
layover after each trip and wait for the dispatcher to find us a
new route, or, finding none, send us back to Rouen. We would
usually stay in Paris a few days, and sometimes for a few weeks.
If we got a trip out we would usually go to Nancy; if not, back
to headquarters in Rouen, in the Champs de Course, at the end
of the Rue Elbuf, which had been a camp for American soldiers
in the 'first' world war.

"What a time I had in Paris! How friendly the people were!
And the women! Where else could one find such delectable
creatures! And in April!—All this I thought as I unconsciously
hummed the popular tune 'April in Paris' . . . lada da da da . . .
Thinking: It was such a good idea to come!

"Was not Paris the center of art? Had not all, virtually all the
great writers been there? Heine, Rilke and Hemingway? What

succulent agony hadn't Balzac, Hugo, de Maupassant suffered in the Faubourg St. Germain!

"I'll find myself a crummy little room in the Quartier Latin, I thought, with an old bed, a writing table with a candle. There should be a fireplace gone to pot. I'll eat cheese and drink red wine, smoke hashish perhaps, and write memorable prose. And I'll have a beautiful but decadent mistress whom I shall immortalize in my stories. I shall suffer . . . I consoled myself, squeezing my black imitation-leather folder with the fat little traveler's checks in twenties and fifties . . .

"I forgot about Le Havre in the dark. I forgot Rouen and Normandy. Fatigue fell away from me and I breathed in the hot stuffy air as though it were as fragrant as the scent of Chanel No. 5, in order to purchase a bottle of which I had 'queued up' with about thirty million American soldiers on a cloudy morning ten years ago . . .

"I got there about nine o'clock at night. When the train pulled in an hour late at the Gare du Nord I was shocked to find that instead of the conquering hero, the 'great liberator,' the object of friendly smiles and earnest entreaties, I was merely another tourist with luggage to be inspected and checked and stored and loaded into a taxi, destined for just what hotel I hadn't the slightest idea. I had to fight my way through a herd of Americans in order to endure this torture! The fighting was all the more tedious because I had to ask everything six times! Those silly asses didn't even understand me when I spoke their own language. The taxi driver who promised to help me find a hotel drove me leagues out of the way—I was sure of that. I had been to the Latin Quarter on a tour ten years before and I knew it wasn't that far from the Gare du Nord. On top of that, when we did reach a hotel it was always full. They were full for hours, and when I found one it was much too expensive. But I was so exhausted by this time that I took it gladly and paid through the nose.

"When I saw the bed I realized how tired I was. But when I saw the little washstand for women (it is called a bidet, I think) in the corner, discreetly hidden by a screen with Japanese ladies preparing their toilette painted on it, I came to my senses. Dragging my tired shipwrecked body down the stairs and into the chilly street, I set out to enjoy Paris, the Paris of old. Names of streets and quarters of the town rang in my ears.

"Now just where was it that we had had so much fun that night ten years ago? . . . There was a club somewhere called the Can Can, I remembered: But where! . . . And a quarter called Strasbourg St. Denis, in which there used to be a large restaurant. We used to eat there. Nearby was a theater. They said it was the largest in the world. Artificial stars glittered when the lights went out. It looked like a real sky . . . with clouds and all. —The Rex!"

"It was coming back to me. I stumbled wearily along with determination. Suddenly the street began to rock from side to side, as the ship had rocked. It made me dizzy. The tendons in my ankles wheezed like ancient leather and the cartilages in my kneecaps scraped together as though they were rusty. Where were my feet? They felt like splintered shank bones stabbing the adamant cobblestones. Nevertheless, I wandered blindly down one dark street after another, searching for soft warm colors and laughter and the smell of perfume and a companion with whom I could share the discreet little toilette behind the silk screen with the Japanese ladies painted on it.

"It started to rain. I was cold and tired and lost. I could not find my way back to the hotel. I turned into an alley near a movie house. In front of it stood a large picture of Fernandel in white duck pants and tennis shoes. He had a funny hat on his head. A woman spoke to me from a doorway. She was old and her hair was dark near the scalp and yellow near her face. A large black mole was painted on her chin—she had three of them. I wondered if it were she whom I was trying to remember, as I stepped into the corridor out of the rain and into a tired musty smell. We drank cognac and I told her that my name was Jimmy . . . And then I tore one of the traveler's checks out of the little black imitation-leather folder and gave it to her. When I found my way back to the hotel it was very late, and when I got to sleep it was almost morning. I slept till noon the next day."

"Monsieur?"

A waiter stood before our table. While I had been occupied with my experiences in Paris my friend had ordered another glass of wine.

"Won't you have one?" he asked.

"No thanks," I replied.

At this the waiter frowned because it was suppertime and we were occupying a center table. He wanted us to leave so that he could arrange it properly and serve perhaps a party of four one of those expensive Mövenpick specialties, from which he might earn a sizable tip. Having once been a cook myself, I felt self-conscious and suggested that we leave. But my companions declared with much enthusiasm that we should stay and finish our talk. The young man, sitting on my right, for whose benefit I was making this explanation, was most vehement in expressing his impatience to know how my stay in Paris had turned out.

"Is that all you have to say about Paris!" he asked. I could see that he was disappointed, and that he was laughing at me for what he felt to be my typically American shortsightedness. I was irritated by his tone, and in order to justify my opinion of Paris I pressed on with a sort of desperation to the more serious part.

The More Serious Part

"OH, I KNOW how you feel about Paris," I began, "—the romance, the magic. *Liberté, Égalité, Fraternité!* The Louvre, Montmartre and all that. I was already convinced before I got there. Remember, Paris is the place of which it is said that all good Americans go when they die. I was just as anxious to enter that heavenly domain as any of my countrymen. But when I tried all day to get a room in the Quartier Latin and failed because the hotels wouldn't rent me a room because they thought I was a North African, I had to reconsider my previous opinion—"

"In Paris!" my companions exclaimed.

"In Paris!" I replied triumphantly. "I met some North African students. They explained it to me. They had lived there for years, they had no language problems and they were at least theoretically French, so they ought to have known—"

"You have a complex!" my companions exclaimed in a chorus.

"It's probably true," I admitted. "I had many complexes. But I don't understand why it was so hard for me to get a room. I made an experiment—"

"What kind of experiment?" asked the young man who had inspired this conversation.

"Well," said I, "I was standing before the information desk at the American Express office when a young and passing pretty white American girl, remarking my French, spoke admiringly of it. I thanked her for her compliment and we then embarked upon the following conversation.

19

"'What are you doing here in Paris?' I asked.

"'I am a journalist. I hope to pay for my vacation by writing articles for the *Herald Tribune*. I used to write for a small paper in my home town back in Ohio. And you?'

"'Oh, I would like to remain in Paris in order to write, too. But the prospects look very bad because until now I haven't been able to find a room in the Latin Quarter. I don't want to live anywhere else. They all *say* that the rooms are full. I don't think that they are full at all. It's because of my color and the racial origin which it implies.'

"'You must think you're still in America!' she cried laughingly. 'This is Paris!'

"'I agree with you as to the name of the city,' I said, 'but this confusion couldn't possibly have happened in America, at least, not where I came from, because I never would have gone into a white hotel in the first place!'

"'You are certainly wrong about Paris, and I can prove it!'

"'How?'

"'By going to the same hotels you went to!'

"I had nothing else to do, so I agreed to go with her. We spent the whole morning retracing our steps. I would point out the house and wait on the nearest corner while she asked for a room. In every case she could have had not only a room, but the room of her choice."

"'I can't understand it,' she said. 'But you shouldn't be too skeptical or bitter.'

"'Oh, I certainly will not,' I said. And we both expressed the hope that everything would turn out all right, that she would be able to write articles for the *Herald Tribune*, and that I would be able to find a room and begin my career as a writer. After that we had coffee and parted."

That held my companions for a minute, after which they allowed me to continue my story without interruptions.

"I finally found a room," I continued, "in the Rue Monsieur le Prince, in the Latin Quarter. It was indeed a crummy little room. It opened onto a dark alcove which was roofed with a skylight, which permitted a dim, filmy illumination to filter down into the room through the window, which was covered with a frayed, dirty-gray curtain. The floor of the alcove, a glass roof which covered the lobby, was littered with garbage, damp yellowing newspapers, dirty rags and puddles of suspicious-looking liquids. The whole floor reeked with the smell of the toilet. The room was furnished with a bed, a little table on which was a cheap wooden lamp instead of a bottle with a candle and a chair. There was no fireplace gone to pot and no decadent mistress to comfort me. The atmosphere was musty and depressing. The sheets on the bed were wettish. When I climbed into bed I was reminded of the sensation I have often experienced upon touching the fungus of a tree. There was no pillow and no blanket, and, though it was April, it was cold enough for a wood fire. The tiny light, a naked yellow bulb hanging from the ceiling, was so feeble that I couldn't read the one book in my possession (the lamp didn't work), *The Odyssey of Homer*.

"I decided to take a bath but learned that I couldn't have one until the following evening, and that in the future I would have to apply for that privilege in advance. I was also informed that I would have to pay 150 francs as well, soap not included. When the eventful next evening arrived I went, freezing with cold, to the bathroom at the top of the building and discovered to my chagrin that the tub was not a full-length tub, but was only half the normal size. I would have to sit upright and wash. I would not be able to stretch out my body and soak for hours on end. Now, all of you sensualists, to whom a hot bath is second only to the rapturous embrace of the one you love, what on earth, I ask you, what on earth could be more disgusting than that! Unless it is what happened to me next: the water was only luke-warm! That was too much. I complained to the manager after my bath, but he only greeted my distemper with a cold, satirical smile. He made some remark which I didn't understand, but which sounded like a supplication to the Good Lord to give him enough patience in order that he might endure the trials of his unfortunate way of life.

"I shivered back to my room. I felt hungry. But then I thought of the tedium of redressing and wandering through street after street in order to find a cheap restaurant, only to puzzle over a menu which I would not be able to understand, and lost my appetite. As I was not able to read in the semi-darkness of my room, I decided to go to sleep. A little sleep will do me good, I thought. After all, I'm only a little tired. After a good night's rest I will awake in the morning refreshed and happy. So I piled every available article I could find on top of the bed for warmth and crawled between the cold, moist sheets. The cool air crept through just the same. And the bed springs collapsed in the middle. My head began to ache. And as the first tantalizing warmth crept over me I discovered that I had to go to the toilet. I contracted a muscle or two and determined to wait it out.

"I was almost asleep.

"Then I heard laughter in the street below: a girl and a boy, or two girls and a boy, or perhaps two boys and two girls. I heard steps on the stair. They passed by my door and paused for a minute. They were kissing. They moved on. The light from the room above filled the alcove and I saw their shadows dance to and fro upon the alcove wall. Then the lights went out.

"Now I'll sleep, I thought. And then I heard a new—and not exactly new, but in fact, a rather old—sound: the quoits on the bed above began to screech, to the accompaniment of sighs and muffled laughter and unintelligible mutterings, followed by a stillness that was torturous to me. After some minutes the stillness was interrupted by the soft sound of two naked feet upon the ceiling: pat pat pat pat, from the bed to the door, down the corridor, until a hinge cried out in the darkness. There followed a tinkling, purling sound of falling water. Then the gargle of the chain and the hissing of the flush-box. Then: pat pat pat pat, back down the corridor, from the door to the bed. And a whine of the quoits.

"Now I'll sleep, I thought. I faced the wall and pulled the sheet about my ears. The quoits whined again. Again the pat pat pat pat of naked feet upon the ceiling, but softer, lighter, from the bed to the door and down the corridor. Then the thin sting of water hissing in a rapid little stream and the gargle of the chain and the slush of the flush-box and then: pat pat pat pat back down the corridor, softly, lightly, from the door to the bed. The quoits on the bed whined, and whined again and again under the strain of twistings and turnings. The light went out. At last all was still.

"I turned and faced the window and tried to sleep. The shadowy forms I had seen and the muffled sounds I had heard called to mind the musty smells whetted by the reek of the toilet and the refuse on the skylight roof. My thoughts filled me with loneliness and despair. As I was upon the verge of sleep, a dirty-gray light crept through the window. It was dawn . . .

"I endured this for a month!" I exclaimed to the amused company. "I walked the streets and visited museums until I was sick. I sat alone, always alone, in café-restaurants in the rain and wind, speaking only to waiters and people who wished to sell me something. I was overcharged for nearly everything I purchased. No one French paid any attention to me whatever. Finally my traveler's checks began to dwindle and I became frightened. I agree with Dostoevski, the Parisians are a materialistic, megalomaniacal people. When I saw signs scrawled on walls and fences, saying, 'American go home!' I was more than ready to go—anywhere and without regrets!

"One morning I met a Dutchman with his American wife on the terrace of a brasserie in the Boulevard St. Michel. They were sitting at a table near mine. I made some feeble excuse to talk to them and started the conversation in which I learned the following: 'Amsterdam,' said he, 'is a wonderful place to live!' He described the waterfront and the canals, and as he was a writer he did it very well. He was a handsome young man with curly blond hair and a little yellow beard and watery blue eyes. His wife was very pretty—dark-haired with large dark eyes—and she knew it. She agreed with me that life in Paris was terrible for a stranger, while he spoke in glowing terms of his homeland. As they spoke I conjured up suitable pictures of Holland which came readily and happily to mind.

"The rosy prospect of visiting the land of Rembrandt and Spinoza and Descartes more than appealed to me, as I looked out over the rainy, gloomy Boulevard St. Michel and saw the endless stream of French-chattering folk who seemed to have no interest save the tedious impetus which drove them up and down the street. As I watched them I marveled that things French had played such an important part in my life, that my veneration for Montaigne, Rabelais and Villon was so passionate. It occurred to me as strange that I could love modern French painting, music and poetry as well as I did. Baudelaire and Rimbaud were intimate friends of mine. Would I not spend my last francs on a Jouvet film! How could I feel all this and yet find the people so unsympathetic? I perceived that something was radically wrong; however, I was in no condition to cope with it at that time . . .

"'But, if Amsterdam is so wonderful, and is such a cheap place to live and since you're having difficulties here and are Dutch besides, why don't you live in Amsterdam?' I asked him with a Missouri horse trader's logic.

"'My wife is Jewish,' he said. She smiled prettily. 'My parents objected to our marriage—'

"'To put it mildly!' tossing her luxurious black hair over her shoulder.

"'We left Amsterdam so that we could live our own lives,' he said. 'Because a writer must be—above all things—free to act and think as he pleases.'

"'I think you are right,' I said. His companion smiled a facetious agreement. 'Your courage has touched me deeply, and you have also given me the solution to my problem.'

"Shortly after that I bade them adieu. I left for Amsterdam the next morning. I don't remember at what time, but it was on the first available train."

A Chapter Which Is Intended to Convey to the Reader the Writer's Fair-Mindedness

IT WAS THE laughter and supercilious smiles of my companions which necessitated this chapter. One or two of them knew Paris very well and had a very different opinion of the city and of its people. I admitted that I had hardly had an opportunity to form a really objective opinion of the place, since my experiences had been primarily of the typical tourist's variety.

"Wouldn't New York or London have been just as lonely?" asked a young man who had not spoken until now.

"It certainly would have been!" said I. "In fact, it *was*, for I have visited those cities several times. And I also realize that generalizations are apt to be dangerous. No one is more sensitive to this danger than I. It is the cliché of our times that 'we live in a generalizing age' and have before us the 'enormous task' of evaluating 'overwhelming masses' of information from many different 'areas' of human experience: but it is nonetheless true, particularly in my own country," I confessed, "a country composed almost entirely of sensitive minorities who are so averse to stereotyped opinion that the most harmless generalization must be qualified in order not to offend them.

"In discussing ideas one of the most frequent qualifications upon the lips of students—the serious and the dilettante alike—is that this or that 'fact' is relative to this or that context. However, they often forget or overlook the real problem which is imposed upon one by this qualification: though the 'fact' may truly be—most certainly will be—'relative' to a specific context, there is the implication of one referent to which all things are not 'relative.' And that is the real problem. We forget that the particularization of experience is merely a convenient device imposed upon us by the intellect, which has by no means reached its potential development, and that if there can be 'relative' parts there certainly must be a 'whole'—even though we cannot *prove* it empirically. You are quite right in censuring me. But allow me to redeem myself by sharing a rather beautiful though sad experience which I had with a young Parisian soldier one night in a bistro in the Rue Monsieur le Prince.

"I had just paid for my Pernod," I began," and feeling that I had paid too much, I asked the waitress for the price list. She pretended not to understand me, so I gave it up and left. I was followed into the street by a young Frenchman in uniform who said to me: '*Monsieur, vous avez trop payé pour votre verre!*' with which opinion I enthusiastically agreed in demotic French and replied in the equivalent of the following:

"'Sir, I have been doing that ever since I came to your cursed city. You French are thieves and cut-throats and you ought to be hanged!

"'*Oh non!*' he exclaimed. 'All of the French people are not like that. You really do not know the real French people, Monsieur. Not the ones in the bars and expensive restaurants, but the *real* people.'

"'I agree with you,' said I. 'I sincerely wish to avoid the tourist pitfalls, but I don't know how because I don't speak the language very well and do not know where to go to meet the real French people. I have found it very difficult to make contact with even these horrible creatures to whom I have been exposed!'

"'Come with me!'

"'But, where are you going?' looking at him a little carefully. Paris hadn't the reputation it had for nothing! He looked harmless enough, but still . . . 'Where do you wish me to go?' I insisted, suspecting that he wished to induce me to buy something, or that he might be in the women procurement business.

"'To my wife. She is just around the corner having a lemon juice.'

"I stopped and took a good look at this fellow. He was much taller than I but very thin. He was dressed in a worn but fairly clean French uniform. His right arm was supported by a black band which was suspended from his neck and his right hand was tucked inside his jacket, as though his arm were broken. Noticing that I eyed him suspiciously, he hastily explained: 'Oh you needn't be afraid, Monsieur! My name is Corporal Henri Pitit!' At this he fumbled with his left hand for papers to prove it. 'I have recently returned from the Tunisian campaign. I was wounded.' He indicated his right arm with his left hand. 'I am very pale and weak because I am only two days away from the hospital. I am taking you to my wife because I am to call for her after her lecture at the university. She is a student of medicine.' He smiled with pride. 'I wish to invite you to my home so that you can see that the real French people are not like those back there. Then you will know, Monsieur, that all French people are not materialistic parasites.'

"I tried to protest that I wasn't hungry, that I had just eaten, but he would not hear of it. To tell the truth I was impressed by the man's sincerity.

"What difference does it make what I think of the French people? thought I. Apparently it meant very much to him. That was why I finally decided to go with him.

"His wife was a pale, half-starved, slightly-built girl with stringy dun-colored hair and large clear courageous eyes. 'How do you do,' she said when her husband introduced me. And she kindly consented when he told her that he had invited me to supper. At that moment she glanced at me sympathetically and then at her husband. I felt like a fool. She paid for her drink and we left the bistro. We took the Metro to a quarter which I had never visited before. We got off at a dreary street and began to wind our way down one alley after another. I thought of the slums in which I was born and the slums of London and Glasgow. At last we entered a dark doorway which led onto a court from which we entered another passageway. A dirty yellow light suspended from the ceiling revealed a dingy atmosphere reeking with the strong smell of urine and decaying food. A pile of rubbish stood in the far end of the passage. Rats gnawed on cans and roaches crawled through the moist contents of the overflowing garbage pail.

"We stopped at the door and entered a room. A young man sitting at a small wooden table covered with an oilcloth rose to greet us. He was perhaps twenty-two, slightly built and stooped. His face was thin and sensitive and his eyes were large and courageous, like those of Henri Pitit's wife. He's her brother, I thought, noticing the thin crop of dun-colored hair which fell into his face. He wore a dark, loose-fitting sweater and a large green knitted scarf around his neck. He had been writing something before we came. A sheet of paper with writing on it lay near the bird cage which stood on the table. There was a small green bird in it. As we approached the young man he smiled a greeting, obviously embarrassed by the presence of a stranger. Henri introduced me.

"'Supper will be ready soon.' Mrs. Pitit looked at me. Then she lit the gas burner, which was supported by a moderate-sized wooden box. The gentle blue flame burned under a large tin can about the size of a ten-gallon lard can, in which was a sort of dirty-gray soup, upon the surface of which floated globules of fat. This I noticed as I accepted, at my host's insistence, the only chair. I had also discerned floating in the liquid a carrot, a potato or two and a little piece of fat meat no bigger than the little green bird in the wooden cage upon the table.

"The soldier sat on the bed. It looked as though they had piled every rag they owned on top of it for warmth. As there was no other bed in the room I supposed that all three of them slept together. The poet stood near the stove and watched his sister prepare the food, that is, add salt and pepper to the soup. There was no bread to be cut.

"Sitting, I had an opportunity to look around a little. The room was about sixteen by nineteen feet square. The small window near the door looked into the dimly illuminated court. The only heat was that afforded by the gas jet upon which the supper cooked. A few wooden boxes which were used as tables stood near the head of the bed on the farther side next to the wall. They contained books and toilet articles. There were no rugs on the dirty tiled floor.

"Supper was ready. My hostess set the table. There were only two plates and two spoons. One of us would have to wait until the first couple finished eating. Of course, the wife should eat first, I insisted, and the husband insisted that because I was the guest, I should join her. He would drink his soup out of a can and the poet volunteered to wait.

"I could hardly eat. The soup didn't taste so bad, but it looked awful, nor was its aroma improved by the stench coming from the toilet outside. I was further disquieted by the fact that a young man who obviously needed food more than I did was waiting for me to finish so that he could eat. Nor could he easily divert his attention from the table, which occupied the center of the room. In spite of our attempts at conversation a tedious silence prevailed. Needless to say, I found it difficult to hide my feelings, which I attempted to do by talking too loudly and too quickly, and by laughing and smiling very often. I think I even convinced them that I had a good time—all except the wife, who knew better. I failed to hide from her serene, knowing eyes my embarrassment due to the glaring irony of my obviously pros- perous condition as compared to theirs. She read the guilt in my face. As she lowered her kind eyes I felt the weight of those dreadful traveler's checks in my pocket (over three thousand dollars)—as I sipped the dirty soup and occupied the only chair.

"I might have given them some of it, but I dared not. For the soldier had been right, these were real French people. My offer could only have offended them and made me feel worse than I already did. So I suffered the evening through and managed before I climbed onto the Metro to exact from them a promise that they would join me for dinner the following week (I had first suggested the next day, but they said that they were busy), apologizing for the fact that I had no home to which to invite them, and that they would have to eat, therefore, in a restaurant.

"'You should not worry about that,' said the soldier. 'We have been pleased to meet you and hope to do so again.'

"'*Au revoir*,' said the young lady with the courageous eyes, very tenderly, and hardly above a whisper, as I boarded the train and sped away, never to return, and never to forget the pathetically beautiful, and yet ridiculous scene, in which I had played an undistinguished part."

There followed a long pause. It lasted perhaps three minutes. The sounds of the random voices of the people in the Mövenpick filtered into the thoughtful silence of the little company who sat around me. My friend who had introduced me to the curious young man for whose benefit I was still defying the ambitious waiter looked finally at me and said in a provocative tone:

"I never knew you were in Amsterdam . . ."

"That!—is a long story," I said discouragingly.

"Tell it," he said, adding, "and have another glass of wine." I accepted. A few minutes later the waiter brought the wine. We toasted each other's health. Then the little group fell silent. I began . . .

Why I Left Amsterdam

"WELL, IF I had had a little more courage during those days," I confessed, "I might have found Amsterdam more agreeable. But as I was new in Europe I found Amsterdam no less fearsome than I had found Paris unfriendly. For Amsterdam presented an old problem and several new ones for which I was totally unprepared.

"The old problem, of course, was that of language. Not knowing the language makes one self-conscious and suspicious. For the first time I experienced the uneasy sensation which results from being looked at by people. But as for friends I fared much better than I had done in Paris. The young writer whom I had met in the Boulevard St. Michel had given me a letter of introduction to a group of his friends. So after spending the first night in a very pleasant but expensive hotel I set out to find them. My friend had suggested that they would help me find a cheap place to stay.

"At the first address on my list I found an amiable young married couple. They read my letter and welcomed me wholeheartedly. The husband was a poet with a considerable reputation in Holland, said his wife. She showed me several small volumes of poems with his name printed on them. And I gathered that she was the daughter of an old but poor aristocratic family. He was tall and wiry and graceful. He wore his hair like the Parisian existentialists of a decade ago. He had a pleasant, sensitive face. While she looked very much like what she declared herself to be. She was tall and rather thin and exquisitely feminine. Her

31

hair was auburn and her eyes were hazel. She was well poised and simply but perfectly dressed. I was delighted with both of them, but especially with her because not only was she pretty but she spoke English perfectly and with a British accent.

"Their apartment was small. It was full of books and personal decorations. There were many poems and signed paintings and drawings on the walls. The little room in which we sat served as a combination bedroom, dining room and parlor, while the little room adjoining it was used as a kitchen. They apologized because they could not offer me a room but promised to help me find one. The hostess offered me coffee, during which I told her how I had met their friend in Paris. She translated what I said into Dutch for her husband, and performed the same service for me when he wished to speak to me.

"'The next one on the list is a painter,' she said. 'His brother was a very successful poet who was killed in the war. He lives not far from where we live. Perhaps you can stay there a few days.' Then she smiled, somewhat curiously, I thought, and added: 'He is very nice—and you will like his girl, too! With the others I don't think you have much chance, but they will do all they can, I'm sure.' When we had finished our coffee she suggested that we go to the Leidseplein, where there was a café which they frequented. 'They should be there now,' she said.

"So we went to the café. It reminded me a little of Paris. Everything was dark brown and not too clean. The atmosphere was smoky and noisy and very familiar. There was much long hair and many beards and thick woolen sweaters. Conversation babbled in a casual manner and many of the young people who occupied tables were not drinking anything. One by one I met first this one and then that one who had been mentioned on the list. But I was greatly inconvenienced by the fact that we could not speak to each other. The young painter with whom I was to stay was very friendly. Luckily he spoke a little French, so we were able to speak to each other a little. He agreed that I could stay with them for a few days until I found something. I was very happy over my good fortune. I went immediately to my hotel after I left the café and got my bags and went to the address which he gave me in the Princegraat.

"The apartment consisted of two medium-sized rooms and a closet-sized kitchen, which was heaped with dirty dishes and cans and coffee grounds and tea leaves and eggshells. The front room, which looked out onto the canal, was very pleasant. There were two large windows. It was furnished with a large round table, a very low bed which stood in a corner. It was surrounded by bookshelves filled with books. There were pictures on the walls, a fireplace gone to pot and odd-looking vases scattered around with flowers in them. Dishes from breakfast were on the table and a worn reddish carpet covered the floor. A stocking here and an underskirt there, hairpins on the floor, a lipstick on the mantel over the fireplace gave the room an enchanted air and filled me with curiosity about my host's girlfriend. When the painter saw my glance lingering upon the empty stocking draped carelessly over the back of the chair he waved his hands nonchalantly at it and said: 'C'est Tania. Elle viendra ce soir . . .'

"Now if I was happy over having found a place to stay that afternoon, I was most certainly unhappy at having found this place to stay by dawn on the following morning! For by that time it was clear to me that I couldn't stay very long in that apartment if I were to keep my sanity. The reason was because, as the painter said, 'Tania will be home this evening.' That is precisely what she did. She was perhaps twenty. Her hair was as red as the sun and she had a full, beautifully developed body. She was a ballerina and she danced at the State Theater. She burst into the room full of enthusiasm about something which I did not understand and flung herself wildly into her lover's arms. Then they tumbled onto the bed and rolled on top of each other and kissed many times, while I stood there horrified and waiting to be introduced. When their joy was exhausted they got up and he introduced me to her. He told her in Dutch that I would be staying with them for a while. She smiled bewitchingly, shook my hand and began taking off her clothes. I started to jump out the window! But that would be silly, I thought. So I held my ground.

"'We're going out!' the poet announced. I took this as an excuse to dash armfuls of cold water into my face.

"We went to the café which I had visited earlier that afternoon. There I met the poet with his auburn-haired wife, as well as all of their friends, with whom I shook hands and smiled and drank many glasses of Dutch gin. Then presently my painter said, '*Viens avec moi!*' He grabbed Tania, who was exclaiming passionately to an unshaven young man, and we dashed into the street and hailed a taxi. After some minutes we entered a noisy quarter filled with roving people. There were many brightly illuminated cafés and nightclubs on both sides of the street. Music filled the air, sambas, tangos and jazz. There were many Negroes, Indonesians and other races about. Seductive women crowded every doorway.

"Finally we got out of the taxi and mingled with the crowd. Then suddenly we entered a street which bordered on a canal. Light from the houses on either side reflected upon the surface of the water. It was green and slimy. On our side of the canal the whole street looked like a shopping district. In front of almost every house on the ground floor was a little storefront. They looked like glass cages about ten cubic feet square. In each window sat a woman. Some were young and some were old. Their hair was mostly blond and they usually wore tight semi-transparent low-cut blouses with no brassieres and short skirts which were very tight. They strained against the women's thighs as they sat with their legs crossed on chairs or stools. Some of them wore shoes and some of them were barefooted. Most of them looked at the floor or at their hands or at the slimy water in the canal with bland, empty expressions. One woman who appeared to be about thirty-six knitted a piece of pink material, while another who appeared to be very young, hardly eighteen, pretended to read a magazine.

"A crowd of drunken men milled before the windows. There were American soldiers and sailors, white and black. Some of the men appeared to be African, while there were others who were obviously English and French in their uniforms. Many of the men spoke German and Dutch. They stood before the windows and peered at the women. They laughed and made jokes as they examined their bodies. Occasionally a man would tap on a window or wiggle his finger for the girl to come out. She would leave the window and a side door would open. The man would go in. A few minutes later the woman would appear in her window and take up her former attitude.

"As we milled among the crowd I began to feel sick. At the same time I was fascinated by what I had seen. I was confused because I could not determine whether I was sick from desire, guilt, or the vulgarity of the scene. I squeezed the painter's arm. 'Let's get out of here!' I spoke in English but apparently he read my meaning in my face.

"We entered another street. There were more cafés filled with people. 'Over here,' he said. We entered a nightclub. A Negro orchestra was playing. The leader played the trumpet and tried to imitate Louis Armstrong. The floor was crowded with jostling couples. The tables and the bar were filled to overflowing with all sorts of people. The atmosphere was bathed in a red smoky light. It was very hot and we were at pains to find a table. But presently a couple sitting at a table near where we were standing left and we took their place. While we waited for the drinks we ordered Tania shivered sensuously to the beat of the music. I tried not to look at her. The painter didn't dance.

"'Dance with Tania,' he urged.

"'The floor is so crowded,' I complained, looking at Tania apologetically. But she, having understood 'Dance with Tania,' had not understood my apology. So when I looked at her she interpreted my glance as an invitation to rise. She rose. Reluctantly I danced with Tania.

"She was round and soft and nakedly dressed in an exquisite red dress. The floor was so crowded that we were pressed against each other. I tried to push her body away but it was no use. Her arm slid around my neck and involuntarily my arm tightened around her waist. I tried to move away from the painter but the floor was so crowded that it was impossible. So we squirmed around in a little inch of space like naked worms in a hot bucket.

"I remembered Tania as I had seen her that evening in their apartment, wild and full of passion. I saw the women with their legs crossed in the windows along the canal. I began to sweat. I shuffled dizzily this way and that while the music droned with a low wail. From time to time I looked at the painter with a weak smile. He smiled back with a strange, amused expression upon his face. Tania was lost in the warmth, in the heat of the music and of my arms. . . .

"We got home very late. Tania started throwing off her clothes the very moment we entered the apartment. I muttered good night hoarsely and rushed to the adjoining room. I tried to shut the sliding doors but they were stuck. I undressed in the darkest corner and lay upon the couch and prayed that I could go to sleep quickly.

"An instant later the light went out in the front room and the nightmare began. The sounds of lovers making love filled the darkness. They conducted this affair as though they were quite alone in the world. With each muffled sound that came from the other room all the passion in the world seemed to crystalize in the darkness and dance naked before my eyes. The animate monster laughed and jeered at me. It divided itself into multitudes and induced the sweat to drip from my armpits and to run down my face. With thongs of fire it warded off each advance of sleep, until dawn.

"As the first rosy light stole through the window I slipped on my clothes and quietly tiptoed out into the street. I walked along the canals until I could walk no more. I sat on the steps of a butcher shop and wearily, enviously watched the town get out of bed. When I got back to the apartment Tania had gone to work and the painter was asleep. I fell upon the couch without undressing and slept very heavily until late in the afternoon.

"During the weeks that followed I spent my days at home sleeping and my nights walking the streets. Needless to say, I made every effort to find another room. My search took me to other members of the little artistic group to whom my friend in Paris had given me a letter of introduction.

"One day I visited a beautiful young lady whose husband was away. She was a poetess and he was—they all said—a great writer. He had gone to England in order to learn English so that he might write in that language because he wished to win a larger reading public and to escape church censorship, which he considered to be discouraging to creative activity in Holland. His wife appeared to be about twenty-three or -four years old, but quite mature, well poised and self-possessed. She was very feminine, small of stature with abundant soft brown hair. Her eyes were large, quiet and blue. Looking at her was like looking at a clear sky from the top of a hill, or like listening to music. When I told her my story and gave her my references she told me that she was sorry that she had no room for me, but that she would help me to find a place. Shortly after that the bell rang downstairs and I was left alone to observe the room.

"It was a large, sunny room with a rather low ceiling supported by huge oak beams. They were neatly varnished and were used as an element of the room's decorative scheme. There was a long comfortable sofa against the wall over which was draped a beautifully woven cover. It looked very old. Pictures and poems in frames hung on the walls. An old-fashioned bookcase with glass doors stood against the wall facing the door. It was crammed with books of all kinds and what appeared to be manuscripts and yellowing periodicals. In the wall opposite the sofa was a window through which a gentle breeze blew. The shutters were open.

"Presently a huge savage-looking tawny cat sprang onto the windowsill and leaped onto the large round table in the center of the room. With a lazy movement he looked indifferently at me and then half leaped, half stepped into his mistress's chair and crouched on his belly. In that position he studied the blazing bar of sunlight which burned the polished wooden floor.

"When my hostess returned several young men were with her. I had seen them before, in the café in the Leidseplein. We greeted each other and I was happy that everyone in the company spoke some English. Upon hearing that her husband was in England

and why, I ventured to sympathize with him for being put to the trouble of learning to write in a foreign language.

"'We—are used to it,' she said.

"I looked at her with a puzzled expression. "'I don't understand.'

"'We're different and they hate us for it.'

"I was more puzzled than before. Who are *we*? I wondered. Had she been a Negro woman I might have understood more quickly. I pondered the mystery in the pause that followed. I tried to remember everything that had happened to me since I came to Holland in order to divine what she meant. Her friends had all been very kind to me. And it now occurred to me that they all seemed very close to each other.

"'It's a pity that the young couple I met in Paris are not here. I would like to know them better,' I said.

"'Family problems,' smiled one of the young men. He was shabbily dressed and very sullen. At his remark the rest of the company exchanged knowing glances.

"'How do you like Holland?' the older and more presentable young man asked. He wore glasses and looked like a serious student of philosophy. I learned later that he was a professor of classical languages at the university, and that his sullen companion was a sculptor. The third man seemed neither young nor old. He sat quietly upright in his chair with his legs crossed and never spoke.

"'Oh, I like it well enough, I guess. I'm still trying to find a room . . . And I can't get used to the way the people stare at me all the time.' Then I told them about my experiences in Paris and why I left. I concluded by lamenting the plight of the Negro who wandered through the world like a child without his mother, a long way from home.

"'They made soap of my parents.' I looked at the lovely young woman who said that. Her gaze was steady and the expression upon her face was calm. Her hands lay gently folded in her lap. Suddenly the savage-looking cat appeared from nowhere and leaped into her lap. She stroked its head gently.

"'Who?'

"They all looked at me incredulously, for at least a full minute. I have often experienced the surprise which they undoubtedly felt when I have spoken with someone who has asked me, 'Who wrote *Hamlet?*'

"'The Germans.' She said the word quietly, as though she had said, 'The Potatoes.'

"By this time I managed to understand that they were Jews. Awareness crept into my expression. The air in the room was deathly still. During the pause I took stock of the universe and tried to place my finger upon the entity that was myself. I remembered that I had seen the smile, which now skirted the periphery of the faces in this room, upon the faces of Negroes when speaking of incidents which occurred during the race riots in Chicago and Detroit, or when they spoke of lynchings in the south or police brutality in the north.

"Shortly after that I brought my visit to a close. I left the little company feeling uncomfortable. The sound of her words, 'They made soap of my parents,' made the bright warm sky look sinister. The gentle, innocent breeze, which wafted through the little park near the house which I had just visited, became an ominous agent of evil. The lovely face of my hostess hovered in my mind like an image of some mythological figure, or like a photograph negative of a beautiful woman who was dead. So great was my association with their pain that I, too, felt Jewish. The fearful monster, *They*, lurked in the dark corners of my mind, and I imagined a perverse and malignant hostility in the expression of every face I encountered. The slightest attention from persons on the street or in public places drove me to distraction!"

At this point the little knot of young men sitting around me in the Mövenpick could no longer contain itself.

"Stop!" someone exclaimed. I ceased to speak, looking around for the voice which had interrupted my reminiscence.

"Yes," said I, somewhat dreamily, noticing that a soft blue color was filtering into the sky. Then someone said—I did not notice who:

"I can understand how the Jewish people must have felt, but it was only natural that the people looked at you. You don't seem to realize that we Europeans don't see a Negro every day!"

"Yes, yes," I replied impatiently, struggling to hold onto my precious thought, and regretting at the same time that I could not stop and take up his objection to what appeared to be my hypersensitivity to being looked at. "You are probably right," I said, "I'll come to that later, but just now I would like to finish with Amsterdam.

"I was trying to describe how the conversation with the young poetess unsettled me. However, the real upheaval was brought on by another gentleman to whom I had been introduced. He was a graphologist. He interested me because of his profession and because he shared my admiration of Spinoza. He was a tall blond man with soft features and a slightly stooped posture. He habitually sat, stood and walked with his head bent upon the ground, as though he bore the weight of some invisible bur- den—which he did!

"I met him through my host in the apartment in the Princegraat. He invited me to his home one day and introduced me to his wife and son. She was a small strong dark woman who looked perhaps thirty but who was perhaps forty. However, she was nonetheless handsome for all that. She was extremely serious and vital in a strange way. Their son was twelve years old and very beautiful.

"He had promised to explain his profession to me because I had admitted to him that I had always looked upon it with a healthy skepticism. But upon my arrival at his home I was swept into his wife's enthusiasm for music. She had a small collection of recordings of Bach, Mozart and Vivaldi, to mention but a few.

"'Music is all I have left,' she said in a grave tone. And I gathered that I was to consider myself privileged in sharing it with her. There was nothing to do after that but listen. We all took comfortable seats around the gramophone. My seat was near the window, through which I looked over the rooftops of Amsterdam. The rest of the time I sat with my eyes fixed fully upon her. She was the center of attraction for us all in a strong, compelling way.

"I learned later that this little woman had been very heroic during the war. She had been captured several times by the Nazis and had managed to escape each time. Her eyes burned like flames as she drank in the music—as though it were life itself, while we participated in the ritual like visitors attending the services of a church not of our faith.

"Then the music stopped. She served us coffee and the subject of graphology flew out of mind. We spoke of Spinoza.

"'We are all the same, parts of a whole, which is God . . . however one chooses to perceive Him . . . That is all he was trying to say.' She uttered her words with great intensity.

"'Yes,' I replied. 'In the edition of the *Ethics* which I read the author included the document of excommunication which was read to Spinoza by the Church authorities. I marveled at the seemingly myriad ways in which he had been cursed by the canons of Church Law. I tried to realize what it must have meant to him to have been an outcast among his own people—and at a time in which there were only a few countries in the western world in which a Jew could find asylum. It made me very sad . . .'

"'You should walk with me a little in the old section of town,' said the graphologist. His wife looked at him and a pained expression filled her eyes. It made me uneasy. 'I'll show you the ghetto in which Spinoza lived . . . The site on which the old synagogue stood.'

"'I'd like to see it very much,' I said, trying to fathom the expression upon the woman's face.

"We finished our coffee and I thanked her for the wonderful music and said good-bye.

"It was a sunny, lazy time of day. We walked slowly to the old quarter of Amsterdam. We passed many houses which were being torn down, and others which stood in ruins. After a while we reached a sort of square with an old stone fountain in the middle of it. 'Here is where we have the market but it is empty today,' he said. We walked on farther. When we had crossed the square he pointed straight ahead and said: 'Over there is where the old church was. It has long since been destroyed. This is the new one.' The walls of the building were riddled with gaping holes from machine guns and mortar shells. Practically all of its windows were shattered. I looked at him questioningly. 'The war,' he said.

"We walked on. Here and there he would point to a building or a house and make some pertinent comment. On one occasion he pointed to a three-story house a few streets from the synagogue and said: 'My family was taken there. They were all killed.' He spoke with a choking, stifled voice. He walked just a step behind me so that I could not see his face. At the sound of his voice I stopped suddenly and tried to shake off the oppressive feeling that came over me. The pained expression on his wife's face came to mind.

"She knew, I thought.

"The sun shone on the dull gray stone buildings and on the stones of the street. It gave off a bright glare. I heard no sound save the sound of his voice, of his breathing and of the silence when we ceased to talk. The face of the beautiful poetess appeared before me. She sat in the sunlit room and looked at me with a steady gaze. Her hands were folded upon her lap. The savage cat suddenly appeared from nowhere and jumped into her arms. She stroked its head and said: 'They made soap of my parents.' I started and swung around and looked at him because the voice which I had heard seemed so loud. I wondered if he had heard it, too. His face grew white when our eyes met. The rimless glasses which he wore made his eyes appear very large and fluid, as though they were peering at me through a glass filled with water.

"'They all died,' he said. 'But I . . . I was not taken. They came early in the morning and dragged my family out of the house. There, by that old post. There were many others. That is where they stood . . .'

"I turned away from him. How could he tell it, ten years later, I wondered. Why to me! Why tell that horrible mess to me! His voice droned in my ear, rehearsing the details until I felt like spitting into his face. I turned and grabbed him by the arm. 'Listen!' I began. But he did not hear me.

"'They didn't take me because I didn't *look* like a Jew. How in God's name does a Jew look!' We walked slowly and silently home. We did not look at each other. As we walked, I thought: 'He confesses to everyone because he didn't declare his identity and die with the members of his family . . . He associates me with himself because I am a black man . . .'

"I experienced a sensation of pity mixed with nausea at the thought of him; not because of what he suffered but because I perceived that he derived some perverse pleasure from telling the intimate details of the death of his family, from the pain which he inflicted upon himself and others.

"We reached the center of the city. His way lay to the right and my way lay straight ahead. We said good-bye and parted. I never saw the graphologist again.

"By now there was a feeling stirring within me which controlled all my actions. I had not been able to find a room. Time was passing and I felt anxious about my condition in the world. Danger was everywhere. I made a decision, which I slowly articulated into action, but in a very indirect way. My first decisive act after I left the graphologist was to visit the house of Descartes. It called to mind his fate at the hands of the church. It was hardly a cheerful reminiscence. As if that was not enough to make clear to me the decision I had made, I dropped by Rembrandt's old residence and remembered how he almost starved to death for refusing to paint the way the burghers wanted him to. It was after this visit that I felt the invisible fires of Nazism, Judaism, Catholicism and Puritanism kindling at my feet. Witch hunts in New England came to my mind. I saw shivering clusters of Dutch Puritans—and Jews among them, no doubt—standing upon the wind-blown shores of Plymouth in the dead of winter. The decisive thought detached itself from my feelings: 'This is the place from which they fled!' Consequently I decided: 'This is no place for me.'"

"So you came to Bern?" exclaimed the young man who inspired my explanation.

"Not exactly. I first went to Germany."

"Germany!" They all shouted in amazement.

I sipped my wine. It tasted very sour. My lips were dry. I looked at the clock over the door and saw that it was late. I should go . . . , I thought, as I thought about Germany, of why I went there and why I left. It seemed a curious thing to have done, even to me. I had often thought of writing a story about it. All I needed was an approach, a first line. Feelings gathered around the tension, which was Germany, and I began to speak without being aware of it or of the members of the company.

Why I Left Germany

"I RECEIVED A letter from a friend. His name was David, a red-headed southerner from Smoky Mountain, Tennessee, who was living in California. He suggested that I visit an acquaintance whom I had met once at a party in his flat in St. James Square in Philadelphia. I felt as Lazarus must have felt when he heard the call which promised him a new lease on life. Obediently, I left Amsterdam three days later, ostensibly on a visit to Bern.

"But on the way I stopped in Germany. Perhaps I will live here, I thought, momentarily forgetting the call which had raised me from the dead. Now the reason I thought such an extraordinary thought, especially in view of what I have just told you about my feelings in Amsterdam, was because I had a roommate in college who had applied to the medical school of a German university. He knew the language very well, having applied himself to its acquisition with the aid of a very beautiful Fräulein. He used to describe her to me in loving detail on dull evenings when we could not afford to leave the campus. Of course, the actual reason he had applied to a foreign medical school three thousand miles from home was because the American schools were very crowded. There were hardly enough places for the legitimate citizens, let alone Jews, Chinese, Japanese, Indians and Negroes.

"The university was in Munich. I would have to pass through Munich on my way to Bern. We can be together again, I thought, remembering the many pleasant days we had spent together in college. Perhaps a pretty Fräulein will teach me German. I would

45

be able to read Goethe in his own language . . . Yes! I will stay in Munich and write and study and enjoy the cathedrals and become cultivated . . .

"He will be surprised to see me, I thought, as the train pulled into the station and I hurried toward the nearest taxi. I got out of the taxi in front of a gloomy-looking house on what appeared to be the outskirts of the town. The mid-day sun shone upon the two scraggy trees that stood in the yard. In spite of the fact that it was a warm day, the atmosphere in the hall, as I ascended the stairs, was cool and forbidding. I felt as though I were descending into a musty, dank cellar. It was very quiet. The windows in the doors of the apartments were of darkly stained glass. Now and again faces peered silently out at me. 'Do you know where—?' I would begin, and presto! the face would disappear. On the third floor a door cracked open as I passed and I heard a woman's laughter. Wearily I climbed to the next floor, examining the names on the polished brass plates as I went. Finally, on the very top floor, I found my friend's name. I rang the bell and waited several silent minutes. I was about to ring a second time when the door opened slightly and a pair of wary eyes peered through the crack.

"Instead of my friend it was Rufus Grey, another student from my college, whom I had almost forgotten.

"'You!' I cried in amazement.

"He opened the door and looked at me, cautiously, hesitantly, before he invited me in. After studying me for some time he seemed to recognize me. He heaved a sigh and said, 'Why, V.O. [they all addressed me after the first two initials of my name at college], what are you doing here!'

"Grey, as I could see upon entering the room, was much altered. He was thirty-three or -four, an ex-soldier, a man of small stature, all muscle and very strong. He was very sensitive and very serious. There were dark red freckles on his yellowish face, just beneath his small, round eyes, which gave a ridiculous air to his serious mien. His ears were comically small and pressed closely to his round head. He was dressed in a plain brown suit, which was badly in need of pressing, though relatively new and of fashionable cut.

"'Come in—come in,' he said.

"I entered the room, wondering what was wrong. He seemed worried. There was a tired, strained expression upon his face and his eyes were red and watery, as though he hadn't slept for days. I asked him where my friend was, taking the seat he indicated with his finger, near the window. He threw up his hands in despair.

"'Look around . . .' He waved his hand at the dirty, disrumpled room. It looked as though someone had packed and left in a hurry. Dirty clothes were strewn everywhere. A pile of dusty books was stacked in a corner. Raveled balls of dust lay like clouds upon the faded linoleum floor and bits of soiled paper were scattered here and there. In the center of the floor was a pile of broken glass and an empty wine bottle, and several food-encrusted plates with knives, forks and spoons lay upon the table.

"'What happened?' I asked him,

"'I thought I'd go mad . . .' He spoke quietly and somewhat distractedly, as he seated himself upon a packing crate which was used as a bed table. '. . . But I won't go mad!' he said. Then he looked up at me, as though a confusing thought had just come to him. 'Why did you come here?'

"I explained that I had come in search of my friend, and that I had considered living in Munich, and that I was surprised at not finding him. A bitter expression came into Grey's face.

"'Are you crazy! They've run him away, man . . . It's hell here!'

"'What do you mean?'

"'The people, man. Look at his room. It costs a hundred and fifty marks a month. Two marks to take a bath! No running water. It's supposed to be heated, but they don't heat it, man.'

"'Can't you complain to the American authorities?'

"'Ha! They don't give a damn, man. The landlady's a bitch, and there's nothing you can do about it. They're trying to beat us down . . .'

"Slowly I learned from Rufus Grey that life in Munich was not very pleasant. It was his opinion that the professors and students at the university were uncooperative, even hostile, and that this situation was complicated more than a little by the difficulty of studying in a foreign language. He said that the people stared at them all the time and laughed at them and that few women would have anything to do with them at all. It was his opinion that the people were bitter and resentful because of the war. 'Nazism is far from dead,' he exclaimed.

"'Perhaps I have complexes . . .' he added thoughtfully. 'Sometimes I think I am still in Georgia.' Then in a very satirical tone he told me that my friend whom I had traveled so far to see must have had complexes, too, because he hadn't been able to stick it out. 'He fell apart like a wet pretzel. He began to drink and carouse in whorehouses. He neglected his studies. He's turned into a dirty, vulgar, slovenly tramp, man.'

I was shocked speechless. I had never known my friend to drink back home, and he had always been a very conscientious student, much more conscientious than I who always had a wild tendency to range through the library so much that I often lost contact with the subjects which were supposed to be the main objects of study. It was I who always persuaded him to go to a movie or to take a day off. Grey said that my friend had also become, of late, very arrogant and overbearing.

"'He was impossible to live with. Even with me and his other American friends. Several of the fellows are Jewish. We all live here in the same pension. The end came last night when he broke a bottle over one of the Jewish students' heads in a drunken rage. You see, for weeks now every white man he sees is a German . . . They fought like hell. Naturally, the Jewish boy didn't like being hit on the head. Especially by a "nigger," he said. That was the mistake he made. But he was just mad. Then they began to throw dishes at each other. If that wasn't bad enough the neighbors crowded around the door and in the street and had a damned good laugh at the two Americans, the white one and the black one, who couldn't get along together even when they left America. It was disgusting!'

"It was very sad and strangely disquieting to me to learn that my friend had changed so. And yet, after much reflection, I can't say that what happened to him was very unusual, for I have frequently noticed, when some old memory of home crops up, or when I am asked to explain to some European the racial problems of the American, I have frequently noticed that such scenes often occur, especially in large cities. The minorities, under pressure from the majority group, in whichever locality they may live or work, sometimes fight each other, out of self-hatred, or fear, or what is more pathetic and yet perversely beautiful, the violent and complicated passion of an inexpressible love. This is probably one of the explanations of the enigmatic southern white-black 'problem,' as one or two American writers, Mr. Faulkner and Mr. Caldwell, for example, sometimes realize. But oh, how difficult a truth it is to accept for these gentlemen and those few others, as well as for myself.

"My friend left Germany shortly after the fight, which apparently had occurred the night before. According to Grey, he simply left a cold, impersonal note saying that he was gone. And that, no doubt, accounted for the state in which I found Grey, enveloped by a profound despair and lonely in what was apparently an unfriendly country.

"What good friends Grey and my friend must have been that he should have suffered so! Whether my friend resumed his studies in America or not, I cannot say. I never wrote to Grey after I left. However, I do know that he is married and is the father of a son and a daughter. This I learned from a friend who later wrote to me and incidentally mentioned his name.

"It is curious that it all should have turned out like that, I thought with a depressed feeling, as I left Grey, sitting on the packing case. My friend had been such a good student. He had long looked forward to his studies in Europe and to becoming a great doctor.

"'Yes,' I used to say, 'you shall go to Germany and become a great doctor.' And he would say:

"'And you must go to Paris and become no less than a Dostoevski or a Proust.' Of these thoughts we dreamed, as we lay in our beds side by side long after the lights were out . . .

"It's such a pity, I thought, as I turned down a broad dull street on which there were no trees. I was beginning to feel a little apprehensive now in the full glare of the sun. As I encountered little knots of people along the way, I remembered Amsterdam with increasing uneasiness and regret—and with longing. I had felt more comfortable there. Grey had advised me not to stay in Munich and I decided to take his advice.

"It was a long way to the center of the town. The sun became increasingly hotter and brighter. I asked a man how to get to the station and he pointed straight ahead and said something I didn't understand and walked away. I followed the direction he had indicated with his finger. After a while I became so tired from walking, and so weary as a result of my depressing thoughts about my friends that I decided to spend the night in a hotel. And as I neared the center of town I grew thirsty. I stopped at what seemed to be a café in order to rest and have a quiet glass of beer. But the café turned out to be a beer hall.

"However, 'beer hall' is an understatement. The place which I had unwittingly entered was a beer stadium!—an enormous room with a damp concrete floor which was perforated here and there with little drains to draw off dropping liquids. It smelled of beer, urine and sweat. Long wooden tables in rows extended the width of the room from the entrance to the rear wall. Seated at the tables on long plank benches supported by thin iron legs were many people of all sizes, shapes and hues of red, drinking beer from giant glasses. Stout waitresses struggled under trays loaded with the brown foamy ooze, setting them down brusquely before red-nosed watery-eyed men and women who thirstily swilled them down in gulps.

"I entered the hall and sat down amid the din. I motioned to a waitress and said, 'Beer.' After a while she set the glass down before me. Just as I raised it to my lips a youngish plump girl of perhaps eighteen, with a rakish smile which revealed a missing front tooth (she looked as though she should have been painted by Frans Hals), sat down behind me and put her beefy hand between my legs. I almost vomited. She said something to me in German which I understood very well, in spite of the fact that the only words I knew in that language were *Ja, Hamburger,* and *Nein.* So I chose *Nein* with a weak smile and rose from the table as soon as she decided to remove her hand. When I finally got out of that place I decided that I wouldn't spend the night in Munich after all. However, as it turned out, I had to because the train left at an inconvenient hour.

"Dead tired I stumbled wearily through the town looking for a cheap hotel. The air was hot and filled with dust from the many buildings which were being torn down or rebuilt. The war, I thought, remembering the ghetto in Amsterdam. After walking through many streets and questioning many militant-looking strangers, taxi drivers, porters, railway clerks—everyone seemed to wear a uniform with epaulettes—I discovered a very charming German lady in the Information office at the station who spoke English very beautifully. She told me precisely where I might find a comfortable, inexpensive room and helped me to decipher the train schedule. I thanked her gratefully and hurried to the hotel which she had suggested. I went immediately to my room, turned the key in the lock and fell heavily across the bed. I awoke at eleven the next morning. Shortly after one I boarded the train for Bern . . .

"As the train pulled out of the station, my anxiety lessened. An old thrill stirred within me, a thrill which I have known since my soldiering days, that of being on the move, headed for some new place. When I was a child it was always tomorrow which held the promise of whatever that something was which I always wanted but could not have today . . . Perhaps that is why romantic and mysterious things have always played such an important part in my life, and why I have always feared that the positivistic tendency which we nowadays mistakenly call "scientific," when expressed in its extreme grotesqueness, would rule out, simply ignore because it is incalculable, the "unknown"—with all its myriad possibilities—which is so precious to me.

"How strongly I felt this as the gloomy barrack-like houses gave way to green fields and pastures, and the landscape softened into the open-air hues of spring! Flowers bloomed, cows grazed, farmers worked their fields. We passed by a stream. I breathed deeply and suddenly a thought came to me:

"I know American Negro soldiers who were in Germany during the war and soldiers in the peacetime army who liked German people so well that they married German women and took them to America—a heroic thing to do! There were those among them who never would have returned to America if they could have helped it . . . So they said . . .

"This thought clashed dangerously with my feelings about Germans during the last twenty-four hours and disquieted me. Apparently in Germany, as in France, much had changed since the war. Could other German cities be different from Munich? I wondered. Or was the trouble with my friends? Or with me?

"I pondered these questions, seeing as I did so, signs scrawled on the walls and fences of Paris, saying, Americans go home! The memory made me shudder. And then a calming thought: Paris is far away . . . Amsterdam is far away . . . The German landscape is receding . . . My senses quickened to new questions, all of which seemed to crystalize into just one question: What will I find in Bern?

"Well," I began, but just then the lights switched on and the Mövenpick was bathed in a dull white light, in a cold dirty-frosty glow which radiated from the imitation glass decoration on the rim of the balcony. It froze the intense green which colored the leaves of the imaginary tree (I smiled as I thought of it), which sprouted from the cash register and the one which stood between the two tables which the waitress had set for supper long long ago. Though the trees could be seen only by me, supper was now visibly being served to a pompous, fashionably dressed lady, wearing a light fur wrap, and her equally pompous husband whose scalp gleamed with the bright pink sheen of a well-nourished stomach. Against the color of this gentleman's head the evening stood out intensely blue.

My companions, especially the newcomer who had been so curious about my presence in Bern, pressed me to continue, but I asked him to excuse the lateness of the hour. Then I pointed out the danger of our remaining any longer because of the angry scowl upon the waiter's face. "I was a cook once. I know just how the man feels," I said. "Besides that, it is becoming almost impossible to speak, with all the noise. Then too, I have an appointment for supper. Friends—a Mr. and Mrs. C—— who live in Wabern [a suburb of Bern] have invited me for a fondue. Mrs. C—— hates it when anyone is late for one of her fondues, for which she has acquired quite a reputation, because if it is not eaten immediately after it reaches its point of perfection, it spoils, the cheese clots into globules of chewing gum. And! since I have no money with which to eat elsewhere, gentlemen, I hope you will excuse me in favor of another time . . ."

I was hungry, exhausted and somewhat depressed as a result of my efforts to retrace my weary steps to Bern. I was also frustrated by the fact that I had failed to get it all in. My man was dissatisfied, I felt. Nor had he liked what I had said about Europe, the French and the Germans. Perhaps he was French-Swiss, German-Swiss, Swiss-German or Swiss-French—I considered all the possibilities, realizing, however, that it was too late to worry about it, since the damage was already done.

"Another time," I said, rising from the table and bidding the cordial company adieu. I walked through the swinging doors of the Mövenpick and stepped out into the Bahnhofplatz feeling naked and very much embarrassed. Fragments of many thoughts were jumbled in my mind and the sound they made mingled with the sound of the traffic. I crossed over to the Spitalgasse and walked slowly under the Loeb arcades, ignoring the fashionably dressed mannequins in the windows under the crystal chandeliers and the crowds of people streaming through the large center doors. Quite unconsciously I headed for Sherrers, a little restaurant in the Marktgasse where I sometimes ate because the food was cheap. I will go there and be quiet and think, I thought. But then suddenly I remembered that I had no money. Madam C——'s fondue! I thought, wheeling around, bumping into a middle-aged man wearing a bowler hat, leading a black French poodle on a yellow leash. "Pardon!" I apologized, realizing that I would have to hurry if I intended to arrive at the C——s' in time. It was a good fifty minutes to Wabern on foot, since I did not have the price for a tram.

What I Thought As I Walked

I THOUGHT VERY little until I got to Monbijoustrasse because the crowd was very thick. There were very many pretty girls with ankles and hips and breasts to watch—every rise and fall—discreetly. But when I swung around to Monbijoustrasse the crowd thinned out, after I crossed the Bundesterrasse on the left side going down past the Olivetti typewriter shop and on past the Rendezvous tearoom. While the people were in the houses with the rosy light streaming through the windows, having their café complets, their Rosti and Bratwurst, and their Apfelkuchen, this is what I thought:

Oh how I miss my own rosy window in the evening! How I miss my pork chops, fried apples and brown gravy, with piping hot biscuits to sop it up and steaming tea to wash it down. I shall always be in some strange city, looking through the windows of other people's houses, eating at other people's tables . . . Then another thought: I did not say all that I really meant back there . . . all of what I really felt. Some of the opinions which I have expressed, however badly, were quite true—once! But oh how ridiculous do they sound to me now! . . .

The evening fell soft and cool as I passed the Wander company. I thought of Little Orphan Annie and Daddie Warbucks and of how surprised—even hurt—I was when I first discovered in an argument in which it had seemed so important to triumph that Ovomaltine was a Swiss product! It's not fair, I thought, continuing up Monbijoustrasse and following the streetcar tracks around the curve and past the Old Folk's Home.

Pale lights shone from its windows. In the large green field opposite a farmer who looked very old plodded heavily through a section of freshly plowed earth, leading a huge gray horse. As I smelled the scent of earth and wet grass I remembered that someone had told me that when the Bernese grow old, when they reach a certain ancient age, eighty-five or ninety-six and two-thirds, I believe, the state gives them a rocking chair free. My informer ventured to suggest this as an explanation as to why the Bernese people are inspired to endeavor to live as long as they can, asking me if I had not already observed that they were a very careful people. How convenient, I thought, smiling to myself as I watched the slowly moving figure disappearing into the darkness: How convenient to live so close to the Old Folk's Home. My smile and my thoughts broke up into ripples of thought which diffused throughout my body as its heat radiated into the evening's coolness. This was due to the effort of walking, and gradually to the music of walking, and when my eyes first beheld the setting sun, breaking through a rush of green to the west, my body discovered its song! . . .

I stopped at a corner to let a car pass. Twenty minutes more, I thought, hoping that I would not be late, wishing that instead of fondue Mrs. C—— might serve simply a little meat and bread, and perhaps a tomato and a green pepper.

But . . . My thoughts rippled again, and presently I was tapping softly upon Mr. and Mrs. C——'s door, saying: "Good evening!" as the scent of cheese and white wine filled my nostrils . . .

That night while falling to sleep in the darkness of my room I reflected that I was really dissatisfied when I left the Mövenpick that evening because I had merely repeated a formula which I had already repeated many times because I had been asked the same questions many times. The explanation which I gave had been far from complete. I had merely said to that young man what I said to those young men who were like *this* instead of like *that*, one of *these* instead of one of *those* types. I was grateful, it was true, not to have been confronted with one of *those* types because they are bastards!—not because their mothers and fathers were not married when they were born—who can talk nowadays!—but because they like to probe into the most intimate parts of my consciousness with their dirty fingers.

One of *those* types may appear at any moment. They may crawl from behind any rock. The exemplary specimen is usually a clever young man who reads American newspapers. He has been to Italy and Paris and Spain, all of whose languages he speaks with a good Swiss accent. He is a man of the world and he intends to let me know it. Furthermore he would like to impress the people wherever he might be that he is *au courant*, that he speaks American and that he is an extremely interesting person who knows everybody. He usually walks up to me and greets me in a familiar manner ("Americans are that way, you know," he seems to say) and addresses me by my first name. He may have overheard it, or learned it from some acquaintance who heard it from a girl with whom I danced one Saturday night a year ago last Christmas at Bierhübeli! He may yell it from across the street from the midst of a crowd leaving the movies at four-thirty, six-thirty, eight-thirty or ten-thirty. Usually he sneaks upon me in a café, but more than likely in the Casino or the Embassy tearoom, as the pretty girls pass to and fro and look and smile and sit and sip their coffee or tea and talk. Once he appeared between sips of beer in the Bali:

"Hi, Wince!" or "Hel-low, Winsen!" he cried above the wrangle of the piano and the glare of the gaudy lights and the nervous laughter of the décolletéed barmaid, extending a sticky hand. "What's new! I'm surprised to see *you!*" He had not seen me when he spoke to me as he was leaving the Sultan tearoom not less than twenty minutes ago! "What! You still 'here' in Bern? —I don't see how you can stand it!"

I looked up at this gentleman with a murderous expression in my eyes. I looked up at this gentleman with a murderous expression in my eyes because on this particular day there was a melancholy humor in the air. I had just received a rejection slip from a magazine whose reader assured me that: "The rejection of your story does not necessarily reflect upon its merit, but merely means that it is not suitable to the needs of our magazine." I was spending my last sixty centimes for a beer with which to wash down that last little nuance. On top of that summer was fading. I had felt it just that day, between half-past three and four-thirty while standing on the little boardwalk overlooking the dam where the river diverts into a channel behind the Schild clothing factory and opposite the Schwellenmätteli sauna and tearoom. Down there I had wished that I were younger and that there had been more sun this summer. I had regretted the changes which red leaves, then no leaves, cold winds and snow would bring into my life. What is to become of me? I had asked myself, looking down into the frothy volumes of ice-cold blue-green water: Do I have what it takes to be a writer? . . . Do I have what it takes to jump? The water looks appealing. If only it weren't so cold! . . .

"Why don't you come home?" my mother had just written: "Your cousin has a wife, a nice job and a nice little house and a doghouse and a dog. He earns eight thousand a year now. You could easily do as well with all your education and traveling experience, etc. . . ."

Let's complicate it:

My last story wasn't very satisfactory. I had to rewrite it. But I hadn't written in a long time—about a month, perhaps two—time goes by so fast! Perhaps it was even longer than that since I had written. I had read a lot of good books and even the fact that their authors were dead afforded me no special satisfaction. Twenty times that day some contentious person, some noisy sadist, had asked me with an eerie smile, "How's the writing coming?" And I had replied:

"Oh, it's coming . . ." wondering when? how? feeling useless and ridiculous because of the clean white block of paper in my briefcase.

"Sold anything?" my well-wisher asked before I could say that I had someplace to go.

More complications:

On this particular day while my man, one of *those*, was wondering how I could stand it in Bern, I owed three months' rent and four coffees at the Rendez-vous tearoom. I had borrowed all that I dared from everyone I knew to borrow from. My friends sped by when they met me in the street. I was a little hungry. I had friends who would feed me but I could not go to them that night because I planned to go to them the following night. The pile of unpublished manuscripts at home gave me no satisfaction, nor did I enjoy reveling in the misery of Edgar Allan Poe and Mozart, a favorite pastime which I usually reserved for the gloomiest days. That day, as summer slipped into autumn, I thought of home, of my mother and father, of my youth and of my plans and ambitions. I thought of the love of a woman and of the domestic life. I had regrets. Doubts overwhelmed me. As I sipped my beer in the Bali I grasped at the last philosophical straw in the hope that it would prevent me from drowning.

Then he attacked me:

"Hi, Wince!" or "Hel-low, Wincen!" he cried above the wrangle of the piano and the glare of the gaudy lights and the nervous laughter of the décolletéed barmaid, extending a sticky hand. "What's new! I'm surprised to see *you*!" He had not seen me when he spoke to me as he was leaving the Sultan tearoom not less than twenty minutes ago. "What! You still here in Bern?—I don't see how you can stand it!"

I looked up at this gentleman with a murderous expression in my eyes. I took the measure of his weak chin, gauging the degree of determination in his harassed eyes and strained to restrain the feeling of sympathy which swelled within me, as I beheld his young, frightened face. With heartless resolution I waited for him to shift to the right or to the left—off balance. He feinted with his left:

". . . But why did you come to Bern anyhow?" grazing my chin with his right. I rolled with the punch. For what he really meant was: Why did *you* come to Bern? That is to say: Why didn't you stay in *America?* And that meant: I *know* why you didn't stay in America, poor devil! Aren't you glad to be in Bern where the people are not mean to you?

I let him have it:

"Oh, I've come to study the decadence of European culture. Look at that!" I exclaimed exultantly, pointing discreetly to a puny young man sitting on the opposite side of the bar. "Have you ever seen anything like that? a grown man drinking beer with a straw! . . . I've heard that Switzerland is one of the most primitive countries in Europe, where the cultural level of the people is the lowest possible and unthinkably decadent."

I smiled inwardly as he writhed in his seat. I did not like him, not because of himself, but because he did not like himself and because he forced me to expose that pettiness within my own nature which made me say nasty things like that. But I could not let him take me without a fight.

"Then too," I added, thinking: I will lighten up a little— "One, if he wishes to write, has to gain perspective, a distance from which to look at his country, his countrymen and himself. So in a way, you might say that I've come to Switzerland in order to establish in my own mind my identity as an American and as a black man in the western world."

"But why Switzerland? Bern, of all places!" he asks, wishing to have his ears soothed with mellifluous protestations of the Swiss democratic spirit.

"It was an accident. I could have done the typically American thing with my three thousand dollars, visited thirty-one coun-tries in fifteen days and returned home exhausted, with an armful of cheap souvenirs, which I could have bought in Macy's base-ment, knowing absolutely nothing of Europe, having seen noth-ing, absolutely nothing that I couldn't have seen had I purchased a good travel magazine and thumbed its pages in my front parlor on a dull Sunday afternoon. I could have done that, but I came to Europe to write, and in order to write you have to keep still. Besides, I thought I could learn more about Europe if I stayed in one city, got to know it very well, and lived with its people. Then, at least, I could know quite a lot about one variety of European, which might help me to understand, by comparison, some general attributes of all of them. Whether Swiss, Dutch, German, Italian or Spanish, there is a point of view, due to certain ways and thoughts which all of them have in common, which is typically European, isn't there?" He agreed that this was true, visibly relieved that the conversation had taken a more trite and yet more objective tone. "Now where else would one stay *than* Bern if he really wanted to listen to the heartbeat of Europe?"

"Come on, you're joking!" he laughed. It was a sudden, accidental laugh. There was a sparkle of pleasure in it, which pleased me, too, because up till now I had seen only a mean grimace upon his face, a frantic expression (though he was rather young, twenty-two maybe, and really a handsome fellow) in his eyes. He laughed as he laughed when he was probably four years old. Also I felt better because the conversation had taken a new turn. My own troubles faded as my thoughts quickened to the crystallization of a new human relationship. An intuitive flash illuminated my mind and I grasped at the words as they stumbled through the light and once more into the dark regions of primitive thought.

"But it's true. Switzerland is the dead center of Europe, and Bern is its capital. In the Kirchenfeld is an embassy or a legation from every major power in the world. Stand in front of the Bahnhof any day," I exclaimed with perhaps too much enthusiasm, "stand in front of the Bahnhof any day, and if two coolies in a rice paddy in upper Mongolia—provided there are rice paddies in upper Mongolia—have a quarrel, you will feel the reverberations of that argument stirring the traffic! Two hours later, when the papers come out, the details will appear in the headlines. Bulletins for housewives will appear, instructing them to gather in their ration quotas. The Red Cross will be alerted. Radical fluctuations in the stock market will jangle over the ticker-tapes. Local business prospects will soar to unprecedented heights or quiver on the brink of catastrophic depths."

He laughed like a delighted child again, and I continued, gladdened by his laughter, swept on in the current of my thought: "Do you know one thing? . . . When President Eisenhower raised the import taxes on Swiss watches, a street cleaner, a pleasant, friendly man, whom I've seen almost every day and spoken to for the past two years now, stopped me on a rainy morning in front of Radio Bern—he was shoveling a pile of horse manure, which must have been recently dropped because it was still steaming—let his shovel fall, and demanded in a most angry tone an explanation of Mr. Eisenhower's economic policy!

"'What are you talking about?' I asked him somewhat timidly because I had to speak French and I wasn't too sure of myself in that language. Then too, I was surprised by his anger, as he had always been most agreeable to me. For a moment I suspected that I had misunderstood him and that he was angry because I had carelessly dropped my pipe ashes on his nice clean sidewalk.

"'What! You don't know what Monsieur Eisenhower is doing?' he cried in a rage, looking at me as though *I* had dropped that pile of manure he had just let fall.

"'No,' I replied, 'I don't know anything about it.'

"'Don't you read the papers!'

"'No . . . I haven't read a paper in months, and politics, since the Emancipation Proclamation which freed the slaves, has never interested me.'

"He stared at me with speechless incredulity.

"'He's—he's increased the—taxes!—on *Swiss* watches!' He spoke with great difficulty, grasping his chest. I stepped closer to the old man in order to assist him should he fall. '*Everybody* knows that the Swiss watch—that the *Swiss watch*—is the *best watch in the world*! They even *admitted* it! And—and—and because the American watch manufacturers are jealous they—they want to stop the importation of Swiss watches. And it is the *Americans* who are always talking about equalizing the distribution of economic revenues throughout the world—and of helping—*helping!* the little countries. Twenty thousand people out of work! The Americans are *idiots!* They don't practice what they preach. Democracy! No *wonder* criminals like McCarthy run your country. And you!' He turned on me with rage in his kind old eyes. 'A *black* man! and *you* don't read the papers!'"

"'Well,' said I, 'I agree with you that the situation does seem a little peculiar. But since I am not in possession of the facts, I am in no position to comment upon this affair. It is also true that the Americans don't always practice what they preach. You're quite right about that. I, too, have considerable proof of that regrettable fact. And it is sure that many of the politicians and government officials certainly are idiots. But, as to the watches, the when and whyfor, I just can't say—as I don't, as I have already said, read the papers much. And I don't think I will begin soon . . .'

"That old man exclaimed against the Americans ten minutes more before I could get away. And do you think that was the end of it?" I asked the young man just as the barmaid dipped low in order to pick up a knife which had fallen from her hand, revealing the deep well between her breasts, which stood up as though they were trained to do so: "Do you think that was the end of it! It was not. I got it from my barber and from casual acquaintances whom I happened to meet on the street. Waiters and waitresses in any café or tearoom had it hot on the breath as well. For over a month it was the sole topic of much frantic conversation!

"Now look," I begged him, "I'll bet you that not one American in a thousand, unless he is directly involved, has the slightest idea that there has been an increase of import taxes on Swiss watches! I'm not saying it's a bad thing that the people are so sensitive, I simply mention it to illustrate my point, that Switzerland is an ideal spot from which to observe not only Europe, but the entire world."

"You'll probably stay and live here always, then?"

"Why should I?"

"Well, you know better than me how it is in the south. Those people must be mad down there. That's something we Europeans just don't understand: how do people think like that? Why doesn't the government, since America *claims* to be democracy, put a stop to it? *I* have nothing against a—a—Nig—a black man. He's—you're just as good as—as me—anybody . . ." He looked at me long and hard, his bewilderment designing his expression, an expression of genuine satisfaction mixed with sadistic pleasure in exposing a sore spot in my complacency. He waited.

"Oh—I can't explain it . . . Not just like that!" I staggered under the weight of the futility of "explaining" why the American government doesn't do something about it to this young man in a crowded, noisy bar over an empty glass of beer, as if the racial conflicts in America could be explained in a word! "America is so big . . ." I said, feeling that he felt that I was avoiding the issue, "and it's so different in many different places."

"But I just can't see how a man, just because he's white, can be so cruel to another man, just because he's a—because he's black."

"Well"—I sighed wearily, in the presence of what seemed to me to be his incredible naïveté, remembering the phrase that jarred my sensibility in Amsterdam, 'They made soap of my parents—' "it's not much different in Europe."

"What! Now come on—"

"No, I mean it. Do you understand the Germans of the last war? that is, those who were Nazis? Do you know how many Jews were asphyxiated or burned alive? how many bars of soap were made of them? This is not slavery as we knew it in America, of course, but that does not matter; it is, as was slavery, an example of man's inhumanity to man, as a famous English poet put it. Tell me, do you understand the English? How many colonials do you think have perished in the diamond mines? or have been slaughtered outright by the Belgians and the French? How many Poles were slaughtered by the Russians? How many Japanese were burned alive at Hiroshima? I range around freely. Choose, if you are not satisfied, an example closer to home, one that you can understand on your own terms. The Swiss mercenary armies were, I believe, is it not so? one of the most terrible armies in the world. How does the saying go, 'Where a Swiss boot has trod no flower stands'?"

"Oh well—in history—"

"Aw hell—now!" I protested: "The coal mines in Belgium, the clochards of Paris and Italy, not to mention the middle and far east and South Africa. Don't get me wrong, I don't wish to excuse America, nor do I wish to overlook the violations of humanity committed by the rest of the world. Read your history, of the crimes committed against the people during the Industrial Revolution; and earlier; choose almost any period in any country you wish. The bones of the needlessly slaughtered would build new worlds. The dust would dry up all the seas!'"

My companion looked at me thoughtfully. I drank the last spot of beer lingering in my glass. It was bitter. Besides, I didn't feel well. I hadn't got down to the point yet! Why I came to Bern was more complicated, more terrible than my personal bickerings or politics or the murder of a few million human beings.

"I've got to go," I said, noticing as I rose from my stool that he felt the tension, too.

"May I invite you for the beer?" he asked.

"It's paid," I replied.

"Well—thank you for the interesting conversation," he said.

"Oh—I thank *you!* . . ."

"Well . . ."

"So long."

We parted, feeling a little sick of ourselves. We had to pass through the same door, so I slowly paid for my beer and allowed him to leave first. I followed carefully in order not to overtake him, or bump into him in the entrance downstairs. I stepped cautiously out of the passage and turned right, and right again, toward the Bärenplatz. The sun was stuck behind the clouds which were thick and heavy. It was a cool wet day. I passed by the Grotto and glanced vacantly at the people who sat and looked vacantly at me. It will rain, I thought. Yes, it will rain before night falls . . . The way it has rained for the past two weeks . . . I passed under the central arch of the Bundeshaus and noticed that the huge chandelier in the lobby was burning. I walked down the stone steps onto the balcony, past the geranium pots. Old men and women, and women with children were sitting on gray benches, looking over the gray walls of the terrace at the Gurten, which was enshrouded in mist. It was almost hidden from sight. While the Aare river below appeared a metallic green, as it wound its way through the trees, under the Kirchenfeld Brücke and swiftly out of sight! To the left the traffic strung lazily over the Kirchenfeld bridge. English tourists, modestly arrogant, strolled past me in sandals and with ancient box cameras strapped across their shoulders. I sat down upon a bench and considered anew the problem of answering the question . . .

That night, in the darkness of my room, my pipe haloing the light bulb with a circle of red flame, I reflected that, having exhausted the more superficial arguments, I had been confronted that afternoon with the more terrible aspects of my state of mind.

I was still irritated because that young man back there in the Bali had implied that I was running away from America for racial reasons. I was further irritated by the fact that if it made me mad there was probably some truth in it. At any rate, it was certainly true that in Bern I enjoyed a freer social existence than I had ever known at home. But that was not it, not really, I reflected:

. . . Did I not come to Europe because I was fed up with the superficial life in America? to see and to write about its superficiality? in order to find myself and get at the truth about the meaning of life? This is why I came, I thought, considering again that when after three years I had not sold my stories I began to doubt. I was busy doubting when I encountered that man back there . . .

Sitting on the Bundesterrasse, looking at the Gurten sweeping up toward the sky, I had begun to wonder, feeling very strange as I did so, as though I were being born at that very moment. I began to doubt that there had really been a man back there (so completely does my imagination take control of me at times!), that he was merely an imaginative personification of my own doubt! A cooling sensation came over me with that thought, but its effect was not altogether comforting. For now I was able to admit to myself that the reason I had been disturbed by the question that fellow had asked me was the same as the reason I had not written for over two months: I was afraid that I had nothing to say, or that I had not the ability to say it. The reason for my fear was even more profound, having to do with moral values, the meaning of the universe and with my conscious relationship to God. Could that be it? I had wondered. So that's why I was so agitated when a little crud accosted me with his naif insinuations. That is why I suffer from anxiety and complexes of inferiority; from embarrassment because my heels are rundown; from hypersensitivity to a thousand and seven tiresome little illusions: because I am not clear about my relationship to God! Now this, I had thought, this throws the matter in another light!

And then I reflected before I fell asleep and as the result of a shift to a more satirical humor that it was a cold, abstract light, which, though it illumined my way, dazzled my eyes not a little! For had I not clambered onto the Bern train in the Munich station like a sinner quaking in fear of hell, wondering what I would find in the city of Bern, knowing in the bottom of my own miserable heart that I would find nothing other than myself!

Unable to keep my eyes open any longer, I fell into a troubled, nightmarish sleep. And I dreamed . . .

Bern

THE STATION WAS a queer, quaint little place with a sentimental niceness in its miniature size. Thin steel ribs nakedly supported the roof of the sheds which housed the small narrow-gauge coaches. Little yellow electric trucks burdened with bags darted here and there like noisy little poodles. The yardmen, dressed in blue smocks that looked like dresses, busied themselves with the train like fussy women occupied with the sewing machine. How unlike the huge sprawling mass of steel and marble which is the Union Station of Kansas City! I thought. And then I thought: What an awful lot of money they must have! impressed by the seriousness of the huge leather purses of red, brown and yellow leather strapped across the shoulders and dangling around the knees of the ticket collectors. The bright-colored posters advertising strange cigarettes in Schweizer-Deutsch, German and Italian, not to mention French, impressed upon me the fact that I was in a foreign country, especially in view of my recent experience with that marshmallowed tongue.

The quays and landings were teeming with people, and as I stepped from the train every one of them seemed to look at me. I straightened my tie, set my hat straight and arranged my coat. What are they looking at! I asked myself, feeling my zipper to see if my fly was open, wondering if their eyes could penetrate my raincoat even if it were. As I made my way through the crowd I remembered the few children who had stared at me in Holland and wished that I was there. Some of the people smiled and whispered as I passed, while some laughed. Are they laughing at me? . . . Why! I puzzled, stumbling up the stairs and looking confusedly this way and that. Suddenly I heard a terrible sound. I broke out in a cold sweat, which was followed by a violent churning in the pit of my stomach: I heard the word *Neger*.

My violent emotional reaction was caused by its similarity to the word "nigger," a derogatory word which has prevailed throughout the lives of all the Negroes in America since the advent of slavery. It has a history, a strong emotional life of its own. Historically, it is a word of hatred and ridicule (self-hatred and self-ridicule among Negroes) whose evolution corresponds with the history of America's national development. It is a sort of negative symbol which is employed to designate the black nobodies who comprise one tenth of the nation's population. It is a word which symbolizes the basis upon which the majority of American white men justify their greed, fear, provincialism and love of this their neighbor.

So conditioned were my ears to that sound that the nuance from "nig . . ." to "Neg . . ." was reduced to negligibility. For "nigger" had become for me a word which was more than a word. It was an animate being which I had invested with a royal if demonic distinction. It was a sort of Satan of words, with its own retinue of Satanically noble words, such as: "black," "kinky" (with which word my hair was often described: it means "knotty"), "flat nose," "thick," "lips," "thickliptips," "red," "bright," "light," "white," "dark," "darky," "blue," "blues," "sing," "happy," "dance," "childlike," and countless others, so many that I could fill volumes with examples of their spellbinding powers. I could give accounts of marvelous feats which they are able to perform, such as leaping into the foreground of my visual field from the anonymity of the printed page of a newspaper and bewitching me out of my self-control, or of dropping from the honeyed lips of the most innocent babes with a dying fall before I could apply my philosophic talisman.

In time, however, as I became accustomed to the word *Neger* —which I certainly had to do because it is universally used in

Europe—I learned not to wince when I heard it, in polite society or upon the lips of innocent ladies or gentle old women who had come to be my friends. I came to look upon it a little less rarely as an objective word, like "apple," "tuberculosis" and "Charlie," and to know that it usually meant merely "black" and little else, and that even that "little else" was of a different quality and quantity than that "little else" to which I was accustomed.

It was like leaving a world in which it is always day and suddenly arriving in another world in which it is always night, or at least, where there is an especially bright evening, an evening which is distinguishable from day, with a little dawn light, a little morning light, mixed in . . . But later it gradually became apparent, as my eyes grew accustomed to the new light, that what I had previously thought were two different worlds was really one world, the same world, but seen from a different point of view. We all, at one time or another, have had the experience—is it not so?—when looking at a map of the world of suddenly intuiting that the various forms which bound the continents look like parts of a picture, which, if one could put them together, would comprise a whole, a sphere, in which form we always see it when we study geography and astronomy. I marveled that it often takes one so long to learn, to really know, the obvious: that the world is one, for example that day is night and night is day! I further remarked with a respect which has often been wanting in me that certain rare persons have, upon surprisingly rare occasions, not only been able to perceive that lack of difference between things apparently unalike, between that which enables them to perform, occasionally, what seems to the rest of us to be miracles, such as walking upon the water as though it were solid earth, such as inducing the "dead" to rise, such as converting a universe into a few bits of canvas. They try to tell us what they see, of the peace which their vantage point affords them, they even tell us by which route they have climbed to their high place, but we seldom understand them, and are seldom appreciative of their efforts. . . . But that is as it should be, I suppose, for we can see only what we can see, hear what we can hear, though the images be mirages and the sounds but echoes in the cavernous hollows of our minds.

The explanation of the quality of sameness within the apparent differences in American racial attitudes is difficult because you who are Europeans will say, as you have already said on a number of occasions, "I just can't understand you Americans. How can you be so primitive with citizens of your own country!" This question cannot be answered in less than one hundred and sixty million volumes, each of which is not less than six thousand pages long. Even then one will only have scratched the surface!

I shall attempt to present for your consideration a historical "explanation" of this phenomenon in several pages, but it will be difficult because I will have to indulge in the grossest generalizations imaginable. I will make overstatements and understatements which will not only seem but be untenable to many Americans, notwithstanding the fact that there are few Americans who are capable of dealing with this particular aspect of American life themselves. It is no accident that the most authoritative work on this subject has been written by a Swedish sociologist who was commissioned to write his book by the American government.

But first a small emotion-conditioning aperitif in order to induce the right mood. Consider the following questions:

Are you Protestant? Catholic? Jewish? Atheist? Are you rich or poor? Could you be by any chance the son or daughter of divorced parents? Did your mother conceive you one moonlight night behind sweet-smelling lilac bushes in the park, as a result of which conception your father forgot to marry her?—are you a bastard? Are you thought to be a little stupid? and as a result are a little maladjusted? Are you too tall?—Too fat? Did your mother and father drop you on some sadistic stranger's doorstep at three A.M.? If you are a war refugee trying to become established in a foreign country, if you suffer behind the iron curtain or in front of the lace one, if you have flapping ears or buck teeth, if you're a blue-eyed boy in a brown-eyed family, I am speaking to you. Are you working as a dishwasher when you should be living the life of a millionaire? Are you the son of a minister? the insignificant son or daughter or brother or wife or husband of a great member of your family? Perhaps you are intelligent but merely lack sensibility? Or are perhaps too sensible? Are you English now that the value of the pound has diminished and the sun is beginning to set upon the British Empire? Do you have Communist worries? If you have any of these petty little problems you will be able to understand, or rather feel, what I shall say about the effects of the word "nigger" upon my consciousness. I cannot speak for the other fourteen million Negroes in the United States. And now my Historical Explanation in the guise of a Little Subjective Sociology:

The United States of America may be described, among other things, as a land of great dynamic tensions. It is a land in which practically all of its citizens are emigrants. Most of the people who emigrated to America went as nobodies and their subsequent history, and therefore the history of America, is the history of their attempts to become somebodies. As to what ideas and culture those criminals, prostitutes, fortune-hunters, speculators, religiously oppressed and land-hungry folk possessed, they brought them with them from England and France and Germany and Russia and Spain and Armenia and Ireland and Italy and anywhere else in the world one would wish to name. Are you surprised? Are you astonished to discover that they are *your* relations, only a few generations removed from the old country? You need not to be surprised: grandchildren, look at grandparents! All of those European nobodies trying hard to become somebodies in a land that belonged to the Indian and the Eskimo—that's America!

Those who arrived first had to work and fight in order to have and to hold what they got. Those who came afterwards had to fight those who previously fought and then fight again to have and to keep what they had gained. That is the story. Those who brought more with them, more money and power, had the means with which to buy men and to buy their services, so some men became "bigger" than others from the start. Some men were strong and more energetic than others, they overpowered the weak. Some men were more intelligent, strong and energetic than others, and they overpowered the merely strong and energetic. That is how things shift around and find that arrangement which sociologists call "society."

Now some of the men who were powerful saw that they could grow cotton in the south, and that there weren't enough people to work the land (people didn't come to America in those days unless they had to), so they got a practical idea, which the Greeks and many other celebrated peoples had had before, of buying slaves and making them do the work. So they bought some slaves and some they stole. They brought them over to America in ships, chained together so they would not escape, men, women and children together in the holds with iron covers on them. It was an expensive operation because so many of them died on the way and had to be thrown overboard. Once they were successfully shipped they had to be housed and fed and made strong enough to work. And they had to be watched because they would often try to escape. The owners made every effort to save their investments.

For what was a nigger good for anyway but to work. He wasn't human. You beat him and he sang; he read the Bible. You sold his mother or his wife or his child and he grinned in your face. He is an animal, a cow or a mule, and must be treated like one: that was the predominant point of view, the point of view which justified slavery in a Christian land. It permitted the slave owners to go to church on Sunday and not be disturbed because they were not really dealing with human beings.

Now the intention of *every man* is moral because man is essentially good. He cannot commit evil without deceiving himself, and he cannot deceive himself for long. The truth will come out in spite of all attempts to suppress it. In this case it came out in the most embarrassing way: from the wombs of black women there issued half-white children; from the wombs of white women—heaven help them!—issued half-black. A word made its debut in the American racial consciousness: *rape*. I imagine that more white women have been "raped" by Negroes than by any other race of men in the history of the modern world! And we know what price was paid for those embarrassing human failings . . .

Meanwhile, America was growing. The Puritans were busy burning the Quakers in the north. Everybody was fighting the Indians. You may see in any cinema in the world the story of how the white man came trading religion and culture for gold and land and human life, if one could call a savage Indian "human." America was moving west and in the south cotton was king. Any history book will tell you the story of how by Lincoln's time cotton was dethroned and the economic state of the nation was at stake, and how Mr. Lincoln made the decision to abolish slavery as an economic expedient, and what the south thought about it.

They didn't like it because it meant a complete change of life, economically and socially. In spite of the hordes of half-white and half-black children which were steadily increasing in number, a nigger was not human. What kind of government would turn niggers loose to mingle with white folks! to go to school and learn to read and write and work and pursue liberty and happiness just like a white man? Such a thing would be disastrous to the southern society. Imagine a big black grinning devil slipping his arms around your daughter's waist. No sir! They would secede first. And they did secede, we all know that, and I doubt that if you or you or you or I had been there at the time, and had been conditioned by just those circumstances, you or I would have been any different. We all are the products of our time and of those places in which we were born. It takes a strong man to be able to transcend the time and the place, and the world has seen very few of them.

Once the Negro was "free" he had a pretty difficult time competing with the white folk. He was behind in his reading and writing and arithmetic. One of his major drives then was to get an education and become somebody. There were many who were in such a hurry that they just could not wait for the place and the time to change and they perished on the way. There were many who waited in vain and they also perished on the way.

While America grew. There were wars. There were shifts of
population. The Negro, as did other minorities, developed in this
complex air with every variety of virtue and vice imaginable. He
succeeded as much as the time and the place would allow, and
some still perished on the way.

The southern American is the product of a hot climate, therefore he is passionate. His hates and loves are violent. If he burned
the Negro alive from the branch of a tree, if he dragged him
through the streets tied to the runners of a speeding automobile,
it was the expression of a love, though perverse, violent and savage, which proclaims the degree of suffering which he, too, must
have experienced. I do not mean to be absurd, we all know that
love and hate are but two aspects of the same emotion!

Therefore, the Negro's assimilation into the general culture
has been accompanied by more dramatic conflicts than those
which other American minorities have experienced. Most
Negroes come north from the south, bringing their intense, complex personalities with them. At the same time other Americans
moved from the north to the south, and from the east to the
west. All of these migrations were marked by varying degrees
of tension which resulted from the social conditioning received
in each respective area. The dynamics of American culture are
intensified even more when we consider the fact that regional
tensions are often opposed to ethnic tensions because, as I have
said, and we must not forget it, most Americans are emigrants.
America is not a country with a fixed social pattern and a pre-
dominating cultural order. It had its first president in 1789! It
has over one hundred and sixty million citizens! Therefore, it is
a land of startling contrasts. Its clashes are violent ones!

Meanwhile the country grows. There are wars, populations
shift, old emigrants fuse into the general society as new emigrants
suffer as their predecessors had suffered. The economic status
of the various minority groups becomes more stabilized. The
pioneering days are over and the new, untapped resources are
becoming fewer. They are beginning to preserve those resources,
to build up rather than tear down. Civilization and culture in the

"old world" sense comes slowly, and with it comes a relaxation of ethnic and regional tensions. One result of this process is the fact that the black folk are becoming whiter and the white folk are revealing a greater variety of physiognomy as a result of ethnic cross-fertilization. And on it goes, as long as there is a pen with which to write it down. . . .

I stood under the marquee of the station and breathed deeply of the cool wet air. As my body relaxed I became aware of the unique scene before my eyes. For some minutes I had been staring at the facade of the luxurious Schweizerhof Hotel, watching the blue train pull up to the little station in front of it and finally depart for a place called Zollikofen, which I almost broke my tongue trying to pronounce. A fine rain sprayed the air and many people swarmed around with umbrellas, red, blue, white, black. A line of glistening taxis ranged in front of the newshawk near the corner in a glistening black cape. He wore a hard round black hat with a flat top and a patent-leather bill and a bright yellow band with printing in large black letters around the crown. Now and again volleys of unintelligible words issued from his mouth with a monotonous, droning sound. It sounded like *Berner Togg Slopp!* . . . *Berner Togg Slopp!* . . . Then I noticed that the taxis were Chryslers and Dodges, and I was pleased to see something which was familiar to me. Presently I noticed that there were many bright-colored flags hanging about, some with black or brown bears with red lapping tongues and red-tipped genitals sticking out against a bright yellow background, looking rather harmless and sort of funny, like toys meant for children, but apparently taken quite seriously, since they were draped upon what seemed to me to have been the most serious facades I had yet seen in Europe. Had it not been for the gray-grim attitude of the church standing in the square on the right they might have given the town a festive air.

After some minutes I noticed an astonishingly pretty girl who came out of the station and got into a taxi. As the taxi pulled away it occurred to me that I should dispose of my trunk and call my friends. They were legation folk who lived in a quarter of Bern which I was later to know as the Kirchenfeld. My friend back home at whose house I had met them briefly in 1947 had told me that they had lived in Bern without meeting any Swiss people. They had complained of loneliness in their letters. That was why it was suggested that I visit them. So I called them out of a comfortable feeling of equality, for I was lonely, too—and frightened.

"Oh!—Who? . . . So. Where are you? At the station. How nice . . . The baby's been ill and we're all very tired because we've had to entertain so many Americans lately. They all seem to be passing through at once. We're sorry we can't invite you to stay with us for a while—but there's no room just now. The house is in a mess. We're not quite settled from moving yet. We're just moving from our old apartment into a new one—a much! nicer one. But perhaps we could find time to have supper together, at least. Fine! Would that be all right with you? Fine! Now let me see, you're at the station! I'll have to get the car and   Oh, all right, good-bye. See you in a few minutes . . ."

She hung up the receiver. I had said three words! It was all settled before I had a chance to say, "Yes," "No," or "Maybe so!" Exactly fifteen minutes later the lady, rain-coated and out of breath, pulled up in front of the station, apologizing profusely for not having come sooner and because Mr. X, her husband (one cannot be too careful about disclosing the names of Embassy personnel) couldn't come to meet me. "What with the Russ Eh . . . He has so much to do these days," she said with an embarrassed, confidential air. "But you'll see him soon, at supper this evening. We're going to eat at a real quaint restaurant. You'll like it. One that's typically Swiss. You'll see. The food is good—and it's not too expensive." She smiled prettily and impersonally, turning her curly head to one side as she zoomed through the misty streets as though hers was the only car in the universe.

We drove directly to their home. It was in a pleasant, flower-spangled neighborhood with a large spacious wood nearby. Once there she gave me a drink and introduced me to the children, a boy of three named Paul and a baby of eight months named

Morty. They were quite friendly and we played amiably together while their mother dressed. Shortly after seven my host arrived. He was tall, intelligent, tired and very friendly.

When everyone was dressed and the maid had put the children to bed we drove to the Kornhaus Keller, a former grain market building where we dined sumptuously on grilled pork chops and boiled vegetables. We had a green salad, coffee and I smoked an excellent Dannemann cigar which costs one franc thirty. The meal was garnished with pleasant reminiscences of America and speculations about my future as a writer. After dinner we drove around the town. The only impression of the town which I remember is that the streets were very narrow and old and strange. An hour or so after nightfall we went dancing at a club called the Chikito, where there was a floorshow and a disturbing number of pretty women. When we finally left it was too late for me to find a hotel room so my host and hostess invited me to spend the night with them, promising to help me find a room on the following day.

Looking for a Room

ON THE FOLLOWING day all the rooms were full. All of them, so they *said*, but I did not believe them. They smiled when they refused me. I could not accuse them of being discourteous. But I had not the slightest doubt that they were merely being prejudiced in the European manner. Strangely, London not America came to mind when I reflected upon the Bernese manner of refusing me. I had been there during the war. A hotel clerk in that great city—in fact, several of them—had informed me that there was no room in the same cold—but infinitely colder—vulgarly courteous manner, and in impeccable English. Though the Bernese hotel clerk's English was not always impeccable, was sometimes incomprehensible, his refusal was equally effective—especially in my state of mind!

What can you say to a man when he tells you nicely that he has no room, even if you would swear that he is lying? If you are a black man from Missouri! Now when you are scowled at, or even thrown out bodily (that is, if you would be ridiculous enough to enter a white hotel in Kansas City!) you can have the satisfaction of being angry, or of indulging in self-pity, or of joining another interracial organization. But when you are rejected courteously, making it a breach of honor not to assume that your fellowman is dealing honestly with you, why there is nothing you can do except freeze in the cold shades of doubt. However, the result in either case is just the same: you are out, you have no place to live. It rains just as hard, dust blows, it hails —and night falls . . .

"But—it's true!" my hostess declared. "The town probably is full-up because tomorrow is Bern's Independence Day. Six hundred years ago Bern joined the confederation. There's going to be a big parade. I should have thought of that." Though I was still somewhat skeptical, I had to believe her because she and her husband were Americans. They were white, but still they knew how things were back home. They could imagine a little how I felt. They advised me to wait a few days and invited me to remain at their house at least until the celebration was over.

"You came at a good time!" said my hostess as we sat down to supper on the eve of the celebration. "We have a friend who has an apartment in the Gerechtigkeitsgasse. The window looks right down on everything. We can see it from there. That's where the important parades usually begin. It's one of the town's oldest streets."

It must be pretty big to keep me out of a room, I thought. I was still a little skeptical when I went to bed. I looked through the window into the night sky. The moon shone brightly. I thought of the events which had occurred during the day. This celebration *must* be important, I thought, . . . if the town really is full-up and the thing really does happen something will have to be changed in the world! A door will open and I will *have* to go through it! . . . A cool, fearful shiver ran up my spine. I pulled the covers around my neck and closed my eyes on the moon . . .

The following day was fair. The clouds were fluted with silver bangles. Bright banners waved from every facade as we drove through the excited town. Bright green boxes crowded with geraniums filled the sills of all the windows along the main street from the Bahnhofplatz to the Gerechtigkeitsgasse. Markers rerouted the traffic with the aid of white-gloved traffic policemen.

"The town's really turned out!" said my host. His oldest son, Paul, peered out of the windows excitedly, shouting to us to look at this! look at that! His mother held his sleepy-eyed brother up to see. The sidewalks were bulging with people. Every shop and hotel window was full of out-thrust heads, like bunches of pink flowers! After many twistings and turnings down special routes we finally contrived to park about eight blocks from the apartment. From there we made our way on foot through the crowd of jostling people.

There were little Bernese flags in every hand and buttons with bears on them in every buttonhole. Men, women and children in bright historic costumes could be seen walking in the direction of the old town. Gleaming surfaces of polished boots, spurs and musical instruments flickered in the sun through holes in the crowd like sunlight flickering on wet leaves. Strange, wild discordant notes shrieked through the air. Babies screamed. Sighs of surprise rippled through the crowd as some fragmentary mystery of the parade passed before their eyes: an Empire carriage, a medieval knight in mail, a distinguished nineteenth-century lady burdened with roses!

We lost little Paul twice on the way before we discovered that it was cheaper to carry him on our shoulders. His father and I took turns. He was delighted. When we finally reached the apartment and climbed the several flights of stairs we were exhausted but Morty, the baby, was fast asleep in his mother's arms.

"Have a drink!" someone shouted as we entered. There were many people in the room, standing before all the available windows, which made it difficult for my host to introduce me to everyone. I smiled a greeting a half-dozen times and shook a few hands, answering, as I did so, a few general questions. Gradually I learned that all the people in the room worked at the legation and knew each other. The room was in an uproar, men, women, children, two dogs and a Persian cat, all talking at once. In fact, they were so busy talking that they almost missed the parade. They would have missed it had not a heretofore anonymous child yelled:

"Look everybody—it's started!" The name of the hero who uttered that famous cry was Bobby.

I shall have reason to be grateful to him for generations to come, for his memorable words catapulted me into another world. I should say two worlds: the first was the world in which all the hotel rooms were *actually* full, and the second was the world of the historic past. For I beheld from the window in the form of a pageant the history of the city of Bern. It unwound before my eyes like a bright parti-colored ribbon! There were knights in armor on bold, prancing steeds majestically advancing through a fairyland of heraldic banners! It was like a childhood memory stepping out of the pages of King Arthur. The feudal world passed in review: peasants dressed in Bernese costumes with laced velvet bodices ribbed with heavy chords of embossed silver, with ornate bonnets fluted with lace and white cotton stockings, carrying baskets of bread and grain—the harvests of the fields—and flagons of wine in their ruddy arms. Proud burghers rode by in luxurious carriages drawn by two, four or six perfect horses, spilling with noble ladies with heaving breasts cradled in fair arms filled with flowers! It was a sight to be enjoyed. Craftsmen from numerous guilds plied their venerable arts on huge wooden wagons floored with straw and drawn by powerful dray horses that moved with the slow cumbersome grace of elephants. They were followed by a general assemblage of characteristic folk from each period in the nation's history. And the civil scene was counterpointed by the military scene. The martiality of the soldiers' stride called to mind the fearless Redcoats who stormed Bunker Hill. How fantastically did they march down the narrow cobblestoned, fountain-strewn streets— each fountain with a colorful statue carved in wood, portraying some heraldic hero, mythological or biblical character—of the old quarter of town!

It was one of the oldest towns I had ever seen, with the exception of the one in Britain, where I looked out toward France from a fragment of the old wall, part of which was a tower from which the Battle of Hastings was fought; except perhaps the little fishing village of Barfleur, in which an old cathedral stood in the rain ten years ago and from which Eisenhower's famous bloody attack upon Germany was launched in 1943. Nevertheless, this old town with its pageant representing the life of a nation, gleaming on a bright summer day, appeared to me in many a breathless moment to have been a chapter torn from the same old book, which is the history of Europe.

What I noticed in particular (it made a tremendous impression upon me) was that the people who participated in the pageant looked so natural in their armor and mail, wielding their pickaxes, shields clapped tight in the crooks of their elbows. This was no mere theatrical staging. The faces and attitudes of the people resembled to an unnerving degree the faces which I had seen in illustrated history books and in historical museums. The air of reality given by the spectacle was intensified even more by the atmosphere of the old town itself: narrow streets, low, stony, heavy, somber with a dank, musty defensive mien.

It was frightening and mysterious, as well as bright and gay. Its brightness and gaiety gave accent to the underlying mystery. Of course, it may have been due to my imagination, but I caught the suggestion in the air that the past could reanimate us and cajole us into parodying ourselves. An irony consists in the fact, I thought, that we feel that we are different from our forefathers, we who watched from the windows over the heads of the geraniums and through the ornate bars of old iron gates. We behold the spectacle as though we are visitors in a museum, or like nursemaids with the children crowded around us, thumbing through the fable book of time which we hold upon our knees. As we turn its pages we are saddened by an era that seems, in retrospect, beautiful and sure. We are saddened by the loss of dignity—when we dare a comparison of the past with the present—fostered by mass living and by the apparent impotence of senile gods of fashion and form . . . We are proud of our gains, though, of our "modernity," as we gaze at the book, proud that we have withstood the changes of time and scene. We are thankful that there is still (or is that only an illusion!) a traceable line—how quickly it fades!—from "then" till "now". . . .

Before I could complete my thought it was all over! The pageant broke up into a million fragments, as though a huge stone had dropped quietly into the sea whose fluid colors and forms rippled out to the far-flung boundaries of that flow of movement which is time, only to converge upon the still point from which the stone dropped—to be witnessed by other eyes . . .

The next day one would not have dreamed, had he glanced into the street, that such a colossal pageant had been held only the day before. The costumes were all put back into their boxes and the boxes stored in the attics, and all the proud horses had ridden away.

"Do you have a room?" I asked the clerk.

"Why, yes, sir. What sort of room would you like?" The young man smiled pleasantly, pen in hand, ready to ratify my fearful desire.

And so on June 21st, in the Year of Our Lord, 1953, Vincent O. Carter, did sign the register of the Adler Hotel (the Eagle) in the very street through which the prancing steeds had borne the armored knights. The street was the Gerechtigkeitsgasse, which means Street of Justice!

Still Looking for a Room and Why

I HAD TO find a private room because living at the Adler, though comfortable enough and relatively cheap, was too expensive for an extended stay. The room cost about eight francs a day, and then I had to eat. I had perhaps twenty-five hundred dollars, but I had come to stay for an indefinite period. Every time I had to tear one of those traveler's checks out of the little black imitation-leather folder the Atlantic Ocean seemed to get twice as wide, fathoms deeper and more perilous than it must have seemed even to Columbus on his first cruise. How many times had I imagined myself stranded upon a salt-eaten raft in midocean, fishing my fare from the deep with frayed shoestrings, the greedy fishes devouring them as an entree to that even more delectable morsel which was myself—literally swimming, manuscripts, typewriter and all, in the gut of some supercilious fish! I had to find a room and a cheap one in which I could cook. It was due to this necessity, I am happy to say, because of the opportunity it provides me of investing this chapter with fascinating lore, that I learned of a few current Swiss impressions of Negroes.

Again I prevailed upon my host and hostess to aid me in my desperate quest. They had the car and as Mr. X was usually busy it fell to my hostess's lot to drive me around town in search of rooms. Upon her advice I placed a want ad in the *Anzeiger*, a very convenient paper devoted to that purpose, and visited the Wohnungsamt, a sort of city house-locating bureau where I got a list of available houses. We spent the first day visiting them but without success. Then two days later I awoke from a deep sleep overwhelmed with letters from a host of aspirant landlords.

"What did I tell you!" my hostess exclaimed, chiding me for my skepticism, while I humbly admitted that I was probably all wrong about racial prejudice in Bern.

"It is very hard to overcome the effects of experiences which one has had during a lifetime—overnight!" I apologized.

All the letters were written in German. Of course, I had not the slightest idea what they said, so Mrs. X translated them and helped me to select the most likely prospects. We started at eight o'clock that morning, and by noon the first ten of the most likely prospects had first opened the door with an anxious smile, but then upon seeing me, had fallen back a pace or two in a mild state of shock. Some had looked, as they screamed for help, this way and that, while others convulsively slammed the door in my face, while I smiled stupidly and waited wherever it was possible for the bolder but temporarily unconscious ones to recover. I had tried to tell them what I wanted, but of course, not all of them spoke English, though a surprising number did. But those who didn't were even more confused by my French. And when Mrs. X came to my aid with the explanation of my presence in flawless Bern-Deutsch, they suffered another shock, it being obvious that she, too, was a foreigner. They simply waved their hands or shut the door, mumbling incomprehensible words in a confused state of mind.

After much perseverance we had managed to push beyond a half-dozen thresholds into the deep interiors of those sacred strongholds of Bernese domestic life. The rooms were semi-private, that is, adjoined to the landlord's part of the house by a locked door draped with a curtain and buttressed with some heavy and forbidding piece of furniture. For this reason, I gathered, the mere thought of living in such close proximity to a strange-looking black man seemed absolutely out of the question.

Nor did we find the situation any better in the Länggasse quarter, nor in the part of the city known as the Breitenrain. The old town was out of the question, apartments there being continually in demand because of the splendid view of the Aare which it afforded to the south, and because it is one of the oldest and most beautiful parts of the city. I found nothing in Muri either. After a while the search became rather tedious. With some of the ladies (apparently the husbands left such tasks to their wives) I got as far as explaining what I did as a profession. They usually wished to be assured that I was financially able to meet my obligations. To the question Do you work? I usually replied, "Yes."

"What do you do?" one middle-aged lady with tired eyes and nervous hands wanted to know.

"Write," I said.

"Write what?"

"Stories . . ."

"Oh . . ." Followed by a pause during which she smiled weakly. As the silence continued a profoundly puzzled expression crept into the lady's face, and she began to study the sunlight falling upon the geranium pots. Everyone had geranium pots. And then she drew a thoughtful breath and asked: "But, what do you *do!*"

I smiled weakly, as a profoundly puzzled expression crept into my face, followed by a deep, studied silence in which I contemplated the light falling upon the geranium pots. Seconds later we both regretted that the room was not really available after all, because there had been a couple, with a baby, in fact . . . "And . . . if you wish to leave your name—or call back later—much later—at twelve or at seven—we will see . . . However, I'm not sure . . . But then—we will see . . ."

One charming lady of forty-three with a roving eye had sighed and regretted deeply that:

"It's *impossible*—impossible, you see, to rent the room to—so young a man . . . I am alone in the house. I have a daughter and, well, I have to be careful. It is exceedingly difficult for a woman who is alone!" blushing coyly.

Just then the daughter, a rather long, lean, dank thing, appeared in the door, on cue, to dramatize the difficulty.

"You are quite right," I said to the poor mother as sympathetically as I could. "I see now," looking at her daughter with a short sweeping glance, "that it really is difficult—as you say. I wish you and your daughter the best of luck."

I'll never get a room, I thought.

But shortly after thinking this thought a happy incident occurred through which I acquired some pertinent and very valuable information. For I made the acquaintance of a very interesting young man who was just beginning his career at Radio Bern, after having had several fascinating failures in other occupations, as a rich student, a prodigal son, a bartender, a kept man, a pimp, a promoter for the Red Cross! secretary to one of the city's most prominent sporting clubs, and, oh, heaven knows what else. Nor can I pause here to reveal the details of the adventures which I have suggested, having already said more than discretion permits. At the time of our meeting this young man had just acquired a very charming girlfriend to whom he later became engaged, and from whom I learned the following facts when I put to her, upon a propitious occasion, the question:

"Why won't the people give me a room?"

"Because you're different," was the English equivalent of what I think she said in Bern-Deutsch, German and French, with a word of monosyllabic English thrown in here and there.

"It's racial prejudice!" I objected.

"It's what?"

"It's—it's because they don't like Negroes!"

"No, it isn't that . . . It's just that the people have never had an experience with a black man before. They think Africans are—"

"Americans!"

"Dangerous. The girls are just simply afraid. They are—many of them—attracted to you, and would like to be with you—probably—if they had the courage—"

"But I didn't want to sleep with them, I simply wanted a room!"

"That is worse. Sleeping with them would have been easier. Because if they rented you a room they would have to worry about what the neighbors would think. But if they slept with you they could slip you out the back entrance after dark. They are afraid of everything—anything—which is different from what they have known. If you had two heads it would be the same."

"For me, too! I'm not a freak!" I insisted a little too heatedly, for I noticed that she moved back slightly when I unconsciously raised my voice. Her fingers trembled and she bit her lip nervously.

"You—know what I mean . . ." she replied apologetically.

"I think so. You mean I'm like a man with two heads."

"Yes!—No!" she exclaimed, stammering now, her English stumbling into French. "Suppose—suppose you were an Eskimo—or an Indian—"

"I'd leave my seal or my buffalo outside—but I'd *still need a room!*"

"Be serious!" she exclaimed in perfect English, and I wondered to whom she had had the occasion to make that admonition.

"I *am* serious!" I replied, in a rage, becoming even more enraged because she didn't, couldn't—nor could anyone, it seemed—realize just how serious I was. She didn't know how many doorbells I had rung, nor how many silly questions I had answered. Besides, there was one other thing, which I shall interrupt this chapter to mention in a special chapter, because it is so important to the appreciation of my state of mind at this time:

EVERYBODY, Men, Women, Children, Dogs,
Cats, and Other Animals, Wild and Domestic,
Looked at Me—ALL the Time!

Continuation of the Little Dialogue Interrupted by the Previous Chapter

"I AM SERIOUS!" I had said.

"Well . . . there *are* stories . . . she said reluctantly, lowering her pretty eyes, sadly, and, at last I saw that she had been holding this bit back in order to spare my feelings.

"Ah ha!" I gasped. "Could there be, after all, a little racial prejudice lurking in the corner?"

"Nig—Negroes—people think, are primitive. There are always pictures in the papers. Showing them as, well, they steal . . . And murderers. They're—well—not educated. Like children, and . . ."

"And . . ."

"Now don't get angry."

"Oh, *I'm* not angry . . ." I whispered hoarsely, suddenly discovering that my voice had abandoned me, wiping the flecks of foam from the corners of my mouth. I regretted the terrible impression I must have been making because I could not stop my eyes from whirling around in my head, no more than I could silence the flames which roared as they shot from my expanded nostrils. "And . . ." pressing her gently to continue.

"Dan-gerous. Only last year there was a process"—by which she meant "trial"—"against a—a—"

"Nee—gro!"

"He was with a girl . . ."

"Rape, no doubt," I exclaimed, but then decided to be objective, asking, "What—did he do?"

"He bit her."

"What!"

"He bit her—here," she said, overpowered by embarrassment, pointing modestly in the general direction of her breast.

"He was in court for that!"

"He bit it off."

"What!" At first I thought she meant the whole breast, but my friend, who was a man of the world, explained that she merely meant the nipple. He had to explain it, because this delicate creature who now covered her own lovely breasts with a jacket flap was so overcome with shame that she couldn't look at us, let alone speak, for several minutes; during which time I agreed that, in this case, the young lady's indignation seemed justified, but that it was a pity that such a reputedly pleasant experience should have ended so painfully.

There were numerous occasions upon which extraordinary manifestations of the negroid temperament had been in evidence, they admitted, more openly now that I seemed less dangerous. Women were known to have died under its powerful influence. One, it seemed, a girl with a fairly strong constitution (she had been known, according to the testimony of her aged father, a wealthy peasant, to milk a hundred cows and chop a cord of wood before breakfast, and then to do a good day's work) had perished in the sinful act, due to the killing excitability of what was apparently an excessive pleasure. The judges had been astonished, she said, by the witnesses' accounts of the peaceful smile which was reported to have been upon her face.

"Ecstatic!" the papers quoted the testimony of the most intelligible witness, "as though she had expired while under the influence of a sublime experience."

"Religious!" said another witness, a doctor, who had performed the examination, the result of which was he proclaimed her dead.

"Martyrs," the local priest testified, "in the days of old,

were often said to have died with that serenity and purity of expression, which I can only imagine by comparing them to this blessed child; though," the good man added, "though their parting attitudes were, no doubt, somewhat different."

At this point I was more astounded by the memory of my friend's girl than by the incredible incidents which she recounted. How her cheeks flushed, how her eyes flashed as she told it! Though I have paused to interrupt her recital with an observation of my own, you must not think that the young lady paused. In fact, it appeared as though she were just getting started. However, I will omit her full account (she spoke for at least seven hours without taking a breath) and relate merely the high points of the last case of which she spoke upon this occasion.

It was that of the dual death of an unknown black man and a Swiss girl. The scene was the little village of Brienz, I think, though I am not altogether certain, it being several years now since I heard of that ill-fated ending suffered by the two star-crossed lovers in the heat—in the very hell—of their passion. It appeared to the coroners that these lovers, in their intense excitement, had literally and lovingly scratched each other to death. They were discovered locked in a bloody and fatal embrace.

"They might have lived to love again," she remembered the examiner had said in the account of the incident which she read, "had either of them been willing to release his grip." Apparently they had scratched in absolute ignorance of their serious condition.

Their discovery was due to the following accident, the details of which I shall relate to you, according to the information given to me by the enthusiastic lady:

"They were only discovered then," she declared heatedly, having lost all signs of her former shyness, "because the neighbors on the floor below noticed a large crimson pool on their freshly painted ceiling. And when the plaster began to crack, and large drops of blood began to drip into the baby's milk, they thought that they should investigate. They called the police and told them about it; and the police went up there and knocked on the door.

No one answered. They pressed their ears to the door and heard sighs and groans and what sounded like the feeble whine of bed quoits. They knocked louder, and this time when there was no response, they broke the door down. They discovered the inseparable couple locked, as I said, in a fatal embrace, but not quite dead. There might still be time, one of the officers had thought— he wrote it down in his official report, which was freely referred to by all the papers—but they could not be separated. Seven strong men tried for the best part of three hours to prize them apart, and failed. They had to be rushed to the hospital on a single stretcher. Due to lacerations of the lips, neck, back, hips, thighs, legs and soles of the feet, they had lost too much blood to be aided by a transfusion. There was a very sad and very discreet account of the funeral in all the leading weeklies of Europe.

"Didn't you read about it in Africa!" she interrupted her narrative to ask; to which I replied that I seldom read the A-m-e-r-i-c-a-n papers, nor any other papers, for that matter. So she finished her story by adding, "And this case became deeply impressed upon the people's minds. It remains, till this very day, one of the strangest in the annals of Swiss criminal history. Is it any wonder that you have trouble getting a room?" She said that she had recently read that a certain well-known Swiss writer had begun to write a new version of Shakespeare's *Othello*, which was to be based upon this incident, and finally, that a famous composer, also one of her countrymen, was devoting his creative powers to setting the theme to music.

Our session soon broke up after that, and I excused myself because I had an appointment to look at a room. I thanked them heartily for the information they had given me, and told them that I would try to use it to my advantage in the future.

Some General Changes in My Attitude
As a Result of My Preliminary Experiences
with the Bernese People

I WAS FORCED to take into consideration the many rooms which I might have rented, but which I had to refuse either because they were too expensive or because the regulations of the house were inconvenient to such a man as myself, a bachelor, a writer with living habits which, though I did not consider them unusual in any way, were looked upon by the ladies who rented rooms as extraordinary, indeed! For instance, I liked to sleep until various odd hours of the night or day and take hot baths, during which I sang at the top of my voice any song which came into my head—for hours at a time. Furthermore, I insisted upon coming and going as I pleased, with anyone whom I might happen to choose, promising, of course, to make due allowances for the convenience of my neighbors. But as the walls of most of the houses were very thin, my coming and going as I pleased with whomever I might have chosen would have been very difficult, if not impossible, not to mention shocking to the apparently delicate ladies, all of whom insisted upon "serious," quiet young men who were expected to live, I gathered, like noiseless machines!

This state of affairs was at times discouraging. And yet, the more I visited Bernese homes in search of rooms, the more I learned to sympathize with those unfortunate persons who had to refuse me, appreciating the need which must have driven them to such a rash expedient. For who would have strangers intruding upon their privacy if they could avoid it? I saw the humiliating irony in my being able to alleviate that need, as well as my own, on the one hand, and of being, by the very fact of my existence, an obstruction to its alleviation on the other.

I now approached the ladies with an attitude of marked humility, and piety, as well, because against my will I confronted them with terrible fears and doubts which had profound, far-reaching moral implications in their lives. I soon realized that I wasn't just *Der Neger*. I was the symbol of a dangerous disturbance, crashing in upon them from the vast, unpredictable world outside. I began to feel after a time the reverberations of a tacit appeal for tranquillity in the air. In fact, their first recommendation in favor of a room was usually that it was quiet, which was to me no recommendation at all because I had never been aware of such a great need of it. The silence of the atmosphere of the town from the very beginning had imposed upon my spontaneous nature a careful, whispering, soft-stepping attitude, which was tedious, to say the least!

I came from a noisy, jostling town where the people sing in the streets, where friend shouts to friend from one side to the other and stranger speaks to stranger—with or without a formal introduction. They fight when they are angry, work and sweat naked to the waist, and complain because the boss is mean. They crush each other to death under the skidding wheels of careening autos and catch the streetcars on the run. Where I live the streets are dark, the police travel in twos and fours and death is a twenty-four-hour inevitability. Ahem! . . .

Finally I realized that I was not in Kansas City. I adopted a "serious attitude" and tried to make myself look as small and as negligible as possible, always proffering my friendliest smile, employing every wile at my disposal to communicate the impression that I was harmless. I now said that my occupation was that of a student and that I also wrote. I strove to discourage the more decadent expressions from my face, regarding the women as though they were nuns, with a pious mien, rejecting the straightforward appraisal of their more pointed virtues for the hyperdiscreet, oblique glance, ostensibly aimed at the hem of the curtain or the border of the rug.

I also polished up on my theoretical work, as a result of which I made the following general observations concerning initial intercultural experiences:

They are characterized by intermittent clashes of opposing provincialisms: the way one does it "over here" as compared to the way one does it "back home," by the comparison of the familiar to the unfamiliar, which usually results in almost universal condemnation of the latter in favor of the former. Thus, even for those who never leave home, the past—let us say—is enshrouded in an aura of rosy magic, while the present is tolerated as a tedious experience which must be endured in the ominous shadows of a doubtful future. That little distinction between the way we do it, as compared to the way of *our neighbors*, may well make them as foreign to us as any foreigner—a thousand or ten thousand miles away—could be.

I further observed that adjustment to the new environment will depend upon the strength of one's character, and upon the degree to which the new environment resists that character. To besiege a city single-handed is virtually impossible at the first onslaught, if not altogether impossible; at any rate, it takes longer than a day; just how long depending upon how long it takes one to "succeed," by which is usually meant in most societies of the modern world, earning money, paying one's own way, as well as conducting oneself in a manner which is generally respected by one's neighbors.

Thus, in *The Odyssey* do we find the wandering Ulysses, time after time, when thrust upon some foreign shore, invited by his host to nourishment and fresh raiment for his weary body, and asked to tell his story, from what land he comes and who is his king, of the deeds he has committed and with what spirit he has committed them. And finally he is invited to participate in the sporting events of the land by which a man is judged. He is pitted against the flowering youth of the nation, in order to determine whether his valor by word verifies his valor by deed. And if the stranger is victorious he is, indeed, a hero, and he is feted accordingly. Even should he fail, but valiantly, he is accepted as a bona fide member of the society:

Now, as a result of this hard-won wisdom, I acquired a room in the Thunstrasse.

What Happened at the Thunstrasse

THE OLD WITCH, my landlady, was "spinning," which means in Bern-Deutsch, "slightly off her rocker." She charged me one hundred and ten francs—much too much—for a rather agreeable front room with two sizable windows overlooking the Helvetiaplatz and the historical museum and with cooking privileges. I had to pay one franc-fifty extra for baths and twenty centimes for each telephone call. There was no running water in the room and the toilet was in the hall. And it soon became clear to me that she did not want me to cook—she pulled a wry face every time I did so, so I gave it up. On top of that I had to pay—I forget how much—for the repair of the gas heater in the bathroom (I broke it all right, I admit that, but it could so easily have been avoided had she but explained its mechanism adequately), which was adjoined to the kitchen on one side and to her room on the other by a couple of enameled, securely locked doors. Since she was always either in her room or in the kitchen she could hear every splash I made! Needless to say, singing under such circumstances was out of the question. Nor could I afford to bathe very often at those prices. To make it a little more tedious she requested that I bathe at stipulated hours and that I inform her in advance each time I ventured to perform this operation.

And I did not dare to make a noise in my own room, nor upon entering or leaving the apartment, so quiet, so funereally quiet was the atmosphere. There the walls were also very thin, permitting one to hear the slightest sound!

The lady appeared to be sixty-three years old, strong and well preserved, except for a nervous twitch of her mouth. She had a large, sensitive, bony face with thin skin. Her eyes were water-blue and tired and they looked as though they had not been closed in years. When her face was quiet it had a frightened child's expression. But it was seldom quiet, her lips mumbled perpetually and her expression was that of one who winced from the pain of invisible blows dealt by merciless invisible hands.

From the neighbors I learned that this lady had been a widow for more than twenty-five years, and that she was known to be very nervous and suspicious, having had difficulties with her roomers throughout the years. I myself had observed that she seemed deathly afraid of me and appeared to be forever on the verge of flight whenever I came near her, though she very often —which was most shocking to me—flounced through the house in thin pajamas, bare-footed and breathless. I sometimes felt that renting me the room had been for this unhappy woman a perilous adventure.

To my surprise it was in this asylum for the aged, libidinously neglected, that I wrote my first three stories, one right after the other, though I could never type at night, the clack clack clack of my typewriter resounding so loudly throughout the building that even I was disturbed by the noise! Therefore, it will not be surprising to you when I tell you that I was pretty tired of this old woman by the time the weather cooled, and that I decided to move. As a result of this decision I was soon to experience real domestic life with a Swiss family, and under pleasanter if not equally complicated circumstances. But there had been one beautiful result of my moving from the Adler Hotel to the Thunstrasse: I discovered the Kirchenfeld.

The Kirchenfeld

Is ONE OF the most beautiful quarters of Bern. It is not steeped and stilted in age and aristocratic tradition like the Junkerngasse in the oldest quarter of Bern, but it is where the embassies are housed and where luxurious villas abound, within whose walls precious things from all over the world abide, for the Bernese are great collectors. It is the quarter where one finds the Kunsthalle (Art Museum) and the Natur-Historisches Museum (Museum of Natural History) and the Landes-Bibliothek (State Library) and the Gymnasium, which is equivalent to our junior college: just a few minutes from the center of town, which is marked by the Zeitglocken, the site of the city's oldest clock tower, by way of the Kirchenfeld Brücke (bridge).

Toss a leaf or a burning cigarette over its rail and watch its airy flight many feet down until it finally comes to rest upon the surface of the swiftly flowing Aare, a thin emerald river which traces a serpentine path through the geographical center of town, skirting the fringe of the Kirchenfeld up past the Tier (animal) Park where the children play among the animals and flowers, while the mothers sit and knit or stroll in the sun when there is sun or watch with anxious eyes the soft feathery hair of merry children in flight! as the teeter-totter rises and falls in the air, reverberant with exclamations of surprise; where the river path is lined with silver birches whose leaves rustle in the slightest wind like a hundred thousand gentle hands clapping, spilling luminous shades of green and white into the air. Oh, I could wax lyrical over this quarter if I possessed the gift, for it was the home of many a peaceful hour.

Most of all I enjoyed the bridge, the entrance of which I could see from the old lady's window. There was nothing special about that old bridge from the point of view of construction. It was supported by three large stone piles, which in turn supported three beautiful steel arches. But that was all, just a bridge. Perhaps I liked it so much because it was the first thing I learned to like in the city, and because I had to cross it so often, going or coming from town, meeting faces which I learned to recognize and feel comfortable with, though they were strange. Then again, I suppose I liked it because there are no nice friendly little bridges in Kansas City, stretching over a clean emerald river. In Kansas City there is only the viaduct, thrusting its mighty body of steel-ribbed concrete over the muddy Missouri River like a grotesque umbilical cord, but nonetheless beautiful, connecting the two Kansas Cities. Factories with neon lights squat beneath it, and the wind carries the low of stalled cattle and the strong smell of hogs, waiting for slaughter and slaughtered, to the nostrils of passers-by. Over its four lanes cars stream endlessly and dangerously in droves, and few pedestrians have the courage to brave its three and a half miles in scorching sun or freezing wind.

However, it is a grand sight, our big bridge, a glorious one in its way, but it is not the same, nor is it similar to this little Bernese bridge—it also has its grandeur—which conducts one from the Kirchenfeld to the town of Bern.

From this wondrous bridge, on special nights, the steeple of the Münster cathedral gleams white against an intensely blue evening—looking like a tower of sculptured frost! while below, a strip of blue-green foam rushes through the little dam, which diverts the main channel of the river into a power station just below the Schwellenmätteli restaurant where on one side, which is parallel to the bridge, one can look directly down upon the bowling court and upon the heads of Italians and Swiss-Italians, aiming their wooden balls with infinite care down the earthen alleys flooded with light.

In the direction of town one sees when looking a hundred feet higher on the same side of the bridge the terrace of the Casino with its velvet-curtained windows and huge crystal chandeliers, dropping like jewels from their vortexes, contrasting the soft patterns of orange light illuminating the green-topped tables, from which tables evening visitors look out over the little valley, sloping up from the shores of the river or into the interior of the dance hall where an orchestra is playing: never so grand a sight as when seen from the bridge at night!—from which, on the other side, looking down, one sees the flawless green surface of the athletic field bordered in white chalk lanes.

As the eye sweeps up toward the town one sees, opposite the Casino, the Bellevue Hotel, Bern's oldest and, in my opinion, most beautiful hotel, where the rooms are large and comfortable and expensive, where the music is good but discreet and where the barmaids can tell you to the penny the value of the diamond ring you're wearing—in at least five languages! It is a hotel in the grand old style, acre-deep in velvet carpets, glistening with crystal light and polished brass. Visiting dignitaries stay there. Elaborate banquets are given in its halls. When I enter its swinging doors a white-coated doorman greets me with a smile. And when I take the five, ten, twenty or fifty dollar note (which my father has borrowed in order to relieve my distress because I have written to him and informed him of it) to the desk and ask the clerk in the Oxford-gray jacket, gambol-striped trousers and powder-gray tie to change it into Swiss francs, he takes it, without a ruffle, without disturbing a hair on his immaculate head, and cashes it with a smile. Though he notices that my shoes could stand a major repair job—for he is an observant man—he does not snigger behind my back, as Mr. Eliot's doorman sniggers—or if he does, he does it discreetly. I walk out through the revolving doors, past the Cadillacs with the license plates of Venezuela and Texas with a smile, which I need not deepen into a humble grin for any man. Nor will I suppress the occasional satisfaction I have had, though I admit it to be sheer vanity of the basest sort, when, upon bumping into the man from Texas, I have uttered an impersonal but courteous, "Oh—I beg your pardon!" in my best Missouri accent, and he has looked at me, a little dazed, I like to fancy, and found that my gaze was firm: that of a man looking into the eyes of another man.

Oh, I like the Kirchenfeld bridge. There are so many spider-webs swaying magically between the light stanchions and the bridge rail. I like all the spiders that weave them. I could wax lyrical about the bridge's spiders if I possessed the gift . . . But wait! I have reserved the spiders for later. Now I must have done with the Thunstrasse once and for all.

I Leave the Thunstrasse

By THE END of the month, as I have said, it was clear that I could not remain much longer at the Thunstrasse—without going crazy. There was no remedy for the situation. The old lady had been a widow too long, her fear and suspicion of men was too great. She was simply a lonely old woman who had been quite attractive in her youth (I saw a picture of her as a young girl once when the door of her room was open), and who should have remarried long ago, but who, because she had not, had developed into an extremely nervous, hypersensitive person, constantly goaded by a thousand invisible fears from the past and the present, as well as the future.

She augmented her income—I imagine she must have had some sort of pension from her husband—by renting rooms to strangers, most of whom were single women. They worked in government offices nearby and were "stable," that is, very quiet, and they had no visitors in their rooms. They arose at seven, lunched at twelve, supped at seven and were in bed by ten-thirty. They were quiet, retiring, serious, hardworking and dull, though one of the young ladies was rather attractive, according to the average bachelor's taste, his taste being broad enough to include most any physical stature and any age between two and ninety-seven, as long, of course, as the body is alive.

Now I was a special case—I was black and much too energetic, hyperanimate and most irregular in my living habits, screeching the doors at all hours of the day and night. After two weeks the landlady became hysterical at the mere sound of my footfall. When I broke the gas heater the die was cast. I broke it out of rage because she insisted that I call her every time I wished to light it, doubting that I could manipulate the mechanism without the benefit of her supervision. Because she explained it imperfectly, or because I did not understand her French well enough, but more than likely because I resented her tacit assumption that I was a savage fresh from the wilds of equatorial Africa and was, therefore, unfamiliar with the artifacts of the western world, I burned out the copper coils by lighting the flame before allowing the water to flow through them first. There were several water pipes to choose from, but the right one, in my overwrought condition, was difficult to locate. When she heard the gentle explosion I thought she would break in two, and while she jumped up and down, waved her arms frantically in the air and stammered incoherently, I managed to make her understand that if she would just send me the repair bill I would promptly pay it. At the end of the month she presented her bill and I gave her the money. Neither of us was happy about it, nor were we happy over the fact that I continued to pay one hundred and ten francs a month for a room and cooking privileges which were nonexistent, since I never used her kitchen after the first week of residence in the little front room. I complained about it as calmly as I could, but she insisted simply that I had agreed to pay it and would have to continue doing so or move. I moved. She was glad and I was glad. When a very nice lady who owned the restaurant in which I ate told me that she had a client who had a little attic room in which I might stay, I took it. At the end of the month I moved in.

The new room was far from ideal because it was too small but it was much better than the one I had just left because the air was freer, more pleasant and more interesting, and because it afforded me my first opportunity of entering a more or less normal Swiss home.

My New Landlord and Lady

My new residence was also in a quiet neighborhood—it would be difficult not to find a quiet neighborhood in Bern. I was still in the Kirchenfeld and I continued to enjoy my walks in the beautiful Tier Park, but now with the added pleasure which was afforded me by the company of my new landlord, an elderly gentleman who was formerly a civil service white-collar worker, but now retired.

The gentleman's health was good considering his age, though he felt the humors of the weather in his bones, and he had consequently matured a philosophy which was geared to sustain him through the probable number of remaining years which he could reasonably hope to endure. His walks with me and the dog, a rather temperamental and somewhat lazy French poodle whose name was, let us say, Diana (I must be discreet here) had a three-fold purpose: health for himself and Diana, which meant for the latter being exposed to the rich variety of succulent trees which the Tier Park afforded, to reminisce upon the pleasant as well as unpleasant memories of the past and to expound the philosophy which was the fruition of three-score and some eight hard-won years of experience upon this hazardous planet.

I mostly listened. Nor will I pass judgment upon the venerable old gentleman's opinions here, a feat which he could certainly accomplish with more accuracy and with a much greater enthusiasm than I can at present work up. Suffice it to say that he was a very sympathetic person, a short, somewhat stout, pink-headed old man with sagging cheeks and wide, drooping eyes. He was proud. He never withdrew his chin from the sharpest winds, even on the coldest days, and there was a spirited, almost youthful spring in his walk, which would occasionally, when animated by a glass of good red wine, lurch into a swagger—though he usually retired shortly after supper and was grateful to the good God who made him when he could report on the following morning that he had had a good night's sleep. However, his parts were dropping away at a discouraging rate. First it was his hairline and then his hair, followed by his teeth. Gradually his hands began to wither like fading flowers and at times his head would sag, it appeared, from the weight of his huge red pendulous earlobes.

As for character, he was honest, considerate and kind. He was patriotic and a good Swiss, a fact which I mention to his credit. But I must also add that he was somewhat limited in his views and in the range of his sensibility, as all good Swiss of his genre must be. That is to say, he had his way of dealing with experience, the "Swiss" way, and as long as one stayed within its frame of reference one was "correct." It took a lot of squeezing but he had managed to achieve a sort of perfection in being typically Swiss in a rather nice way. A staunch Protestant, he was not exactly intolerant but not especially enthusiastic over believers in the Catholic faith. Once during a meal when there was talk of a butcher selling cats for rabbits he suggested: "The dog who did that *must* have been a Catholic because no good Protestant would do such a thing!" He was studious and could trace his words to their Greek and Latin origins, which impressed me, since most of my countrymen are deficient in those two venerable tongues. Finally he possessed the virtue of curiosity, for he was tirelessly interested in discussing new ways and new thoughts—if they did not threaten the ways and thoughts to which he was accustomed: very much like your father and my father, only Swiss. We got along very well on our walks because I said very little while he did most of the talking. We would have been on the best of terms even now had my money not run out.

But the gentleman's wife was another matter. She was per-haps ten years younger than her husband, "feminine," complex, proud, sensitive. She still retained a semblance (my taste is broad) of her youthful good looks. She had dark eyes with long sweep-ing eyelashes and an abundance of dark black hair mingled with silvery gray. A downy mustache haloed her full-lipped mouth, about which a suggestive smile played. Her figure was still intact, in spite of the fact that in recent years she had grown a little stout. I often thought when I saw her dressed to go out that she must have been quite a beauty at sixteen!

After her first husband died she had been looking for some nice man who would simply be good to her. My landlord was certainly that, and since he had lost his first wife, a good but strong-minded woman, they both agreed, he had been looking for someone who would simply be good to him. So they mar-ried and were as happy as any man who is not a skeptic could expect them to be.

Now she had reached that age from which for a woman there is no turning back, and it was from the shock of that realization that she was suffering when I came to live at her house. The lady was very much aware of her body because it waxed intermittently hot and cold. She had dizzy spells and sleepless nights, during which she remembered much of what she had experienced in her youth.

Alas, the past was past. Fortune had turned his head the other way. So her thoughts ran. But she had a helpmate, a friend. Oh, how sadly wonderful it is to be saved, she seemed to be saying on the one hand, and on the other: Life is a bitter draught at best. But I will, I *have* to make the best of it. I will try . . . Oh, but the chance that got away! . . . If I had but known *then*, could have guessed, could have had only a hint, a little sniff! of what I know *now!* The ironies of the lady's reflective thoughts would often make her laugh bitter-sweetly, and sometimes when the dizzy madness stirred within her breast she would weep.

There were three problems which complicated my relations with this lady: language, her extremely subtle and unconscious antagonism to me due to her sexual state (of which even I am aware only upon reflection) and that irretrievable past which she strove in vain to recover. She spoke just enough English to be confusing, while I spoke no German or Swiss-German at all and my French was negligible. Because she translated directly from German into English when she spoke, quite often a correctly pronounced English word would render a meaning foreign to the lady's intention. Many a harmless quarrel arose over words. And, of course, we discussed everything. I was impatient with views which were a hundred years old and rash in my judgment of them, while she was impatient with ideas which were "new," especially on her bad days, on which days she was impatient with God for making her an old woman. However, much bad feeling between us was prevented by the old man, who acted as arbiter. He was more objective than either of us and more often correct when he made a statement of ostensible fact.

What did we discuss? Mostly politics and social forms, which amounted to little more than the differences between how we do it over here as compared to how we do it at home. Naturally, each of us was an ardent advocate of his own method.

"The Swiss are stupid because they beat their rugs every day and close all the bars at eleven-thirty. Both of these practices are very irksome to me!" I heatedly declared. And she retaliated by saying:

"You Americans are stupid for letting McCarthy intimidate the *president* of the United States! Americans are primitive, uncultivated, persecutors of black people, Indians and Jews. And to have the nerve to tax—it's criminal—Swiss watches which are superior to their own. They even admitted it!"

And then I declared: "The Swiss are stupid because of this and this! and that and that and that!" While she maintained that Americans were asinine for the following reasons:

"That and that and that!"

Neither of us read the papers much, she rather superficially and I hardly at all. The old man supplied the facts, of which there were many to support either view. But in general that gentleman was inclined (I felt strongly) to agree with his wife, for which I certainly cannot blame him since a quiet life above all was the chief desire of his waning years.

But we had a more serious, though more agreeable problem: the lady's past. It had a decisive effect upon my stomach, as well as upon my dwindling fortune. She had owned with her first husband a prosperous pension which had flourished during the Great War. I was in Barfleur at the time but she told me at least seventy-six dozen times of how Bern teemed with soldiers from practically every nation on earth during that war. There were Germans and Nazis and Italians and Fascists and British Colonials and Canadians and Americans, Poles, Czechs, Eskimos, Laplanders, Chinese, Yugoslavians, Senegalese and Pygmies, Indians American and Indians Indian, Old Frisians and Indo-Germanians, Afro-Americans, Moors, North, South, East, West and Central Africans, Phoenicians, Masons, Greeks, Ku-Klux-Klanese, Iberians, Carpet-baggers, Jews from at least a hundred countries, Turks, Russians, San-skrits and Polynese, Brahamen and Atmen, Australians, New Zealanders, Ainus, Tasmanians, Arabs and Aminites and Dutch-Tunesian and Dutch, Mormons and Celestial Guards from Father Divine's Heaven and the Heaven of Daddy Grace, forty thousand Salvation Army foot soldiers, Catholics, Protestants, Back-biters and Back-sliders and Excommunicees.

My lady's pension accommodated only the cream, the top leaves of this militant, migrant crop of humanity. They crept within her doors under the cover of night and crept out under a veil of secrecy, never to be heard of again. Night fell, the moon rose and doors opened on oiled hinges. World-weary mouths were fed in secret. Diplomats! Generals! Heroes! Scoundrels! They all stole silently within her protective ken. And she had lavished upon them a mother's affection.

She was the cook and the cook was busy around the clock. She was the maid and the bed quoits never rested, the bed linen was a mountain of whiteness turning gray with the dust of the weary earth that waxed and waned like the gathering, dispersing mounds of desert sand.

And how she had fed them. "I am a gifted cook," she often said, and she did not lie, she was a wonderful cook. That is why this episode in my life was so painful. She had worked for impossible hours at a time, shouldering the whole responsibility, shouldering it with magnificent stews, with pies and Berner Platten and Rösti and Bratwurst and tender green salads, which she composed from the choicest vegetables, which only she could induce from secret plots of earth accessible only to her connoisseur's instinct. The best wines were poured at her table, the richest ales and beers, the creamiest Ovomaltine and Schalen-Dunkel.

Her calling nearly killed her. Filling the world's stomach frayed her nerves and hardened her arteries. It calloused the soles of her pretty feet, which were so bruised from standing on cold stone and waxed wood that she had lost a toe, which now made reflection while walking painful. Yes, she had done it, she had done it all, and for what!

The war ended, as wars will, and all the hungry people went away. Secret missions became public missions, and the world-weary faced the rising sun of a still day. It was on such a day that her first husband died. In the whirl of death calculations flew like dead leaves. Profit and loss rattled in the mouths of disinterested lawyers like false teeth. Man-hours dwindled into exaggerated aches and pains, and were paid in gray hairs and tears. The black wagon rolled slowly down the street. All was lost save the memory, save the permanent pain etched into her aching body, save the rent in her bruised heart.

It was no laughing matter, though she laughed more often than she cried through the tears which flowed from her dark, heavy-lidded eyes. And the laughter, articulating the irony of her predicament in forgetful moments, say, as she lipped the brim of the wine glass, made a raucous sound, while the bottles, emptied of their contents, jangled a morbid air.

It was this memory which gave me indigestion and an extra layer of fat. For I had to tax all of my ingenuity in order to create fresh excuses for not eating the wonderful food which that lady cooked, for being just one and a half minutes late for that soufflé, which had to be eaten the very instant she whisked it out of the oven.

Oh, she was a heavenly cook, that was true, but the eating schedule was terrible! In her house one ate at eight or nine, twelve, four and seven. The morning meal was a light one, consisting of only bread, butter, jam, cheese and coffee. The twelve o'clock meal was a complete and an excellent one with a perfect soup, one or two kinds of meat, appropriate side dishes (at least two), salad of the most mouthsome vegetables in season, wine, cheese in several varieties, coffee and fruit—every day!

Imagine writing a story after that! But more, as she was a wonderful cook, she exacted the tribute of a reigning culinary queen. One had to say, "Oh!" and "Ah!" with the long aspirate exhalation after each mouthful, and say it with gusto, and smile as one ate with enthusiasm, or the lady would frown menacingly. None of this would have been difficult had I possessed the appetite of a giant tapeworm, and could have lavished my praises voluntarily, but that lady had a look which said, "Well? . . ." and Lord help me if I did not give the right answer!

She and the old man did not eat much, they were usually half sick, so I had to eat most of the food. If I did not, she would complain that I was wasting both food and money. I agreed and suggested that she cook less, but she objected on the grounds that a healthy young man like me should eat a lot. So the board bill continued to be expensive. It was a pity because the little room upstairs was cheap enough, and the laundry for a whole month was seldom more than six francs—she repaired everything excellently and did my shirts better than most laundries. However, in all fairness, I must admit that she did not overcharge me, the luxurious meals which she served were cheap considering the money I had to pay. I could have done worse at the Café du Commerce where the food is famous, but it could have cost me less, I could have eaten for half the amount had she but cooked according to my appetite. I know, because I have eaten since then for one eighth the amount, though, obviously, with some difficulty! But this lady could no more economize on her dream than most of us can. She was the young, energetic mistress of the pension of old, and I was the world-weary guest who stole into her motherly kitchen, half-starved, death-hounded and secret. This dear lady—at times she was very dear—almost killed me. The only reason she did not was because my money ran out.

There were one or two other little things that did not go too well with us, but which were mostly my fault because they clashed with the way we did things "back home" as I have suggested, the Swiss eat a light breakfast, a roll and coffee, etc., and a heavy lunch. Then they listen to the news or read while they relax on the sofa. The hand-workers, secretaries and low-salaried people begin work at two, the white-collar, semi- and executive workers begin at three, the latter having a four o'clock snack (*Z'Vieri* pronounced "fieri"), usually coffee or tea and a roll or a sandwich. Then at seven in most houses in the city they have supper while they listen attentively to the evening news. Supper is coffee-complete—milk-coffee, bread and butter, jam or "Chueche" (apple, pear, apricot, plum, etc.) and cheese, or any of a variety of light dishes, hot or cold, sour or sweet. The days and nights are interspersed with beer, *hell* (light) or *dunkel* (dark), strong (Münchner) or normal (domestic), hot or cold, and red, white, foreign or domestic wines (the Vaud and Tessin sections of Switzerland are the principal wine centers and the wines are very good). Two thirds of the population goes to bed at ten and rises at six-thirty, paydays and weekends excepted, when the people spend as much as they dare and take a little longer to do it. This living and eating schedule almost ruined me, and made work virtually impossible. I worked very hard, but my stories suffered, I think, from the tedious overstuffing of my stomach, and from the strain of the tension under which they were written . . . Then too, I suppose they would have suffered somewhat anyway because I did not write very well, I was only in the fifth or sixth month of my "literary" career!

I was not regular enough in my living habits. I slept too late. The lady could not do my room at her accustomed hour, between nine and ten. It was inconvenient for her to do it later because she had to go to the market and wash and iron on scheduled days. She had to prepare her elaborate lunch, the dog's elaborate lunch, go to the coiffeur, the doctor, and do all the things that your wife and our mothers have to do. I was able to appreciate her position, so I told her that I would do my room myself. But she protested that it was not a man's work, and I lost stature in her sight because I practically forced her to let me have my way about it in order that I might sleep as long as I wished. She insisted on shining my shoes, to my embarrassment, and when I complained that I would shine my own, explaining that in America men cleaned women's shoes, or at least cleaned their own, she was angry because she felt that her womanhood had been violated. Shining shoes was woman's work!

Though we slurred over these difficulties, they made a deep and lasting impression upon her, which I often discovered later when references to them would emerge from her thoughts in all manner of perverse shapes in the heat of our arguments. However, to our credit, we never lost sight of the fact that our difficulties were superficial. I would possibly be with them still, if not dead from overindulgence in some of the best food I have eaten since I left my mother's kitchen, and had I been able to sell at least one story for a reasonable amount.

The Public Life

My life in Bern during the first year was for the most part a public one. As I was usually very lonely, I went to the places to which a lonely man goes in search of company, wherever there was a crowd. It was a bitter-sweet compromise. I saw people, but strange, cruel, hostile people, I often felt. Children pointed at me on the street and shouted, "Mommie! Look—there goes a *Neger! Ne-ger! Ne-ger!*" while Mommie giggled amusedly.

Now, I could well understand that children are curious and often indiscreet—I was once a child—but I could not understand why their parents did not correct their manners. And more, why they indulged in the same childish behavior themselves! I would have been severely reprimanded for pointing my finger at an old friend, let alone a stranger, when I was a child. But not so on the streets and in the restaurants and tearooms of Bern.

How boorish! I often thought, as often when I passed a group of adults on the sidewalk they permitted me to hear what I guessed to be some depreciating remark.

It is true, I did not understand the language, but the language of scorn and ridicule has an intonation which requires no knowledge of vocabulary or grammar. In time, entering a public assembly became a torturous experience for me. I wanted and needed friends, and yet contact with the people was unbearable. I had to force myself to face the town. I walked straight, too straight, I think, with my head high, too high, like a drunken man who wants to conceal his drunkenness, or like a pretty

Italian girl who works at the Mövenpick, passing a knot of leerie-eyed men on her way home at twelve-thirty A.M., umbrella clutched in hand, ears closed to their vulgar suggestions, eyes peeled for the lurking auto, ready to ward off the indecent attack, with her pride and her dignity perched on her shoulder, daring them to knock it off. I have seen that pathetic sight many times, and I have understood her feelings because I have felt the way she felt. And often, though she knew it not, I have been ready to defend her.

I roamed through the streets of the town by day and by night. In this way I got to know it very well. Oh, I didn't know the names of the streets, though I had read them dozens of times in many different states of consciousness. The truth was that I did not take them seriously, nor the town itself. It was like a little elf land. Everything looked so small. The people made such important gestures. Irony piled on top of rage when they pointed and laughed at *me!* Why, *they* were the funniest little things I had ever seen, with their curious peasant costumes and those queer, dwarfy old men who sold the *Berner Tagblatt* with their big hats, barking that strange monotonous jargon—and the wiry twisted ones, with the beards that hung down to their knees! The pious expressions of the Salvation Army folk brought a reminiscent smile to my lips, since that famous expression plays so great a part in American life. But they did what no American holy soldier ever did, they gave me a little pamphlet in English to read asking, ARE YOU SAVED? They broke me up into little chunks.

The terrible, painted figures on the fountains I never took seriously. The heraldic flags looked like the props of a Hollywood movie. The knights with shields, coats-of-arms and all that represented on some of them, belonged to my childhood, perhaps to the tenderest part of me. That's why they embarrassed me a little, just as I am sometimes embarrassed when I remember the romantic dreams and illusions of my childhood in which I was the hero of many a heroic scene. They were the symbols of a world I had merely read about and projected myself into, a world in which I, it seemed, had no heroic part: I was not the vassal of a great and powerful king who fought the Christian's battles in the far east—the crusaders, though naïf, cannot all have been looters and mountebanks! No golden-haired Guinivere ever languished in my arms, nor did I slay the dreaded dragon, except in my childish imagination.

But wait: once, when I was ten or eleven years old—I was on my way to the movies—I passed by an alley just off the main street. I heard someone moaning. I went to see what it was. It was an old white woman sprawled on the stones. Her lips were parched and her head was clotted with blood from the countless falls she had taken in trying to gain her feet. Her matted hair fell into her face and her eyes were glazed and watery and only half open. She smelled of whisky, but as I drew near to her I couldn't really tell, because she was sweating, and she looked feverish. She motioned to me to help her. I didn't want to do it at first because I was in a hurry to get to the movie; then, too, I had my good suit on—she looked sticky and she smelled very bad. I started to leave her, but she called out to me. I could not move.

I'll help her as far as the end of the alley where someone can see her, where some of her own people can see her, I thought. And then I thought, Why should I? She's not colored! I felt ashamed. I helped her to the end of the alley where some of her own people could see her . . .

It was about eight-fifteen on a beautiful summer evening. The traffic literally sang along the busy street. It was Troost Avenue, on which the swift, streamlined streetcar ran; just below Twelfth Street, where the people transferred to lines going east and west, the Troost line running north and south; so there were many people, and many cars speeding by, and pedestrians walking this way and that. The old woman cried out to them, trying to get to her feet, but falling back down every time. Her hair would fall into her face and she would feebly sweep it away with her dirt-clotted hands. No one looked at her. She braced herself against the curb and began to cry. Then suddenly she grabbed her stomach and vomited on the sidewalk. The foul-smelling stuff ran down the front of her dress and streamed from her mouth like the rent strands of a spiderweb. White and black people looked at her now, in disgust, and passed on. Some of them stepped over her, while others crossed the street . . .

I watched it all from the corner. It looked as though no one would pick her up and take her home. And I could not go to the movie because they would not.

Why won't they? I wondered, in a rage, because it was getting late, and the old hag just lay there befouling herself. I will have to do it, I thought, there's no one else.

I went to the corner of the alley where she lay and asked her if she were all right. She mumbled something I could not understand. Then she motioned for me to help her to her feet. I bent down and extended my hand, and she threw her reeking arms around my neck and began to cry. I tried to hold her away from me but I could not because she shook so much.

"Where do you live?" I asked her, looking nervously around, wondering if people were looking. Gradually I learned, as we walked, that she lived in the apartment opposite the garage on the corner of the Eleventh Street traffic-way. I knew the place well because I passed every day going and coming from school. I would have to cross Twelfth Street, past the heavy traffic and walk up Troost Avenue to Eleventh Street; past the grocery store where I knew everybody, past the cleaner shop where I took my parents' clothes and past the numberless trams crowded with people, most of whom were white! But there was no help for it, there was no other way.

I tightened my grip on the old woman's waist and tried to hurry her along, but it was impossible because she was so sick and tired and old that she could hardly walk. We had to stop every two or three minutes and rest. Twice more she vomited, the last time splattering my pants with it. I dragged her on. The movie had already begun; perhaps I could be in time for the second feature . . . After what seemed like ages I got her to the apartment.

But it was a white apartment and I was afraid to go in. I tried to stop a man but he brushed past me; and then a woman, but she ignored me, too.

I'll have to do it, I decided, and take what comes. I almost had to carry her up the stairs, frightened as I did so, because she was so thin! and into the lobby of the building. It was empty. I put her on the elevator and got off at her floor. I half carried and half dragged her into her room. I bathed her face in cold water and brushed her hair out of her face. She looked different, like an old child, hardly older than I. I folded her arms upon her chest and took off her shoes and the frayed remains of her stockings. Then, as I threw the blanket over her, I became frightened.

What if someone should find me here, I thought. They would never believe me. What if something were missing? . . . if this old woman came to in the morning and missed something and said I took it? The whole world saw me dragging her to her apartment! I wiped the vomit off my pants as well as I could, and stole out of the apartment as quickly as caution would allow.

I went directly home. It was only ten minutes away, but I made it in five. "What! You home so early?" my mother asked me. My father was gone to the barber shop.

"Yessum. I don't feel good . . ."

"Whew! you smell terrible," she exclaimed, examining my clothes.

Knowing that I would catch the devil if I had told her what I had done, I told her that I felt sick in my stomach. She made me take a bath and put me to bed and made me eat a bowl of tomato soup. A little while later someone knocked on the kitchen screen. It sounded like Mrs. Higgens who lived across the alley in the house that faced Troost Avenue—our house faced Harrison Street.

She saw me! I thought, trembling in my bed.

No sooner had I pulled the cover over my head than my mother came into the room and sat down on the side of the bed and kissed me. There must have been tears in her eyes because when she went away my face was wet . . .

No golden-haired Guinivere had ever lain in my arms, nor had I slain the dragon and saved the realm, except in my childish imagination. And yet, there were heroic kings in Africa from ancient noble lines, I have been told, though the facts were never written down in the history books I had to study. There were, doubtless, black Guiniveres . . . and lions, as big as dragons and twice as real. But I will not break my pen bemoaning the ironies which marred the dream I had chosen. Indeed, it is strange how a little thing like a flag with a dragon or a lion or a knight on a horse painted on it can cut through the surface of one's personality, down to the vital, essential self, which sleeps and projects its dreams into that much more fanciful outer world, which only a pessimist can call, with any seriousness, "Reality."

I visited practically all the bars and all the more accessible tearooms. In time, I found many of the more obscure ones, which, however, I was inclined to avoid at first, feeling more secure in a crowd.

I had seen the city at four A.M. and at six A.M. I had heard the first streetcar rumble down the street and beheld with wonder from the center of the Bahnhofplatz the last magical moment when all the streetcars stood in the station filled with the home-bound who had been to the movies and to the tearooms or dancing or to choir rehearsal, strolling or working late, huddled in a tight little group under the shelter when it rained, and ranging freely, leisurely, under the strain of a pleasant fatigue when the moon shone and a warm breeze wafted them on: waiting—having boarded now the streetcars, paid and pocketed their transfers —for the signal, a short blast of a whistle. It blew! as the bell in the tower of the Evangelical church rang, and all the cars moved silently in the eleven directions from the heart of the city, while the buses coughed and whined through the shifting crowd of pedestrians which dispersed like sparks of fire before the wind.

No city silence is ever so still as that of the city of Bern at twelve o'clock and one o'clock and two o'clock, on a Monday, Tuesday or Wednesday night, or any night during the Christmas week when all the families huddle in rose-tinted rooms behind heavily curtained windows. In the silence of the summer's or winter's night I have often not gone home, I have walked under the Loeb arches in the Spitalgasse and stared at the elegant mannequins in their cold forsaken splendor, glaring emptily out the windows. And though I have looked up at them they have not looked down at me. I have walked under the low arches of the old town and heard the water purling between the intermittent sounds of my footfalls. How lonely the electric lights seemed with no company save the blind stones! Sometimes I have seen another man walking close to the edge of the curb—as I stopped at the Bärenplatz and viewed the empty marketplace or looked at the vacant seats before the Grotto, where, hours before, people with vacant faces sat—who, upon seeing me, drew near, hesitated with a questioning tremor and then passed quietly under the arch; so as not to awake the pigeons asleep on the ledge above, beneath the clock, underneath which, hours ago, the streetcars passed.

Now, at this point, when I had money, I would turn left and amble toward the Neuengasse, down the Neuengasse past the Frisco Bar, opposite which a knot of watchful women stood facing the door. Others sat inside on the tall red leather stools around the bar, watching and waiting and watching, and some neither watching nor waiting in vain, though oftimes vainly, for I have looked at them a time or two and have seen their dignities poised dangerously upon the penciled edge of a self-assertive eyebrow: while the barmaids and the barman danced attendance upon the frequent demands for beer, whisky and pretty red liquids in small thin glasses with lemon rind floating on top; while the birds within the glass cage along the wall innocently conducted themselves in a manner which reflected the overwhelming desires of the people staring at each other from the rim of the circled bar. However, innocence, as far as the bird watchers were concerned, was a bird which had long since flown away! It occurred to me once, on a "long Wednesday night," when the drinking lasted until three, that there was irony in the fact that the birds and not the people were in a glass cage. It appeared to me to be unjust somehow. And I remembered looking at the hungry-eyed people with the uneasy conviction that something had gone wrong.

And This Theme Has
Another Disquieting Variation

—FOR, IF IT really were a "long Wednesday night" the orchestra would be playing downstairs in the Chikito, a pretty good orchestra usually, one that played a variety of musical styles tolerably well and sometimes excellently: jazz, German and Viennese waltzes, tangos, polkas, sambas, fox and slow trots, which they sang in three or four or five languages. And there would probably be a floor show, though not necessarily.

As I would enter this pleasant atmosphere, men and women would smile at me for various reasons unknown to me, all of which I interpreted as questionable. Occasionally a roving eye accentuated by a raised eyebrow would ask me a tacit question, and I would contrive to take a seat, if I could find one, facing it. This I accomplished with a casual mime, as though I were the devil and this was hell. When the waiter would come and hand me the voluminous beverage list I would take it and without reading it order whisky, patting my foot discreetly to the rhythm of the music lest I exhibit too much emotionalism. And I would reflect that I had sought such diversion at least fifteen years ago because then as now I had not enough courage to rush across the floor the moment the music started, bow slightly and ask the pretty girl with the roving eye (who would have then as now already answered yes to all my little questions) to dance with me.

She probably wouldn't . . . probably won't . . . What if she didn't! I would argue as I sat in my chair and sulked resentfully and complained in a most ungentlemanly fashion: The drinks in this place are too expensive. She's probably a prostitute . . . or a husband-hunter . . . or a snob anyway . . . And then I would find myself wishing that I were once more in Paris during a war. Then I would drink my whisky slowly, thinking: Seven francs for one drink! . . . Twenty in the Kursaal last night . . .

The music would start again.

I should go now, I would think, but hesitate, as she smiled and slipped her naked arm around the other man's shoulder. And I would think, He who hesitates—didn't the man speak the truth!—is lost . . . Lost but with a practiced, nonchalant air . . . Lost and lonely, with my dignity intact; lonely in my throbbing sensitivity to the rhythm of the music and to the memory of the tune which I used to sing when I was in high school, an old Jimmie Lunceford number . . . What was her name? . . . What was that girl's name in high school when I used to sing that tune?

The pretty girl with the tacit question in her eyes would dance by and cut a glance at me over her partner's shoulder. She *would* like to dance with me, I would think, but it's too late now. I've missed the right moment . . . He who hesitates is . . . I mustn't let them know I care . . . Then I would yawn, discreetly; while the music played.

After that she would seldom look at me again. Her companion, the man who asked when I hesitated, would order wine. She would make some droll remark about me, I would assume, because now they would look at me and laugh. After that when she would dance near me she would press her body close to the body of her partner. Shortly after that she would leave. Then I would make a novel speculation:

It's late, I would think, yawning discreetly, and wearily now, pouring the rest of the soda water into my glass so that it would appear to be full, after which I would become thoroughly interested in the shape of the violin player's nose. He would be playing a tango in the soft hour-before-closing light. The dancing couples, warmed by the whisky, emboldened by desire and last-minute desperation, would snuggle embarrassingly close to one another; at which a rather plain-looking girl sitting in the corner opposite me would look at me with a daring expression upon her face, and I would drop her glance to the floor, where it would be trampled upon by the feet of a hundred men and women . . .

When the soda water was gone I would catch a glance at myself in the mirror on the other side of the room and behold with a feeling of ridiculousness the brilliant sheen upon my face and the rose glaze of my eyeballs. Overcome with humility and shame I would rise from my table, forgetting to pay the waiter, who, remembering, would remind me, and then I would remember, flush with embarrassment and fumble nervously in this and that pocket until I found the note, which detained me. He would return the change, which always seemed a mocking gesture, since there was so little left, and I would finally leave the room; walking too gracefully—I felt it—climbing the stair, uttering a self-conscious good-night to the hat-check boy, avoiding the full-view mirror as I climbed swiftly the second flight.

Sometimes laughing couples would follow me, and I would pause before the door in order to let them pass, thinking, What a good impression I'm making, as I followed them out the door. I would watch discreetly the woman's pretty ankles disappearing into the car, and watch the car disappear, as I pocketed my hands or lit my pipe, and walked slowly toward the station, taking the left turn past the Schweizerhof, Loeb, and the travel bureau, where I would often pause to look at the darkened windows containing travel posters advertising voyages to Rome, Egypt, Africa and America. I would ponder the rates in dollars and cents as I crossed the Bundesterrasse and followed it down to the Kirchenfeld bridge. Perhaps the moon would be blue . . . falling silvery-white upon the water. The water would rush quietly, the bridge would be empty, and the streets would be empty, all the way home.

During that first year I became so familiar with the public places of entertainment in Bern that I knew their various clientele by heart. I knew, for example, who frequented the Perry Bar, and when; and if he or she were with his or her husband or the "other" man or woman. I knew, I thought, every prostitute in Bern, what streets she walked or what bars she frequented, and when her "route" changed—though I never spent a night with one because they were usually too expensive! I knew hat-check men and women, waitresses, policemen, streetcar conductors, bus drivers, garbage men and street cleaners, kiosk clerks and Salvation Army veterans. I noticed every new spiderweb which appeared on the Kirchenfeld bridge and gave the spiders names, though I knew practically none of the people's names. However, after a time, we met so often in the streets of the city that decency demanded that we greet each other, on which occasions precedents were established which have lasted till this day . . .

For some reason, perhaps because my American friends had taken me there during the first week of my visit, I frequented the Perry Bar. I would usually arrive there about nine or ten or ten-thirty if I had gone to the movies, to the Capitol or the Forum, close by. I liked it well enough at that time because it catered to a companionable crowd of professional and semi-professional folk, among whom were a few Americans from the Embassy who usually came out on Thursdays and Fridays. I found them agreeable because they could drink without getting drunk, or get drunk without getting vulgar—a very hard thing for many of us to do!

Often I was invited to a table with a family, or with a party of young folk, and sometimes with a man or a woman who had traveled long in an English-speaking country and who, feeling out of sorts in Switzerland, were anxious to talk to someone whom they felt might be able to sympathize with his or her point of view. Well, whatever the reason—and there were certainly more than I have indicated here—I was introduced around the table and feted with wine. And although the dominant reason for the invitation was curiosity, their motives were also friendly ones as well, and mixed with perhaps pity because I looked so forlorn, so lonely, so nobody-knows-the-trouble-I-see-ish.

I accepted their invitations because I really was lonely and because I, too, was curious. They want to observe me, I thought. And my attitude was, Well, let them. And while they're observing me I can also take a few notes. The thought would cause me to smile inside like a Missouri horse trader. However, sometimes I accepted an invitation merely out of an embarrassing inability to say no, because not all the ladies and gentlemen who invited me to drink with them were to my liking. But even on the most unfortunate occasions things usually went better after the second glass of wine.

Often I had a wonderful, hilarious evening. We drank and sang, and hazarded harmless opinions in each other's languages. Sometimes the company was predominantly masculine and sometimes predominantly feminine. Sometimes the pianist was a happy man who played merry tunes which we all sang together, German songs and Swiss songs: "Im tiefen Keller," "Die schwarze Rose," "O mein Papa," and, of course—it was a Swiss song, too, they said—"Old Man River." Often when the party broke up we went somewhere else because we were having so much fun that we hated to stop; to the Casino until twelve, and from the Casino to the Perroquet or the Chikito or the Bellevue—wherever the night was "long"—and from there to someone-with-a-car's apartment, where we stole quietly up still flights of stairs, opened fresh bottles with a "pop!" and lounged on sofas, while the wine gurgled with the innocence of a child. At this stage we exchanged confidences, and awakened slumbering children in order that they might see *Der Neger*.

Some of those people I never saw again. Others I saw often, but in another place and under other circumstances when the mood was different. I soon learned that I had to be able to distinguish those subtle nuances of attitude caused by a shift in time and place. The charming brunette who drank with me last night might not greet me at twelve noon in front of the Bahnhof, or if she were with her mother or her boyfriend. Or the daring blond lady, turning thirty-five, who squeezed my hand under the table may miraculously appear in the guise of a dedicated mother of triplets on the following Saturday afternoon, as I ran across her, *par hazard*, in the Tier Park. I had to learn to separate the lambs from the sheep, the sheep from the goats and the foxes from the wolves. And on one or two occasions I had to learn to separate the hearts from the stones.

Hearts and Stones: Introduction:

MANY OF MY adventures I would recount to my landlord and lady the next day at lunch or supper. They became the subjects of many a bitter argument, for we were still fighting the old battle: how we do it back home as opposed to how you do it over here. Neither side had managed to convince the other. I insisted that the Bernese were as prejudiced as hell, but only in a different way from the Americans. For the Bernese I was "different" but the result was just the same, I was isolated. I claimed that the women were sex starved and sadistic because they openly flirted with me in the presence of their husbands, but ran like turkeys when they were alone in a public place in the broad open daylight. I said that most of them, a good eighty percent, were neurotic and that you could see it in their eyes; which meant that their men were, if not impotent, then certainly insensitive to their women, stealing their own pleasure and leaving the women unsatisfied. For I had observed that the women were most sadly neglected by their men, being little more than housemaids, since they could not vote and played no serious role in the society. "They are merely toys for the men to play with," I said.

While she insisted that I had no right to complain because I could simply go back to my own country. "Go back home!" she exclaimed passionately, "where they would kill you for even looking at the very women you're talking about. You Americans are children who have made your country into a circus. Look at your elections! Huh! And those loud ugly clothes . . . Especially the men. They're effeminate because they've given up their manhood to their women. And the women! They're flat, uninteresting, mass-produced creatures who all look alike . . . And who can't sew, can't cook. You live out of cans and spend all your lives in front of television." That is the gist of what she said.

The old man said that we ought not talk like that. And it was true, the little half-truths interspersed in all this verbiage hurt us and embittered us, though we pretended to laugh it off, while in reality it merely inspired us to strain our resources for fresh, piquant insults to hurl at each other.

Occasionally I would have an incident to report, in which I felt the racial implications were not to be denied. For instance, I told them of Mademoiselle let us say, Z, whom I had recently met one evening at the Chikito. First of all she was a *nice* girl, that is to say, the body was warm. As she sat next to my table, I finally worked up the courage after the second whisky to ask her for a dance. She accepted—a fact which made me a little suspicious. After all, why should she! I thought. Another uncalled-for advantage was that she spoke perfect English without accent. I was happy as a screwdriver, charming and witty, which I can be sometimes, and as smooth with the music as a greased eel, which I am most of the time. When the evening came to an end I offered to take her home, but she refused to allow it because she said she had to return with her brother. And it was true, I saw him sitting at the table with his girlfriend—they were engaged and she later became his wife. I told her that I was sorry and that I thanked her heartily for a very enjoyable evening, as I pressed her cheek close to mine for the last four bars before the music stopped.

But I was in luck, I felt, because I was able to make a date for the following week, on a Thursday night, at the same place. We had worn our dancing shoes, the wine poured freely, and the tangos were unusually succulent, so again we had a nice time. And I was secretly cheered by the fact that she had come without her brother and his fiancée. On this night I learned her first name but she was rather evasive about her family name and she would not tell me exactly where she lived, referring merely to the general quarter. Now, I felt this to be a little curious. An uneasy feeling came over me. It could be that her family wouldn't approve, I thought. A defensive attitude crept into my consciousness. I began to observe her more carefully. I wondered why she was—apparently—always alone. She was a very pleasant-looking girl with a much more than passing good figure. She was of average stature, had soft brown well-groomed hair, and several charming little mannerisms, of which—I had the impression— she was not aware; such as looking at you twice, in two staccato glances, when she spoke to you, especially when she asked a question; and of gripping your hand when she shook it, as though it were a pencil. And there are some women in whom shyness is as precious an asset as a perfect waistline is to others—she was such a one. She drank her wine with that carelessness which marks the attitude of one whose family has a wine celler. As I have said, her English was excellent, and as she had spoken of having visited many European countries, as well as America—several times—I gathered that she was widely traveled. I was simply delighted and somewhat astonished when she told me of having met on some occasion Langston Hughes. I was also puzzled. Who was she? Why wouldn't she tell? She had a story, I could see that in her eyes and in her nervous movements—what was it!

Oh, I didn't press her for explanation, I merely watched her a little more closely after that because—well, she was alone and I was alone . . .

And so the second evening ended, pleasurably, though a trifle more self-consciously. Once more I offered to take her home and once more she refused to allow it. And this time with no explanation at all. Now, I did not like that, nor was I enthusiastic about what happened when we met the following week in the Embassy tearoom. She arrived about ten minutes late, which would have been all right, but she passed my table as though she had not seen me. That was impossible, since mine was the only black face in the place and every eye was trained upon me. When I called her she stopped suddenly and looked around, as though she were surprised to see me, speaking in loud, excited tones, accepting the invitation—which I did not offer because our rendezvous had been previously arranged—to join me!—as though the idea were delightfully novel.

She wants all these people who are looking at us to think that our meeting is an accident, I thought. Is she ashamed to be with me? . . . Will we always meet in some public place? and leave separately? . . . And then I reflected that, so far, we had always met in a public place, and under similar theatrical circumstances. I got mad. Oh, I tried to hide it, realizing that I was hypersensitive, hoping for my sake—not hers—that I was wrong. However, I played the game and swilled the hot, tasteless tea, and decided that we would soon be ripe for a crisis.

She proposed that we go dancing at the Chikito the following week. I insisted on calling for her at her home and upon meeting her parents to whom, I explained, I would be responsible for her. But she refused because, said she, "It's impossible!"

Well, thought I, this won't do. So I told her, "Either you are out with me, or—you are not out with me. If I don't call for you at your home and take you back there, we are not really together." Why, she doesn't respect me! I thought. And then I thought, If we can't meet in the broad daylight, in the open air, we can't meet in the dark, thinking of all the women who had already made such proposals, directly and indirectly, becoming angry all over again, hating the vulgar nocturnal implications of a liaison instead of a clear, normal, respectable relation with a woman.

I explained all this to her as well as I could. And all she did was to become angry and leave in a very agitated state. The next day I received a letter from her written on her family stationery in which she declared her love for me and still maintained that what I had suggested was "impossible."

"You don't know Switzerland," she wrote, "what the people are really like," and then she broke off into distracted statements which I was at a loss to understand. I was also confused and resentful of what I felt to be a downright prejudicial situation, which was all the more ridiculous because of her strange declaration of—love!

How could that be! I thought. There hasn't been time . . . But not only that, there is a certain magic aura around a true realization of love, which need not be questioned. It doesn't surprise us, it fills us with awe . . . as when the first single, solitary star appears in the evening sky! Out of deepest respect for her I wrote her a kind letter, returning her own, advising her to be a little more discreet in the future. I repeated the conditions, already mentioned, under which a future meeting would be possible for me if she were really serious. But the young lady was merely insulted again. She wrote me another letter, and this time a bitter one. I was astonished.

Now when I told my landlady about this she, being an extremely curious woman, looked up the address on the letterhead in the telephone book and discovered that the young lady was rich, very rich indeed, and advised me not to be so rash, thinking, no doubt, of the wonderful life which had escaped her in her own youth, and now projecting her cherished ambitions into this situation.

But upon the discovery that the young lady was really wealthy, and from one of the "better" families in Bern, I became all the more furious. Why was I furious?

Because I have always had an almost instinctive dislike of rich people. They are the ones who have but do not need what you do not have and obviously need very much—all your life. And why? Because they were once in the position to exploit someone: you, me—anyone. I will not lie, I envy them, too. I am jealous of their power of movement within and without the social, ethical and moral frontiers of society. And I am angry because of their power to move me against my will. I envy the respect which society pays them, a respect which they do not always merit. I expect of them the intelligence, cultivation and gentleness of sensibility which their rich surroundings afford. I feel cheated—and quite often—when I find the rich only rich in money, reigning like lords of the realm, dropping their crumbs in the mouths of a dutiful middle class, the lower members of which accept their lot with puritanical resignation.

—I get mine in a can at the supermarket without the conso-
lation of an interview, though my "class" has never been known
to be wanting in religious resignation . . . Such were the thoughts
I thought. And then I thought, She just can't have me any way
she wants me simply because she—or her parents—have money.
What's Hecuba to me!

Now I might have suffered less from such narrowmind-
edness had I been able to rid myself of that popular illusion,
made famous by well-meaning persons like Rousseau, Marx,
Wordsworth and Whitman, that the poor are, by virtue of their
poverty, simple, earthy, honest, virtuous and grossly misunderstood. It saddens me to reflect now that I who despised weakness in others was not free from weakness myself. For, to tell the
truth, I had always expected more not only of the rich, but of
white people in general, than I had a right to expect of them, if
I had but known it. My attitude may be summed up thus:

They have the world. Why then are they not the wisest, the
noblest and the most perfect of God's creatures?

It slowly dawned upon me that, for all that, they were not the
wisest, the noblest and most perfect of God's creatures. Far from
it! There were many of them who were far less wise, noble and
perfect than I. And more—most of them were, in fact—and this
was hard to digest: just like me! How much easier it is to suffer if
your master is really your superior. No man's dignity suffers who
is slain by a falling mountain, or who is boiled in the lava of an
erupting volcano. Ahab dies a heroic death! But to learn that the
person or thing which kills you is just as you are, especially since
you do not really like yourself—let us face it honestly—because
you are black, having been taught since birth, and having observed
by your "position" in society that black is an undesirable color.
Why, it is too much to bear all at once. And now—what a chance
I had to show them, all of them, the white *and* the rich—at one
and the same time: *Your color and your money mean nothing to me!*

Now hear me, my dear, wherever you are, and to all of you
badly used white folk, wherever you are, forgive me—I beg of
you—for being an ass!

My landlady was a little sad about it, for she understood us both—I must give her credit. She could actually feel a little of what I felt. Oh, not the racial feelings, but the thing which she, as a European, was even more sensitive about, if that is possible, being rejected by the rich and being confined for money reasons to her class, though fundamentally there is not much real class distinction in Switzerland, a little more than in America, Europe having had a stronger precedent than the snobbish nouveau riche Country Club American tradition, and much more historical justification, since the European aristocracy has had a function in Europe which it has never enjoyed in my country. So, this lady, putting herself into my place, imagined herself as Cinderella. The hour came and the clock struck, but there was no happy ending. The past was mocking the present.

I, on the other hand, was strangely relieved because I now reflected that Mademoiselle Z—— was more than likely a little confused, and in a strained and somewhat restless state of mind. She had always been nervous, always "jumpy." I remembered the little things that used to bother her when we were together. For example, she always looked this way and that when we danced, and could never really enjoy the music for worrying about being in step. She could not keep in step because she could not relax. I began to understand, or to think I understood, those impish little mannerisms, which I mentioned earlier and which, at the time, seemed quaint. Now the impression grew in my mind that she had always seemed to have had something on her mind which she could never articulate into words. She seemed so bored with life in Switzerland—so she told me—that she spent some months of every year in Italy. But then she was bored in Italy, too. She went to America and was bored in America. Now she is white, twenty-five and rich, I remembered thinking, why should she be bored! Gradually I began to feel a sense of something tragic and perhaps decadent stirring beneath her character. It appeared to me that I, as an individual, was not very important to her, but that I represented the manifestation of some sort of protest she was trying to make against perhaps her parents or

Swiss society . . . Whatever her motives were, it seemed quite clear to me now that I was just a symptom of some complex emotional or spiritual malady, which neither of us understood any too clearly.

Upon the receipt of her last letter I, in the bright light of a puritanical self-righteousness, nobody knowing the trouble I saw, maintained an adamant silence. She did not write again. A few weeks later I learned from an American medical student who knew her that she had returned to America. I have never seen her again, although I often see her brother and his wife on the street or at the movies, but I have never dared to ask about her . . .

Hearts and Stones Continued,
or: A Barroom Ballad:

MY LANDLADY AND I were disheartened over this affair for some weeks. I felt that I had almost persuaded her to my way of thinking, at least regarding racial prejudice in Switzerland, when she protested that merely exclaiming "racial prejudice!" was too simple, repeating her old conviction that the people's attitudes toward me were based upon the fact that I was simply different and nothing more.

"But that's enough!" I exclaimed furiously, but there was no changing her. So I decided that I would tell her of the following experience which I had with a pretty barmaid in town:

She was the kind of girl of whom you would say, had you grown a little callous, that she was neither this nor that; a small, dark little thing, frizzled about the head, with a lip line about a size too large—she thought it improved her face. Her body she left to its own devices because, as she well knew, mother nature had done well by her, providing the eye with artistic surprises from almost any point of view. I mean simply that she had a good hip. When the hip is good one can usually assume the rest. Only in her case the assumption was not necessary, for she showed one just a little more than our grandmothers would think decent, which is the mode nowadays.

She worked in one of the friendly bars which I frequented. She smiled sweetly when she brought me my cognac and

Dannemann cigar. It was a difficult trick, but I managed to smile back and puff at the same time, as she lit it, though I was a little embarrassed when the smoke spurted out of my ears. As she was shy it took her several lightings to get around to telling me through the piano player that she was "interested in me." I was no less shy, but I managed to respond in less than a cool minute after I got wind of the news; breathlessly!

You mustn't judge us too harshly, we were young, these are lonely times, and we were lonely . . .

"The Bernese are so cold and grasping and unhospitable!" she told me. She said that she was French-Swiss and not Swiss-French, as I had suggested upon first noticing her excellent accent, which most Bernese do not have.

"French-Swiss!" she had insisted, arching her penciled eyebrows with pride, and I was saddened by the fact that she had all but plucked out the real ones, the lovelier ones, the ones her mother had smoothed back with a wetted finger when she was a girl. Which lady had recently died, she said sadly when I asked her if she had a family. "And after that I left home. There was nothing to do . . . Her father was an old man. In Bern she hoped to finish her apprenticeship and get a job as a barmaid and be successful like the very successful, very popular barmaid who was at that moment busy eyeing the boss's wife's diamond ring—I noticed it as my barmaid spoke. "One can earn a lot of money that way," she said.

All of this she told me over coffee that night after the bar had closed. And I could see, with a tinge of pity, the influence which her superior had upon her—in the line of the lip and the daring dip of her dangerous décolleté and in her cold mechanical laugh, frozen by the stony glare in her eyes, which was as hard as a "whore's heart." At least, as hard as such an unfortunate woman's heart is reputed to be by those who consider themselves to be connoisseurs of that famous organ.

But there was one thought which cheered me a little—my barmaid was still young, her sensibility had not been crusted over with callousness yet. Nor had she fully mastered that superficial city sophistication which stamps the members of her profession. Though she was applying herself to her homework, she was practically ignorant of the ways of the world (why else would she waste valuable time with me!) and she knew it, so she was, as you can see, intelligent.

"I like the way you talk," she said. "You're different."

I asked her if her name was Guinivere.

"No," she said. "It's Mimi. What's yours?"

"Vincent," I said.

"Ah—Vason! It's French!"

"I suppose so—if you say it that way . . ." I suppose that is what I said, my French was so poor. Then she said that she liked the way I dressed.

"You're cute," she said with a smile.

I told her that I liked her, too.

"That's nice," she said.

She said that I understood her, and that I was different from Swiss men, who wanted only one thing from a girl, and then didn't know what to do with it when they got it. She dropped her eyes and then her head and blushed prettily.

"Yes," I said sympathetically, agreeing with her that it must be awful when one had to work in a place in which the men expected only one thing of a girl, and that it was no less than tragic when they, upon getting it, did not know what to do with it. "You're cute," I said. And then I told her that I had noticed that she had a very nice leg, if she would permit me the liberty of saying so, adding discreetly: "Of course, from an aesthetic—"

"A what?" she interrupted suspiciously.

"An artistic point of view," I hastily put in, gazing disinterestedly upon that marvelous limb.

The liberty was permitted, she said, delighted that I had been inspired to praise it; but I would have to wait until tomorrow night because it had to be arranged.

Now I accepted this voluntary intelligence with a restraint which betokens the highest commendation. I practically slept on the spot where she proposed that I meet her because the boss did not like the girls to meet friends in the bar. When she arrived she told me that everything had been arranged. A happy thrill tingled through me. I had had such a feeling before when I was a soldier. A soldier of fortune was I! I thought, With a gal in every fort. "Bravo!" I cried foolishly. "Bravo, old soldier! waxing waning, militant thing! old cannon fodder; folly fodder. One taxi for two brave soldiers!" I shouted, and a taxi skidded up to us. As we got in, I hardly noticed the queer way in which the driver looked at us. Perhaps I thought: He's her old daddy. "Be gone!" I cried, rearing back in the seat, puffing my cigar, while she told the driver where; which I suspected to be unnecessary, as I squeezed my lady's hand with a modicum of certainty, and she uttered an open-throated squeal, as the car swerved around the corner . . .

The next days were serious days, in which I repented of my folly on the night before, the money I had spent and the general waste of effort and energy. I became absorbed in a theme for a story about a virtuous young man and a virtuous young woman who had loved as children. It aroused within me a consciousness of the need to recapture something that was lost in me. I took long walks and long looks at the city. I made many trips over the bridges and looked through dazzling spiderwebs at the sloping, gossamer-ribbed, life below.

During one of my walks, on a beautiful day, I had the following intuition, which I shall now relate:

The spider is, as far as spiders go, a perfect creature, I thought, as I watched one of those busy fellows modestly swinging a heavy girder of gossamer from the stanchion to the railing of the Kirchenfeld bridge . . . It is perfect because it is perfectly equipped to perform its highest level of activity—

At this point I was distracted by a very pretty girl, about twenty, I guessed, wearing a narrow skirt. Her hips swayed this way and that as she walked.

—instinctively! I thought; and then I thought, Yes, instinctively, because in that creature thought and action are completely integrated. It no longer needs to think what to do, nor does it have problems with more or less isolated feelings. To feel for him is the same as thinking, and thinking is the same as acting. He *is*, and yet he is always *becoming*. The work which results from such a highly integrated consciousness, which is the same as saying "unconsciousness," since to be perfectly conscious is to be perfectly "unconscious," the work, then, which results . . .

It became increasingly difficult to concentrate because this happened to be a busy hour, and girls wearing tight pants and sweaters kept swishing around me!

. . . is necessarily perfect; and how astonishingly beautiful!

Thus, the spider becomes a transparent entity, a perfect form, and yet formless through its integration with all of creation, like an ice cube afloat in a glass of gin. It is one with the whole, though it must suffer the fate of the immediate part, which its own peculiar form represents. It waxes and wanes, it changes, but its perfect self-consciousness ("unconsciousness," perfect integration of "feeling-thought-action") does not change. It is at rest, at peace with itself, like the hub of a spinning wheel, like the axis of the spinning globe, which is this world . . .

With the light of these thoughts shimmering in my eyes I looked at the skies and the trees, at the birds and at the river below, and made many new discoveries about myself, and about my relationship to the world at large. My spirits soared, as a result of which, I made a momentous decision: to revive within my breast my youthful enthusiasm over the Good and the Path of Virtue. For I had been, as a young man, attracted to the Holy Life. Now I would reinspire myself to dwell upon the mysteries of religion and upon the metaphysical problems which evolved therefrom, one of which I felt I had solved upon this wondrous day, the problem of Free Will and Divine Grace.

I had now decided, in view of my activities during the last few weeks, especially of the previous day, and in view of the luminous intuition generated by the moral palpitations of my sensitive heart, that the Will is Free only if man adheres to his form, and exploits his potentialities on all levels as completely as possible. That is, as my mother used to say, "Be yourself, boy!" This can be achieved only by the strictest adherence to discipline, to law—any law will do, they all lead one to the same end, which is the revelation of its own aspect of truth, from which, as with the spider, one may, in a way which I cannot describe, comprehend the universe. Now one can possess an unyielding discipline if he has willpower. Willpower is achieved through determination. Determination is an attribute of character. Character depends upon the taste of your mother's milk and on whether or not your father takes cream in his coffee, as well as a few other incalculable "accidents." But when one splits the thinnest hair he finds that the entity known as Free Will depends upon the Grace of God.

Reassured by my newly discovered wisdom, I vowed that I would seek out the Way, and that I would never flee in the face of moral danger again. Furthermore, I would accept the most terrible thing of all, to face myself. At this point I strained over the bridge, in order to see if I could see my reflection in the water about a hundred feet below, saw that I could not and felt sort of silly, but succeeded in convincing myself that my decision had filled me with respect for myself and for my fellowman as well: What matter if he laughed at me as I walked down the street! I would love him, in spite of all! For, after all, was not love the final answer?—cool, objective, undifferentiated love?

I wrote and rewrote many pages on this theme. But as concentration grew wearisome, and the tedium of typing with two fingers exhausted me, I sought relaxation in some harmless diversion. I decided to go to town and have a glass of wine, and to enjoy a well-earned holiday. Of course, I had partly decided upon this course because I had by no means forgotten my barmaid. I thought of her very much . . . I planned to visit her bar and talk to her. I would show her that I was still friendly, that I still respected her and that I was not one of "those," of whom Bern was ostensibly full, who wanted only one thing from a girl, and then, which was worse, didn't know what to do with it when he got it. I would show her that my "objective" love for her as a human being transcended the moral condemnation of society because of the highly conventional, extremely natural, though notoriously unlawful, act which we had committed.

I arrived at the bar somewhat earlier than my usual hour and took not my usual seat, but one in the corner near the door. One of the waiters sniggered as I filled my pipe. The head barmaid glanced at the pianist with a smile, and he began to play "Nobody knows the trouble I've seen," very softly. My barmaid rushed over to me. I looked up at her and smiled uneasily.

"I have to talk to you," she said imperiously.

"All right," I said. Then I ordered wine, thinking better of the cigar, for I had a faint premonition that I was going to need all the money I could get my hands on, and soon!

"What are you going to do?" she asked me a little while after the bar closed. We had found a lonely spot in the Tier Park. We sat on a bench under a tree by the Aare. The sky was not very clear, but the night was warm. There was a slight breeze. "What are you going to do?" she asked aggressively; while I watched the ducks floating backwards downriver, diving for worms, and marveled how they could see backwards in the dark.

"Are you sure?"

"What do you mean, am I sure!"

Mimi's words haunted my mind the whole of the following week. We decided to wait on the doctor's report. Then she would tell me. Then we would do what we would do.

"Are you sure?" I asked her a few days later, on the same bench, under the same tree that stood by the Aare. She did not answer; while I observed that there was not a duck in sight, and marveled that they all had flown away.

The decision is all mine, I thought. A bird screeched in the night, and the vision of a bright sunny day on the Kirchenfeld bridge came to mind, and my heart was filled with the noble resolves which had inspired me to seek out the Way of the Good. To live the moral life, I thought; to walk in the middle of the road, in wind, sun and rain; and not run for cover, but see and feel the vicissitudes of life in their sameness, and to not look back! . . . A virtuous feeling overpowered me, as I took her by the hand and said:

"Well, Mimi . . . if you're sure . . . I'll take you for—I mean,

dear Mimi, may I have—the honor—to ask you to become—
my wife? And if it's a girl I'd like her name to be Guinivere. I
mean—"

"What!"

Her mouth flew open wide, as though I had slapped her in
the face with a stone about the size of the Matterhorn.

"But—isn't that what you wanted?"

"You want to *marry* me!" Unconsciously she brushed her hair
back. A furtive smile rushed into her face and quivered tremu-
lously upon her lips. And then she jammed her finger into her
mouth, crushed with happiness, I supposed. She looked into my
eyes for a long time, as though she would discover my meaning.
I dared not look away. Then she looked away, across the river
and into the trees of Wabern.

"But . . . I can't. I'm still young. I've got my whole life before
me . . ."

Her words flowed dreamily over my mind, so engrossed was
I with the vision of moral righteousness and purity I had conjured up on the bridge while looking at the world through a
spiderweb. My determination not to run away from myself was
unshaken. To walk in the middle of the road, I thought, and take
the weather as it comes, and not look back . . .

"What about Guinivere?" I asked her.

"Who?"

"The baby?"

She looked at the river. Then she smiled and looked at me
and I could see that she was imagining the baby within her. And
I imagined the baby within her, whose name was . . . Suddenly
she shook her head and rose from the bench. Tears smeared the
black stuff around her eyes, as she told me that she knew a man
who would give her something to take to get rid of it. I told her
that it would mean risking her life.

"You don't have to do it!" I cried. "Have the baby and give
it to me. It would be nice if it were a girl. We could name her
Guinivere and—"

"My mother's name was Marie," she said tonelessly.

"We could go away and have it. Nobody would know. I have seven hundred dollars left. We could go to the south of France."

She said the man had promised her a job in another town. This was her big chance. He would make her a partner . . .

I turned down the river path and walked a long way without looking back. After a while I sat on a bench and watched the white water roll under the bridge . . .

A few months later when by chance I entered the bar where she used to work, the pianist asked me, during the intermission, if I had heard anything of my barmaid. I told him that she had a job working in another bar in another town, and that she was a partner, but that I had not heard from her, and doubted if I ever would again.

"The 'bar' is a whorehouse!" he said. "One of the waiters went to Munich for his holidays and saw her there. She looks a mess. They've got her and she can't get away. She'd give up her kneecaps to get back here now, my friend. You're a lucky man!" He patted me on the shoulder and gave me a confidential smile. "Have a drink."

"No thanks," I said.

I left the bar feeling—what? A little sad? Yes, and a little ashamed of the self-righteous feeling within me that I could not suppress. I felt a little sick of myself for feeling that I was what the pianist had said I was, a "lucky" man.

Lucky? Lucky—because we had had absolutely nothing in common but loneliness, a loneliness which is fed upon that food which makes one lonelier still. We would have been miserable together, I thought, in an effort to console myself. People usually are when there is no love between them. At the same time I felt a resentment against her which bit into my heart like acid, and for which this "revenge" was but sour-sweet. For I was thinking: Would she not have been better off with me?

But there was something deeper still which pained my heart, the thought: She would not marry me because I am a black man . . . Had I been white it would have been different. I'm glad! something profoundly evil and perverse within my nature said with a frightful clarity. I tried to suppress it, knowing that I went too far! but it rose to the surface of my mind in spite of me.

I was a deeply troubled man for some time after that. I was troubled not by what had happened to her, but by what had happened to me because of it. Or have I always been that way! I wondered, feeling that for all my moral pretensions there was something unclean in me. I now appeared more repulsive in my own eyes than the old woman I found lying in the gutter on Troost Avenue—even when she fouled my clothes! . . . Nor could I think these thoughts away, they simply had to wear away. They had to break up into fine filaments of light and shift in the aura of nervous tension in which I moved and felt. They could merely cast rays of speculation into that "future" in which I might, if I were able, absolve myself. Meanwhile, life simply went on.

How many times I passed that cursed bar and was not able to enter it. Nor can I go there now when I understand her better and myself, as well, and have forgiven us both.

I had told this story to my landlord and lady as an indirect means of confession, but to my shame, in my perverse desire to hurt others because I had been hurt, I presented it in its negative light, drawing from it a "general pattern of Swiss! behavior," pointing up many hurting little ironies which I had acquired not a little skill in locating. As you can well imagine, my story did not endear me to that lady, although there was nothing which she could say to contradict my interpretation of it. However, it was a petty triumph, and I lost much by it. My time in the Kirchenfeld was running out. My money was seeping through my fingers like grains of sand through the hole in an hourglass.

The Radio

Now, I HEAR you asking me a question which I have asked myself a thousand times, and which I am able to answer only now because only now is the answer clear and sharp against the background of the events which followed, in which perspective it can also be seen more roundly. The question which I imagine you to be asking is this:

Why did you endure it all? Why did you stay? You *said* you came only on a visit. What changed your mind?

Had you questioned me thus in the Kirchenfeld era I might have said, "Oh, I don't know . . ." dreading the task of analyzing so many complex details which I hardly understood myself. Now, however, I would say this: I arrived a few days before the six-hundred-year celebration of Bern's membership in the Federation of Switzerland. My host and hostess encouraged me to see it, and after I had seen it they encouraged me to stay a few days longer. Then one evening we went dancing at the Bellevue, where we met friends of theirs, a Swiss couple, a Mr. and Mrs. J—— who were planning to have a party in two weeks. They begged me to stay for it. They said, especially Mrs. J——, that it would be such a pity if I did not. And as the lady said it very charmingly, reinforcing her appeal with the warmest and most wondrous of smiles, and as I have always had a weakness for wonderfully smiling women, I stayed, as you see . . .

But the party was postponed a week, and then another week, and another. Meanwhile, my host, a very clever man, one evening when I was having supper at his home (it was a rare occasion because he was always frightfully and somewhat confidentially busy) suggested that I write my impressions of Bern as a tourist and sell them to the radio. "The Swiss like that sort of thing, he said. I thought it was an excellent idea, but a rather frightening one. Though I had come to Europe in order to write, I had thus far done little else than fill up notebooks and project fantastic plans for epic works which would, according to my speculations, shake the literary world to its foundations.

"I'll think about it," I said.

The very next afternoon I went to Radio Bern and told them that I was an American visiting Bern who would like to write his impressions of the town. The switchboard operator, who later became a faithful friend (I believe I still owe her money), called a Mr. R— and told him that in the lobby, standing before her, was a *Neger*, a Mr. Carter, an American, who would like to speak to someone about his impressions. Shortly after that Mr. R— came down. He was a pleasant, dimple-chinned man of possibly forty-three, of not quite medium height, with the expression of a sincere child. I told him that I was visiting Switzerland and that I would like to write my impressions of Bern.

"What would you say?" he wanted to know. "Generally . . ."

"Oh, I would just give my impressions . . . of the people and the sights"—and then I got an idea—"as seen through the eyes of an American Negro . . . who . . . who compares—as he looks at your city—his corresponding, and yet contrasting experiences in America . . . In his own town!" Mr. R— smiled sincerely, which caused the dimple in his chin to deepen. He touched it thoughtfully with his finger.

"Yes . . . that might be interesting. Why don't you write something and let us look at it."

I returned to my friends in an elated mood. I was astounded because it had been so easy. "Imagine!" I told them, Just imagine—just walking right in through the lobby of the Continental Hotel, taking the main elevator to the top floor, going into the radio station and saying, "I'd like to write my impressions of

Kansas City. Never!" And then this frightening thought came to me: Now all I have to do is write it!

Three days later I returned to the radio station with I forget how many pages of manuscript, containing my impressions.

And they bought it! That is to say, they would buy it when it was translated into German and broadcast in about a month, then they would pay. Of course, it was not much, compared to what one might have earned in America, but that didn't matter, what mattered was that I had sold something, the first thing I had ever written. I would always be grateful to Bern for that!

The following week Mr. R—— introduced me to a bright young man named Mr. S——, who had been to America and who spoke English very well. He translated the manuscript into German and directed the program. It was quite a success. It was so "fresh," they all agreed, so "naïf," "childlike" in its simplicity and "quaint." For I had spoken of how quaint and fairylike Bern seemed, as compared to the raucous complexity of America.

"Here all the land is cultivated," I said. "From the steepest hills down to the skinniest little strips of earth by the railroad tracks." I observed that the woods with their nurtured trees were more like gardens than woods such as those which I had known —wild and rambling, with thorny undergrowths and untamed thickets. Bernese trees looked much too domesticated to house the ferocious bobcat and the night-probing coon—and where were the wild dogs? I wondered in short, meaty sentences.

"From the landscape the character of a people is in evidence," I opined, in my "child-simple" way; "for the land and water make the people and the people make the land—and water. And they build the bridges [I had the Kirchenfeld bridge in mind, of course] which connect the valleys as well as the spirit of man to worlds eternal"—here I made reference to the rather wonderful old cathedral (the Münster) sticking up out of the center of the old town.

Then I paid them back for pointing at me and making exuberant exclamations when I passed them on the street—with a simple little thrust of my forefinger into what I hoped to be a sensitive rib, twisting a little as I commented on the pageant I had seen on the day of the federation celebration, wondering, in a mildly satirical vein, if the faces dressed in ancient garb, in armor and mail were the same faces I had seen in the pictures which hung on the walls of the historical museum, into whose garden I looked every morning from my window in the Thunstrasse. And I paid them back for occupying all the hotel rooms and burdening my sensitive spirit with suspicions of racial prejudice:

All of which seemed curious to my auditors—quite curious —and quaint, delightfully quaint, since nothing like that *could possibly happen in Bern!*

I had tried to be as interesting as I could be. The theme was threaded with a question, Why had I come to Bern, having run so far and fast through several reputedly interesting European countries? I explained all with music, with the Negro spiritual and with the "blues," in the realistic atmosphere provided by the sounds of the city. We tried to capture for the listener its voice speaking to me the language of the European mentality as opposed to the American mentality. It was quite successful. Everyone was enthusiastic.

Now: why did I stay here and endure it all?

"Oh," as I explained it to my American friends, "if I can profit by the experience which I am able to acquire at the radio, why, I'll stay right here and do it. If I can sell, say, one program a month, and if in the meantime I can break into the American market, why, I can stay indefinitely!" That is what I thought.

My friends wished me luck and explained that my only dif-ficulty with the Bernese would not result from racial prejudice, but would be a result of their "sensitivity" to persons, things or ideas that were "different," and that meant, primarily, "not Bernese." I figured that nothing worse than I had already expe-rienced could possibly happen to me and I decided to stay and accept the challenge. For I had decided that I would never run away from life or myself again . . . To walk in the middle of the road with the wind full in my face, accepting the weather, foul or fair, and not to look back, that was my idea.

So I bought ribbons for my typewriter and paper clips. I bought a good English-German dictionary and a good English-French dictionary, deciding to wait at least a year before I added a good English-Italian one to my collection because I had no more intention of neglecting Dante on his own terrain than I had of neglecting Goethe and Gide on theirs. Of course, my Shakespeare was always with me, my Eliot and Donne. I dusted off my Kant and Hegel and polished my Nietzsche. Flaubert was never far from reach and Jowett's translation of Plato shielded Montaigne's essays from the dusty drafts which blew through my window, the ashtray resting calmly and securely upon the older philosopher.

Why did I endure it all?

I hammered away at the American editors. Just one acceptance, I thought, and I'm made for six months—a year! I wrote stories in volleys and mailed them in single file. It was expensive. I had to wait for the readers to read them, pen their rejections and return them. It took time. Poe had waited, Faulkner had waited, Hemingway had to sell his own on the boulevards of Paris, and we all know of the trouble which Jack London had, not to mention Joyce. I, too, will wait, I decided. And while I waited I reveled in the more tragic biographies of famous men, and felt romantically trodden upon by Fate. How I enjoyed the idea of being trodden upon, as I sipped my landlord and lady's wine, and drowned my sorrows in the nocturnal humors of the city, whetting my thirst for fame upon vintage Chopin, Bach and King Oliver. Meanwhile, my money was running out, and I pressed my friends at the radio with ideas for new programs.

Through Which "Pressing" I Encountered Ideas Which Were Shocking to My Delicate Sensibility!

Now, IT WAS universally agreed that my programs were good; the director said so, my colleagues said so and the public said so. I thought they were pretty good myself. But they were not really to my liking because they dealt with slavery and unpleasant attitudes, interspersed with plaintive, though beautiful, Negro spirituals. They represented a concept of the American Negro which to my mind was not entirely true, and which was, I discovered, gradually, by and large the only concept which Europeans have—that of the suppressed but happy, suffering but profoundly religious Negro; a relatively primitive, simple-minded creature. So naturally when I proposed new programs with new themes, themes which they did not usually associate with the Negro, they were rejected in spite of the fact that they were often admitted to be good ideas and well written.

"This is all right," they would say, "but if we have a *Neger* writing material for us, we want things which are typical of him and of his people." And when I would inquire into the nature of the "typical" Negro, they would refer me to spirituals, which were written two hundred years ago.

I was enraged at this, though I admit now that it was silly of me. But at the time I felt that they were calling my identity into question. Perhaps, and I think you think this, too, I would not have been so agitated had I been more sure of myself. Be that as it may, I was agitated by what I felt to be an innocent conservatism which has always stereotyped the Negro, and which is and has been so dangerous to him. I was a desperate man, fighting for his right to exist!

Our main difficulty would always center around the music which I used, in order to intensify the narrative, for background and for purposes of unity. We often used Negro spirituals, of which the radio has a considerable library. I chose music which seemed to harmonize with the themes of the programs and which, of course, represented what in my judgment was the best in Negro music. In all fairness I must say that my friends who were usually collaborators and directors of the programs wanted the same. The only trouble was that we did not agree as to what was "best" in Negro music.

I would always prefer, say, Marian Anderson to Mahalia Jackson, or the Hall Johnson Choir to the choir of the First or Second Baptist Church of almost any American city! This difference amounted to a preference for the disciplined, trained expression of Negro music over the undisciplined, untrained expression, which my friends euphemistically termed "natural expression." The "natural expression," they argued, was closer to the deepest sentiments of the Negro people, the primitive simplicity and rhythmic intensity of Africa, while the trained product of the conservatory was a "Europeanized" debasement of its "purity."

Now, as I was the first American Negro most of them had ever seen, much less spoken to, I was astounded that they knew so much about the "deepest sentiments" of the Negro people. "For I would be at a loss," I admitted, "to expound the deepest sentiments of the Swiss people, though I would have more justification in trying, inasmuch as I have been a guest in your country for several years. But—we'll let that pass . . ."

The issues were clear. There were two questions: What is art?—"pure" or "folk art," as differentiated from "sophisticated" or "cultivated," "fine" art? and, what is the "true" nature of the Negro? The first question is elementary and the second is meaningless, so I suggest that we consider the former first.

Now, I am no musicologist, but it is my opinion that the work songs of Negro laborers in the fields of Alabama and Georgia are a far cry from the superbly finished expression of Marian Anderson, notwithstanding the fact that they are both vital and rich. To my mind, the workman's song is merely the beginning of art, a primeval outburst of song, which is right because it is sincere and because it sings from the very heart of an intensely human experience. It may be sad, it may be gay, but more than likely it will contain a mixture of these opposing humors. It is a beginning of art, though a complete expression on its own level, which may fling the singer into the far world of eternal verities, and it will move us profoundly.

But the greatest art, "fine art," is that which is passionate and yet restrained, an expression of the greatest freedom within the strictest limitations of form. When it is truly great it is like a cloud which passes through the sky, it moves us without involving us; it is like a flower, quietly violent in its perfection—perhaps unseen, but nonetheless great for all that—blooming in the dark!

The workman's song—and we have to be there, on the spot, in order to catch it—has intensity, vitality, sincerity—everything but that degree of perfection which is the result of a perfect balance of form and content, which is the result of experience sifted through a nurtured sensibility and reexpressed on the highest aesthetic level of the culture from which it evolved, extending that sensibility even beyond its own awareness. We all love the early ballads of pre-Chaucerian England, of Italy, of France—they are moving! But no one would deny—or would they?—the superiority of a Shakespearian sonnet; Boccaccio is Boccaccio; Villon piped a tune which is as light as air and as mighty as a spiderweb; there is no need to quote verses from Goethe, whose accents fall like sunbeams upon these troubled times!

The art of Marian Anderson represents the acme of what the Negro's expression can reach. But what I have just said is ridiculous, for if this great lady can elevate the Negro music to the level of "fine" art, how then can I confine her excellence to her race?

Is it not the main attribute of a work of art that it transcends itself through the very medium which it employs to express itself!

Now the workman may because of the depth of his feeling and because of the completeness of his self-awareness achieve qualitatively just as much as the master of "fine art," *for art is not an end in itself.* Hence, Louis Armstrong at the top of his powers produces a music which is qualitatively as great as that of any classical master; Ellington may be compared to Stravinsky; the artistry of Lionel Hampton in his best moments may suggest to the listener those terrible tensions with which Beethoven assails our senses. How does one classify the virtuosity of Art Tatum! And yet I would not underestimate Lipatti's interpretation of Chopin in order to support any theory.

A new question evolves now: just how far can genius, trained or untrained, take one? I refer to Armstrong for the answer. Now, that gentleman may have started out on a river boat (that "cat's" been everywhere!) but he has managed to pick up along the way the training which some of us who are less endowed with musical ability struggle for years to learn in the conservatory. And strangely enough, the quality of utterance which moves us in the end is not musical at all. Music is only the by-product of that powerful, general impetus which is the man himself. Armstrong would have been great had he never left the river boat. And how the dishes in the kitchen of the Anderson home must have tingled, as she sang to amuse herself while washing them!

So the controversy boiled down to a disagreement over the difference between the more and the less highly developed intuitive sensibilities which are trained to economize their forces, so as to achieve the highest effects, in all their rich contrasts and nuances, which "fine art" demands. It cannot be denied that the latter is the greater, though more difficult to achieve and the least likely to be popular with the majority of music-loving folk. For "fine art" is harmonious, often severely subtle, unobtrusive, uncompromising, complete from the first detail to the last. It is as free as air, and yet, as restrained as a brick wall! It is so easy and natural in its simplicity that it appears to the sensibility of its audience to be a thing naturally and therefore easily achieved. Hence, it is often said of great artists that they are "children of nature" who are "inspired" to "reveal" its wonders; that they are "different" from other people, having been "chosen" by God or the Devil! However this may be, I am sure that Shakespeare did not hatch his plays over a glass of ale. I have seen no less than thirty revisions of a single paragraph from a manuscript of Balzac's. It took Joyce fourteen years to write *Ulysses*, and Da Vinci has not finished the *Mona Lisa* yet!

And What Did They Have to Say to That?

WHY, I COULD hardly believe my ears, but, when I had finished my long, pedantic argument-crushing discourse on art, this is what my friends at the radio said to me:

"You are ashamed of this music because you are ashamed of your own people. You are ashamed of being a Negro."

A nauseous sensation rose slowly and deliberately from the pit of my stomach. My heart pounded wildly and a dizzy coolness wafted my wet forehead, as though I were falling from a great height. A tedious desperation crept into my voice—I could hear it!—when, struggling for control, I protested weakly and unconvincingly: "How—unreasonable you are! Simply because I refuse to accept what seems to me to be a noisy insincere rendition of the Negro spiritual!" I was further irritated by the fact that the one who acted as spokesman for the others seemed so little inclined to listen to what *I* said, especially since *I* was the person in question, and since the music which we were discussing was *my* heritage. And not only was a simple opinion about a genre of music at stake, not merely the egotistical satisfaction of being right, but the meaning of my very existence was being challenged—I felt it desperately.

Girls in tight skirts wiggling over a bridge between light stanchions housing spiders building webs on a sunny day came into my mind. I saw myself looking over the rail in an effort to catch my reflection in the water flowing far below, and feeling ridiculous because I could not, while my thoughts of moral solicitude soared as freely as light through the visionary air! I had resolved to walk in the middle of the road in all the weathers of the year. But now my friend's question had caused a veritable hell to break loose in the sky of my consciousness. Thunder thundered! Lightning flashed; I trembled like a solitary leaf on a very solitary tree.

He looked at me in righteous silence. And as I returned his look, I thought I heard him say: But—why did you come to Bern? A loud raucous laugh echoed down a long dark cavern. At that moment, though I knew that my mind was merely playing tricks upon me, I realized that the old question had still to be answered. A tinge of irony permeated my thoughts as I reflected that perhaps there was only one question in my life, and that the myriad questions which had thus far passed through my consciousness were crystalized into that one question. Again I saw myself straining over the bridge rail, feeling a trifle ridiculous in the presence of the heroic spider, silently building his web, and tried to catch my reflection upon the surface of the waters. At that instant a curious thing happened, which I believe to have been one of the greatest events in my life: the sun emerged from a heavy cloud and flooded the bridge with a wondrous light. Even had it been night I could have divined the colors in the pupils of the eyes of the fishes that passed beneath the bridge! Without straining my imagination in the least I could clearly discern a rather neglected shoe resting on the river's pebbly bottom. I fixed my attention upon a shoestring which unfurled from its eyelets. And then I spoke to the man:

"Perhaps you are right . . . Perhaps I am ashamed of the Negro people . . . of being a Negro. Heaven knows he has caused me enough trouble. He is so black and controversial. So—polymorphous that it is hard to hold onto him. Since our discussion has grown out of our disagreement as to the true nature of the Negro spiritual, perhaps it would be better to start there, to go to the scene of the crime, as it were. It is always best, is it not?, to have a starting point, from which, if one perseveres, like a spider, say, he cannot help but discover at least one aspect of the truth—if I may use the word. And that aspect may, *par hazard* or by the Grace of God, lead him to a world of truth which is void of mere aspects.

"Your suggestion that I am ashamed of my people and, therefore, of myself disturbs me greatly. I am convinced that there must be some particle of truth in it, otherwise I would not be disturbed. Now I beg of you, allow me to retrace my steps in order that I may look a little into the history of the Negro spiritual and discover just where the element of shame comes in, for I swear to you that at this moment I do not know it.

"Now, as well as I can remember, when those stalwart Africans got off the boat the first thing they did was to check their modest luggage, roll up their sleeves and go to work. For they were an order-loving folk! And we both know that they found ready employment, and in abundance because the south was in a mess. Men with vision and strong backs were needed to raise the cotton and tobacco and build the roads and lay the rails, which would one day connect the eastern and western shores of the United States of America.

"And we also know—we have heard—how in the cool of the evening when the day's work was done instead of whiling away their time over a volume of Shakespeare, or reinforcing their spirits with the *Ethics* of Spinoza; instead of going to the theater and concert halls every night, which then as now were expensive, they made up their own music. It took a few days to become really good at it because they did not know the American language, and formal instruction was expensive. However, there were from time to time religious folk—some of them were Swiss, no doubt—who instructed them in the religion of the western world, the religion of the Jews, Moses, Abraham and Jesus.

"Because this new religion was a religion of farmers and hunters and fishermen and men who tended animals, of kings and fools and men who were wise, the Africans because they had also been hunters, fishermen and tenders of animals, having been kings, fools and men of wisdom in the old country readily understood the new teaching, especially since they were more or less

"naturally" endowed with a philosophical disposition which had
long since been tempered in the fires of an ancient passion for life
and that species of romantic humor which causes the rhinoceros
to run with the grace of a gazelle!

"Very soon then, in a matter of a few weeks perhaps, they
discovered that the new religion had much in common with
their own. Furthermore, they were able to sympathize with the
world-weary Hebrews who, as did Ulysses, wandered from land
to land in search of peace, even eating with sad reluctance, as
did Dante, the "salty" bread of strange kitchens . . . So in their
spare time and purely for their own edification they set the new
western religion to music. They gave it the old rhythms of Africa
and rhymed it. In order to relieve the tedium of work in the
fields and the heaviness of the loneliness which stole upon them
now and again, they sang the new religion as they worked and
when they felt particularly sad. The song which they sang became
known as the Negro spiritual.

"But you know much of this already," I said, feeling suddenly
the need to check my history for shameful elements. By shifting my head from the right to the left I managed to disturb the
image which quite unexpectedly filled my mind, that of flesh-
filled skirts worming over the bridge at the busy hour, while a
dauntless spider swung a gossamer boulder from a stanchion to
the bridge rail . . .

"I've found nothing in the quality of the Negro spiritual
which disturbs me," I reflected aloud. "In its formative period I
think you will agree with me that it was unmistakably great. 'Go
Down Moses' is, for example, as powerful as any church music
which has ever been written. Now I am certainly not ashamed of
Moses, nor of the song which the fellows sang about him. And, is
not working in the fields one of man's oldest and most venerable
occupations? The shameful thing eludes me.

"What is it!" I asked my companion, but he only looked at
me as though he were the animate manifestation of my own conscience. At that moment the sun sank into a huge cloud and I
was drenched in a coolness which sent shivers through my body.

But in the next instant the sun reappeared and I looked at my auditor thoughtfully and said: "Wait—wait a minute! I must go back and start all over again because I've just had an idea."

The idea came to me when the sun sank into the cloud and drenched me in shade. I shivered. A profound gloom came over me. Fear and hopelessness assailed me, for it had occurred to me that it was neither the song nor the work which irritated me, but the weather, the circumstances under which the work was done; that is to say, the condition of slavery.

"The spiritual," I began with great difficulty, "was written while the Negro was a slave. The work which he did was not voluntarily done. He was unhappy about it and he asked the new God to help him because he had learned that He had helped Moses, Abraham and Jesus when they were in trouble. Through the medium of a powerful necessity to live expressed as faith he created a song which transcended the limitations which slavery placed upon him, he became free! That is, those who possessed the genius which permitted them to objectify their suffering became free. The others had to make their adjustments as well as they could. Therefore, I am proud of the spiritual because it is great music, and I am ashamed of the rest because it reminds me of slavery. You see, I do not like to be reminded of my former undignified position in the world, nor of my present one, by stereotyped opinions which well—and ill—meaning people continually wag before my nose. And I do not enjoy being the victim of my own sense of conditioned guilt and inferiority because of it. When you play Negro music which I must choose, you will play that music of which I am proud and which represents the best which my people have attained. For I feel responsible for every one of them who was ever born, for every man in the world who is black. Because whenever he does something in the world, good or bad, I am blamed for it.

"The irony of it all is that I realize that my position is a false one. I am not every Negro, nor am I every man. You are perfectly right in pointing your finger at my weakness. Keep on pointing until I can't stand it any longer. Because when I can't stand it any longer perhaps the pain which I shall impose upon myself and the pain which you impose upon me will be so great that I shall have to cry out from that region of my awareness which lies beyond 'pain' and 'pleasure,' and I, too, shall perhaps utter a beautiful sound which shall set me free of both you and myself . . .

"But on the other hand . . . my position is not altogether false," I declared, wishing to rob him of the illusion that my problem was an easy one. "I was a slave, but now I am legally free. And what is more, I have become educated and sophisticated in the towns and cities of America and on the battlefields of foreign countries. It is my educated sophistication now which struggles with that general diffusion of intellect and feeling which is known as the sensibility. As a result there is a new song in my heart, or rather the old song, the same song, but in a new key. Because with the acquisition of legal freedom I inherited as a legacy a new slavery, freedom from which can be attained not by federal proclamation but only by the attainment of perfect morality. For that attainment I am responsible to myself alone and to what gods I may conceive. Thus you see, friend, we have —have we not?—made a complete circle. Freedom is forever the issue, in order to attain which I must sing a song which is the song of myself. In order to read that strange music I must look deep into myself—and beyond. Such was the song of slavery, such is your song, the song of every man, which is the song of Marian Anderson."

My friend looked at me a long time and then he asked:

"What would you say of jazz then?"

"Blow, man!"

"What!"

"Blow! That is the cry of the jazz enthusiasts back home. And that is my cry, too. It is meant as an encouragement to the musician to transcend himself and reach that level of pure music which is typical of all music. Isn't jazz the offspring of the spiritual! Armstrong will shake hands with Mozart and Ellington will converse as an equal with Stravinsky—if not today, then tomorrow."

And when I said to him, in order to illustrate my point, that Marian Anderson sings the music of Bach magnificently there was another argument because his reply was, "Yes . . . but why should we hear Bach from Anderson when we can hear it by German artists who can sing it better?"

"But can they?" I asked. "Bach belongs to the world. Any true and trained sensibility can interpret Bach. Have not the Jews proved to be the outstanding interpreters on any number of instruments of almost all of the great composers?"

"As a singer of Negro spirituals, she is peerless—"

"May she not also be peerless as a singer of Bach?"

"No!"

"That, my friend, is intellectual prejudice!" I cried. And then a curious thing happened. While I was saying the phrase "intellectual prejudice" another term was resounding in my ears. It was a term which in essence means the same thing, but which is broader in scope, signifying a meaning which includes not only racial prejudice but any kind of limited point of view. The term which came to me was the term "provincialism!" Joy leaped through me as I vaguely realized the significance of my discovery. It opened the doors to many emotional rooms which had heretofore been locked. The word "provincialism" lifted the burdensome weight of the feeling that I was isolated from my fellow-man. It converted me into a mere member of a larger group of persons, the reaction to whom could be classified with a word which was valid in any limiting context. My thoughts about this marvelous word became clearer as the conversation continued because we began to speak next of Andrés Segovia in connection with this theme.

"I'm glad that you mention Segovia," my friend said, "because he is a good case in point. I find it regrettable that he plays so many European composers and so little Spanish folk music on his guitar. After all, the guitar is a folk music instrument and not an instrument upon which classical music should be played."

"But—what is the end of either performance?" I asked heatedly.

"To play music, of course!"

"Then what does it matter upon which instrument it is played, as long as it is played well! Is it not reasonable to believe that in spite of the fact that the guitar did not exist in Bach's time he *might* have written for it had someone invented it?"

"But Bach wrote for the organ, the spinet—"

"Do you know that much of Bach's music which was originally written for the organ is played upon the cembalo, and that to many persons—myself included—it sounds better upon that instrument?"

"That is another matter!"

"Yes, you are right," I said, suddenly remembering that Bach did write for the cembalo. "Bach wrote for the cembalo. But that doesn't negate the principle underlying the question we are discussing. You can't simply deny my existence because of a convention. Instead of the words 'Bach' and 'guitar' substitute 'Negro' and 'classical music.' The analogy is obvious. One plays jazz, which is loud and noisy, upon a Negro, and Bach or any classical music—preferably by a German—upon a European. Segovia is no less wrong for playing the classics upon the guitar than Marian Anderson is wrong for singing music which was composed by that classical master!

"No sir! Man's thought progresses from the consideration of particular, differentiated things. All of his endeavors, whether vain, futile, wise or foolish, tend to that end. To deny him that possibility—which is impossible anyway because nature is dynamic and will not be killed—is to distort that which is most vital in his nature. On the other hand, sometimes that very 'distortion' results in an act of assimilation, of incorporating into himself the vital opposing element which threatens his existence, infusing into the new being nature's incorrigible will to survive. Often this drive becomes so powerful that it overreaches the mere ethnic impetus—in this case—which motivated it and the particular environment which nurtured it, and engulfs the then known world. It rides upon the air's strong currents as song, it pounds within the chargers' hooves as conquest, or it quavers within some prophetic throat as religion. When the great wave recedes a new page must be added to the history of human beings . . ."

"Yes, yes," he said, "perhaps there is some little truth in what you have said. I am sympathetic to your oratorical efforts, but there are many qualifications which your argument calls to mind which should be taken into consideration. The question is an interesting one, and profitable as a subject of discussion, since it is always to one's advantage to learn the point of view of an outsider.

"But, as to the theme which you have presented for a program, we will have to consider it seriously. It is very difficult, you see, because it is different here from in America, where the radio is—is a privately owned and purely commercial enterprise. In *der Schweiz* the tendency is to be a little, shall I say, conservative. We must educate as well as entertain our listeners without shocking them with racial views . . ."

At this point I hastily suggested that we go somewhere and have a beer. While we drank it I tried to remember what we had spoken about, but I could not remember a word. I merely felt tired and weary, as though I had climbed a long steep hill and stopped without reaching the top. Finally I said good-bye to my friend. I had to go and he had to go.

I stepped out into the street and was assailed by the world. I walked heavily toward the bridge. It was late afternoon. The sky was a severe metallic blue and the clouds were hard and sharp and white. I looked at them and fragments of the discussion sprang out of oblivion and mingled with the myriad sounds and colors around me and with the weariness within me. But only for an instant or two, because after that I became lost in the memory of the words and feelings with which I had struggled so futilely to answer the question. I had to laugh when I thought of how it had come disguised as a feeling of shame! By the time I reached home I had completely reassembled the argument in which shame had lain buried.

I repeated it over and over to my landlord and lady during the Indian Summer of my stay in the Kirchenfeld. And I was surprised to find them—especially my landlord—so sympathetic.

"I can understand how you feel very well," he said.

"How?" I asked, believing him to be so absorbed in the life and tradition of his country as to be totally ignorant of my problem. "How could that be!" I asked unbelievingly and somewhat brusquely because it is always a little disconcerting to be understood.

"With the choir." I knew that he was member of one of the city's oldest and most distinguished singing groups. "It was two —perhaps three—years ago. We were going to London on a concert tour. Dr. Dumbkopf—he's dead now—made the embarrassing suggestion that we wear Swiss Alpine costumes on the stage. He made me crazy! Imagine wanting to give foreigners the impression that we Swiss wear Alpine costumes every day and carry Alpine horns around in our hip pockets!"

I shook with laughter, while the old man became so upset at the mere memory of the proposal that my landlady and I were at pains to quiet him . . .

What Happened in the Weeks That Followed

I TRIED TO write about the problems which had occupied my thoughts during the previous weeks because I thought them to be of vital importance. Needless to say, I was unable to write a decent line because my emotional involvement in them was so great that I could hardly see straight, let alone write clearly. But not only that, I had another hectic problem. When I tried to tell how hurt and angry I was I felt (it had often occurred in the past but never so frequently as now) silly and even ridiculous, as I had felt that day on the bridge in the presence of the spider. After I had "defined" the "problem" and explained all the reasons why and why not and run several times up and down the scale of pathos, the "problem" seemed to disappear! My life, your lives, life! seemed to be in the best possible condition. I took a good look at myself in the mirror and was forced to admit that were I God I would not change a thing! And yet, this conclusion did not make me happy either. The result was that I had to give up writing about race problems altogether. I had to (excuse me) leave the nigger in the woodpile to take care of himself, while I busied what was left of my "self" with other and less dangerous themes.

But how can a man write with only a fragment of himself? Well, I tried it, and the editors were sorry. "Very sorry," they said, though they assured me that their rejection slips did not necessarily mean that my stories were bad, but merely that they were not suitable to the needs of their magazines.

Meanwhile, the little black imitation-leather folder with

the traveler's checks grew thinner. I had long ceased to smoke Dannemann cigars—four or six a day!—at a franc apiece, having discovered the Stumpe, upon which discovery it occurred to me that Switzerland had achieved what many high-minded Americans have long proposed as a solution to at least one of the nation's most vital problems, the production of a good five-cent cigar! I also plucked up my courage and braved the terrible Brissago, which to my surprise I liked very much, though they were a trifle strong as compared to the cigars I had previously smoked, but happily, like the ones I had previously smoked, with the exception of the Dannemann, it was cheap.

I not only altered my smoking habits, I drank less wine and danced less and visited the Chikito and my few favorite bars less often. As my fortune dwindled and the likelihood of revitalizing it by selling programs to the radio diminished, I began to worry.

I had serious conferences with my landlord and lady and the bags beneath my eyes swelled with apprehension.

"It is apparent to all of us," said my landlady, "that fame and wealth will not come to you immediately. You should get a job and work!"

"My work is writing," said I.

This reply strained my position considerably with these two venerable persons. I had broken one of the *Ten Commandments of Switzerland*: Everyone must work! by which is meant, "work for which one is paid"—by the week, biweekly, monthly, with a graded increase in salary and a pension at the age of sixty-five, all signed and pat and stamped!

"Perhaps my father will give me a little money," I said.

"He might," they replied. "But how shameful!—A strong, healthy young man like you, asking your parents to give you money when you are perfectly able to work yourself!"

"We're sorry!" my mother said in her letter some months later, and I could see the tearstains on the paper. "We're sorry but we—your father and I—just can't afford to send you any more money. We're deep in debt for what we've sent you already. You know we would if we could. It's not as if we had it and wouldn't

send it . . ." There had followed a description of the family circumstances which I knew very well. And then she had said:
"After all, you're a man. You're thirty years old already and we're
forty-six." She had not completed her thought, there had been
no need, so she ended her letter with some loving words which
only mothers use. I cried like a baby, right there in the middle of
the Bahnhofplatz, as I read it. When I finished the letter I folded
it carefully and put it into my pocket and took it home where it
is now, in a drawer among the rejection slips.

But this had not actually happened before I went to Paris,
and before my money finally ran out.

Paris the Second Time

WAS FUN. I went with Mr. and Mrs. C—— from the radio. Mr. C—— had to represent Bern at an Inter-European Radio Conference, which had convened for the worthy purposes of improving the relations between the various European radio services, and the discussion and exposition of new technical methods recently discovered and employed in order to produce sound magic for the greater delight and spiritual elevation of its listeners. I was fortunate in having been invited to go along with the C——s, for they were my friends. I would not have to be alone in Paris. Another advantage was that they spoke French much better than I did, although my ability to speak that language had by this time considerably improved, so I was not inconvenienced by that problem, as I had been on my first visit.

Now that I look back upon my experiences during the second trip I am amazed by the contrast which I perceive when I think of the feelings which I had when I first got off the boat in Le Havre, and when I finally arrived in Paris only to be robbed of all the paradisiacal illusions which I had conjured up in my mind. When I arrived this time it was September, sunny and warm. There was no problem about accommodations, we had reservations in a nice little hotel in the Latin Quarter. My room was cheap, sunny and reasonably clean, with subtler toilet smells and quieter bed quoits than those of the room which I had formerly occupied in the Rue Monsieur le Prince. We were just off the Boulevard St. Michel, about four minutes from the Metro.

There was a comfortable, cheap Greek restaurant around the corner from the hotel, so we ate our French meals in Greek, and very good they were. Singers came in while we ate and sang songs of the folk of today and yesterday the way they felt them, which was sometimes good and sometimes bad, but always moving because sincere. Some people gave them money, while others did not look at them or listen to them. The food was very good, especially the bread.

We often visited a Turkish coffee house near the restaurant after dinner. They sold things other than coffee there as well, at a secret-looking bar behind a curtain. Two beautiful Arabic-looking girls who also looked like sisters sang Turkish, Arabic and Greek-sounding folk songs as they danced, swaying their soft brown bodies which were bare in the middle, with fillips of spangled gold dazzling their breasts and the triangular spot just below their navels—orientally. They danced to the gypsy beat of tambourines which they whirled from the tips of their lacquered fingers. Men with sheens on their faces put money into them, and more money, causing the music to play with greater intensity to the whirl of the bodies, swaying between the waist and the thigh, with the aid somehow of the knees and the tremble of the toes. Their golden breasts cooperated with the general movement by rolling sensuously, but not vulgarly, ecstatically, while a fine foam of sweat crowned their brows like coronets of pearl.

In the heat of the dance their lips parted and they moistened them with their wet tongues.

The violinist played the violin as though it were a bass fiddle, accompanied by funny-looking string instruments which I have often seen in movies in which the heroine's name is Tania. She is up to her pretty red lips in intrigue with enemy agents, for which intrigue she must—regrettably—be killed in the end, but not before she has discovered the God-given virtue in the bright and shining American Way of Life!

There were ornate red rugs all about and shiny brass things with polished surfaces and lacquered things with questionable inlays. All of the people who were there, except the C——s and myself, looked like what Europeans think American gangsters look like. I often went to this little coffee house even when my friends did not come with me.

Gradually, the city revealed some of its charm to me now. With someone friendly to be with and to talk to I could relax and regard the city more "objectively." So I took my time and had a good long look at the city of Paris. I tried not to but I could not help being influenced by all the descriptions of Paris by the many famous persons who have published them. They were all forced, it seems, to pass their impressions on to posterity. Therefore, I looked at the Seine, for example, with a literary glint in my eye at first, and then I felt silly, terribly silly! and gave it up. I looked at the Seine again and thought: It's a funny-looking little old river. All those grown men with such great big poles! tempting those poor innocent little fish out. Can't eat them but it's fun to catch them: I understand that . . . I must have watched the fishermen for hours. Near Notre Dame. I took a look on a wet rainy day. It was cold inside but the white candles were bright. There were many strangers saying, "Oh!" and "Ah!" They bought postcards with a picture of the church on it. Many photographed it. But I simply looked at it quietly, and skeptically, as though to say, as the legendary Missourian is supposed to say: "You've got to show me!"—and was overcome by a beautiful feeling which stole upon me quite unaware. I like Utrillo's painting of it best, I thought, because it describes best what I . . . what a temperament such as mine feels when it is exposed to such an old romantic beauty . . .

On another day I admired the sweeping approach to the Place de la Concorde. When I returned to the hotel I met Mr. and Mrs. C——. As we had a glass of wine at a nearby brasserie I told them my impression of it. "I thought it so grand and free! And then I felt so ordinary as I thought it. Probably because that is precisely what everyone else seems to think. They certainly say so. I managed to control my literary impulses and enjoy the place quietly and nobly resisted the temptation to pee against the balustrades!"

I took a walk through the Bois de Boulogne on a sad

afternoon. I do not know why I had reason to be sad, except that I often find myself sad on a beautiful afternoon in autumn without knowing the reason why, not exactly. But of course, I never have to explain to myself the reason why I am sad, I must provide a reason only when I attempt to explain it to somebody else. On this particular afternoon I was thinking about a young man whom I did not even know, to whom the Bois de Boulogne meant a lot, apparently. He went there one evening when the sun was setting, I imagine, when the redness of the sunset mingled with the red coloring of the leaves and shot himself with a revolver, out of a desperation which originated in the seat of his grandmother's (or perhaps his mother's) nervous sensibility, more than likely. I thought of him as I walked, searching for a way which he knew he would not find again, like a boy searching for a ball that is lost, kicking the dead leaves with the toe of his shoe, not really caring about the ball now, the real reason for his melancholy lying hidden, deep down somewhere in the bottom of his consciousness. I tried to guess why he had chosen just this spot, why he had traveled many miles from his own land to do it. Romance . . . I thought. I looked suspiciously at the fading flowers and at the trees, and wondered if they knew what I was thinking; if He knew, beneath the red and yellow stains of the trees, from beneath the blades of rusty grass beneath my feet! Overwhelmed by a respect for the unknown, I walked softly and carefully upon the earth after that—and away from the Bois de Boulogne.

I was getting the "feel" of the place now. I was grasping it with my fingers, smelling and tasting essences, which I slowly remembered having experienced under the crazy conditions of war. They filtered through the memory of ten intervening years and were reinforced by a rumor of chaotic vitality which had echoed through the abandoned graves of generations.

I was constantly assailed by the conviction that I had actually been here before: just here, at this particular place, at this time when the sun shone as it does at this very instant! Or there! having smelled precisely that peculiar scent before, and

seen that color, which is really more orange than red, whizzing
past my eyes from the vortex of the tail-light of a passing auto.
A feeling of familiarity followed me through spacious gardens,
under arches and even into the Louvre, where I watched Jesus
being crucified in an innumerable variety of excruciating ways. I
remembered how tiresome it was, stretching my neck up and up,
and higher still, only to have my exertions rewarded by confusion
because I had always imagined that one should look back sort
of over one's shoulder and down at history, through all the pain
and suffering, the way a hump-backed man, from the elliptical
mouth of a cave, silhouetted against the sky, looks back into
the darkness from which he has ascended. A few minutes later
I laughed aloud in the subway and surprised myself, suddenly
feeling embarrassed because an old lady and a pretty girl looked
at me. I could hardly get off the train fast enough because I had
also the impression that I had known the old lady and the pretty
girl all my life!

In Paris I discovered that the nice thing about being with
friends in a foreign city is that they make one appreciate being
alone, which is quite different from being alone because there
is no one to be with. Often Mr. C—— was busy with his conferences and Mrs. C—— and I pursued our pleasures separately.
However, we usually ate lunch together at the United Nations
building, as well as the evening meal, which we usually took at
the most convenient restaurant, when, of course, we were not in
the vicinity of our little Greek restaurant near the Turkish coffee
house girls. We did a little shopping together. Mrs. C—— bought
a huge bottle of eau de Cologne, which I smuggled over the border because the customs officer did not (just as Mrs. C—— knew
he would not) look into my bag. She bought powder, which
they blended to just the "tone" she wanted from mountains of
colorful powders, pink and beige and mauve and violet and red.
As I watched the charming young lady mix and weigh them I
imagined how wonderful it would be to make bread from flour
of such wondrous colors. A bright orange loaf, piping hot! for
breakfast.

One of my greatest pleasures was derived from simply walking through the streets at night and not from looking at all the historical buildings and monuments, which I viewed with some pleasure, I must admit; nor from the French people or the naked women in the nightclubs (I went to one or two of them and they were sort of interesting, fascinating in a promiscuous, guilt-ridden way, but they did not provide what one really might call a personal, private pleasure, a pleasure which satisfies because you yourself have created it, spontaneous and rewarding because unlooked for) but by simply walking through the streets and looking at what was to be seen.

All the streets were interesting. That dirty alley over there with the cracked windowpane painted blue, what was behind it? I wondered. A yard crowded with wooden circus horses painted white and red and gold, accompanied by a rusty diving helmet and an enormous shoe which was as tall as a very tall man! I walked through short black little streets that glistened in the rain, one with a candy store with windows filled with colored jars and with a pile of baling wire jammed against the door—why? That light!—What was up there? Soft shadows dancing behind a shuttered window.

In Paris I was the stranger (as I was in Kansas City, Detroit, Philadelphia and London) who stood on the outside, looking in, discovering what? at odd hours of the day and night. It was always the strangeness, the unpredictableness of the shapes and colors and sounds that fascinated me, which aroused within me an insatiable curiosity. Every object was a new world, and I was Columbus!

There must be other places as lovely as Paris, but I had never seen a city which was so filled with loveliness—in the guise of surprise. Follow the Seine or climb the great hill in Montmartre, or should you suffer from an access of happiness, stumble through the honey-combed maze behind the Hôtel de Ville. There is a lusty hell if I ever saw one, with all the eyes glaring out of the windows looking for sinners, looking for me:

"Sorry . . . sorry . . ." I muttered hoarsely as I brushed past them, wondering if the young girl with the strange eyes had ever been young once in Kansas City, grown old, and fallen with the weight of age onto the sidewalk just below Twelfth and Troost, when I was a boy of ten or eleven.

On an odd night I visited another quarter where the poor people lived and I felt at home there because it reminded me of Kansas City. I walked past the people who slept under the bridges on the stones.

"Sorry . . . sorry . . ." I muttered to an old man playing the violin.

And to the man whom I passed the next day, lying in the middle of the sidewalk in the Boulevard St. Michel, while hundreds of people walked around him without giving him a second look. They stepped over him, too. He might as well be dead . . . Sorry . . . sorry . . . Paris might just as well be Kansas City . . . But it isn't. Because I'm no longer . . . Was I ten or eleven?

After fourteen days we returned to Bern. We were glad to get back because we needed a rest. Gradually, as the tensions (which resulted from the shocks which I had received through many vital violent experiences in Paris) relaxed, a profound depression sank me in misery.

Why I Was Depressed and Sunk in Misery

WELL, I WAS depressed and sunk in misery because I had begun to reflect seriously once again upon my position in the world. Thus far I had sold none of my stories, and I was not really sure that they were good. Though there might still be a few opportunities to write for the radio, the prospects did not look particularly encouraging because they wanted me to write only about the Negro, that is, the Negro of their imagination, or to play Negro spirituals with a little pathetic narrative thrown in, in order to make their texts more comprehensible, or they wanted a little but not too much jazz.

Now I had many other ideas which I felt to be good ones, with new themes, requiring novel radiophonic techniques and exploiting more general areas of interest—literature, poetry, philosophy—in a simple, amusing way.

For example, I did a little thing for which I had great hopes, a program called "Come Fill the Cup." I got the title from a movie which I had seen about an alcoholic, but my theme was different from that. I wanted to show how things, which seem utterly different, even entirely unrelated, are very much related indeed. I wanted to compare the creative process, as exemplified in jazz, especially its improvisory aspect, with the higher intuitive process, as described by no less a personage than Immanuel Kant, whose *Critique of Pure Reason* I had sweated over as a student.

I chose him especially because he was German, he represented a high point in the German culture, which was the heritage of the German-Swiss people. I thought it would be sort of cute to show what happens when the intelligence is informed by the intuition and thereby inspired to overreach itself in the projection of a creative idea.

And what better example could one find than music, which represents man's highest form of creative activity, if one wished to avoid pedanticism? and what better music than jazz, since it is a genre which I know best, as interpreted by Fats Waller? with his robust, at times, Rabelaisian humor—if one wished to freely exploit the novelty of such a comparison!

I took Kant's classical example of the cup or water glass submerged in the sea. The glass symbolized the "form," which was equated with the perceiving intelligence of man, while the sea represented the "formless," undifferentiated, ubiquitous "truth." The brim of the glass marked the limit of the perceiving, thought-articulating intelligence, at which point something mysterious happened, the infiltration of the unknown into the area of the known by a process which has never been discovered, which Plato elucidated in the *Ion*, and which "Idealist" and "Materialist" philosophers alike, throughout the long arduous history of western thought, have had difficulty in "explaining," except through poetry, and abstruse symbolism, as embodied in such words as "intuition," "inspiration," contact with "the unknown," and so forth . . . I wanted to bring them into the parlor so that Frau Schmidt could enjoy the novelty of an intuitive experience, which I would recreate, using the music of "Fats" Waller as a point of departure, analyzing the tensions which catapulted him out of the written score into an explosive spray, a phosphorescent shower of beauty!

But my pet project never saw the light of day, although they bought the manuscript by accident! However, it was quietly shelved when it was read more closely and the program was never produced. I was even more depressed when the money which I had earned for it was spent. How would I get more? I wondered. My father could send me a little, but not much, nor could he send it indefinitely. It was a few months later that I received my mother's loving letter.

"You can go to work!" everyone said with sly smiles.

They said it with sly smiles, I thought, merely because they had to work. I fancied that they were secretly jealous because they thought that I lived a wanton life of leisure and was not willing to pay for it. From their point of view I was on a continual vacation. "Writing—work!" they exclaimed, their smiles deepening, thinking: Writing is no work. Writing is writing. I watched them trying to remember how little effort it took to write a letter or a grocery list, and then remember with a frown that even these slight tasks had been difficult enough, remembering with a deeper frown the mothers and friends to whom they owed long overdue letters, which memory they managed to discard with a flippant toss of their heads.

Why else should they continue to hound me about working? I had the feeling that they were glad that I had run out of money, not out of meanness, but out of their desire to see me conform to the apparently inescapable pattern which governed their lives. Was it not a sacrilege not to bow down to the God of Work? Wait a minute, I can give you a clear example of how I think they felt from an experience I had when I was a soldier:

It happened in Liège, Belgium. My train crew had escorted a supply train there. Upon arrival we were ordered to wait a day or two until we could get another train returning to our home base, which was Rouen, or perhaps take another train to a depot farther along the line. When we got off the train we were very dirty and very tired. We rushed to the hotel to which we were assigned and washed and shined ourselves in order that we might more presentably avail ourselves of Belgian hospitality. I had heard that there was a famous cathedral in the city, so I decided to go out and have a look at it.

We were ordered to carry our weapons with us because the front lines were not very far away, so I slung my rifle over my shoulder and headed for town. I was happy to be free for a few hours and I was happy to be clean for the first time in over a week. Furthermore, I was going to see a famous cathedral, after which I intended to sin just as hard as I could and make up for it.

I walked casually down the street, looking this way and that, gradually becoming absorbed in the complex pattern of sights and sounds and smells that was Liège. I thought, as I crossed a wide, sweeping boulevard, that I had heard (just where, I failed to remember) that the same engineer who planned this beautiful city had also planned Washington, D.C. I was busy trying to imagine what Washington must be like (I had never seen America's capital city) when I came—quite suddenly—upon a knot of soldiers standing around a truck from which they had apparently just descended. They looked as though they had just come from the front because they were muddy and weary-looking. Their eyes were bleary from lack of sleep and their faces were strained into ugly expressions. As I approached them they looked contemptuously at me and I felt a little self-conscious in my clean uniform and polished shoes.

"Look!—at that shining nigger!" one of them yelled just as I looked away and started to cross to the other side of the street. Another one, a very big Pfc., leaped quickly in front of me and pretended to look at himself in the buttons on my jacket. I squeezed the sling of my rifle but left it on my shoulder.

"You go'n to a party, nigger?" he asked. "Look, boys, this nigger's go'n to a party!" He flipped my tie out of my jacket. I stepped back from him and looked anxiously up and down the street for a way of escape. In an instant they were all around me. I took my rifle off my shoulder. They began to laugh and rail at me, moving closer all the time until they were almost upon me. Encouraged by the others, the big one grabbed my tie as though it were a rope and jerked it. I fell to one knee, jerking my rifle from my shoulder as I fell. The big one who stood closest to me kicked it out of my hands and, as I struggled to regain it, a calm southern voice rang out over the others:

"Leav'um alone."

The men grew quiet. A short, lean little man wearing sergeant's stripes walked toward me. The men fell back silently, respectfully, as he approached. He looked dirtier than the rest and there was an unlit cigarette butt clamped between his parched lips.

"Where ya from?" he asked, looking at me with a sympathy which I hardly expected.

"Missouri," I said. I spoke as calmly as I could.

"Missouri . . ." He repeated the word very slowly, as though he were thinking of Missouri very hard. "All right, you guys, break it up!" he said, still looking at me with a comfortable, confident authority until all the men had returned to the truck. Then without another word he turned from me and walked away. And I resumed my search for the famous cathedral.

I did not feel bad about what had happened. The experiences which those men had just gone through were clearly written on their faces. What soldier has not felt the same way, right or wrong, at one time or another. I was comforted by the fact that it might have been worse. After I had walked a block or two down the street I suddenly had an idea. I returned immediately to the hotel and put on my old uniform, the one I had taken off. Thus attired I went out and found and thoroughly enjoyed my cathedral. And when I had finished I returned to the livelier part of town and sinned very hard in order to make up for it. I had a hell of a time! . . .

Why else should they continue to hound me about working? I wondered. How many times had I heard the accusation in their voices when they would exclaim:

"You can sleep, but *I* have to get up early in the morning!" in which statement I heard the further implication:

"You sluggard!" when, say, some rendezvous would be proposed at an odd hour of the day or night.

"How lucky you are that you can afford the luxury of doing what you want to do!"

Writing was all right, they guessed, but:

"Can one make a living that way? If not, what then?"

"One must work," they all agreed, "and have a 'place' and *then* write. Write in the evenings, during lunch hours, on days off. Whatchacallum—what was his name?—he was a *great* writer, and he did it. And you can do it, too—*if*—you *really* have something to say!"

I was terrified by such talk. And what was worse, I suffered from guilt because in my heart I believed that they were justified in speaking as they did, even though I knew on other levels of consideration that they were wrong. All of my guilty feelings revolved around the question, Do I have enough talent to justify asking my parents to support me?

I was afraid of devolving into a sort of part-time hobby writer. How many would-be writers had I seen end up that way! How many had I seen in factories with college degrees, with professions, earning that safe weekly paycheck instead of enduring the terrible beginning which all independent creative effort demands! Then too, if working was my aim, could I not work more easily in America. "I did not come to Europe for that!" I protested to my landlord and lady and to my many well-meaning friends and acquaintances. "There must be a solution to this problem," I opined, and I felt confident that I would find one.

I wrote to my parents. They agreed to send me a little money from time to time for as long as they could, explaining that they could not do it indefinitely for reasons which I well understood. They did not really understand my point of view, that is, why I had left my home and family, which was a happy one, in order to subsist in some foreign country simply because I wanted to write stories. He must have another reason, they thought. I could tell by the tone of their letters, though they never said it in any tangible way. They thought that I possibly wished to escape racial prejudice in America, I thought, or that I was in love with a white girl, if not secretly married already. "He was always a strange boy," was the way my father explained it, according to a letter which my mother wrote to me, telling me what he had said to friends back home. Nevertheless, they would help all they could. They would make sacrifices and borrow money—they would have to do it—in order to help me.

"You are our son, and we love you," my mother had said. "The rest is simple."

Their love and devotion made me even more ashamed of myself on the one hand, and caused me to feel like a martyr on the other. Feeling like a shameful martyr, I in turn felt ridiculous, which feeling reinforced my former feeling of shame because the problem was so simple. I had merely to find a way of earning money so that I could write without losing my sense of dignity and without imposing upon other people.

It was all nonsense, I knew, my pride, my inhibitions. My state of mind irritated me not a little because now my old resolutions to live the good, moral and courageous life came to mind. I was embarrassed because I trembled so in the face of a little bad weather. What respectable spider would be discouraged merely because the weather was bad! It was the thought of my distinguished colleague that caused me to make a momentous decision.

The Momentous Decision

THE MOMENTOUS DECISION was to give English lessons. It was a momentous decision because it initiated a new and exciting phase of my existence in Bern. My position changed from that of an independent tourist, having merely an abstract, commercial relationship to the town and its people, to that of a resident with a "place" in the social and economic life of the society. I entered many new homes and made many new friends and acquaintances, many of which I have kept till this very day.

However, giving English lessons did not provide an ideal solution to my money problem. I earned about five francs an hour (about a dollar and fifteen cents in American currency), which was more or less the standard price. I had only three or four lessons a week at best. It was difficult for them to come to me because my room was too small. Another reason was that they were afraid that people would not understand their being in a room alone for a whole hour with a man, and such a man. And for the same reason it was often impossible for me to go to them. The result was that most of the pupils who came to me were determined young ladies who wanted to learn English for some definite purpose, such as preparing for a trip to England, or to qualify for a position requiring a passing knowledge of English. Others came simply because they were bored, having nothing better to occupy their time, and because they thought it would be novel to be in contact with a strange black man. And then there were others who came because they wished to earn the reputation of being radical, and who wished to defy their parents or the prevailing provincialism which cramped their freer and more spontaneous impulses.

Needless to say, I was a great disappointment to most of them because, after all, a verb was still a verb, no matter who taught it. It usually turned out that my pupils stopped coming after the novelty wore off, and I found myself at pains to eat on the money which I earned from the three or four lessons which I more or less managed to keep. However, there was many a week in which I had only two lessons, or one, or none at all.

Fortunately, several of my friends who appreciated the intensity of my desire to write frequently invited me to dinner. Among these were the ever-faithful Mr. and Mrs. C—— from the radio. They were interesting, well-read persons who shared my love of literature, art and music, and were a constant source of encouragement and joy, not only because they extended to me their hospitality, but because they did so without condescension, and because they respected my ambitions.

I also frequented the home of Mr. and Mrs. S—— with whom I shared similar experiences. And finally I came to know a Mr. and Mrs. M—— whom I had met at a New Year's party. They took English lessons twice a week, on which occasions I was their guest for dinner. In time they opened their home to me and I became a sort of standard friend of the family. With the aid of these few friends and with my English lessons I managed to survive. My decision had been a momentous one because it really had initiated a new and exciting phase of my existence in Bern. In less than a month after I left the quiet little attic room in the Kirchenfeld I had become a sort of migrant mendicant, in which role I was able to resolve my feelings of shame and guilt for not being able to maintain my economic independence.

And—believe me!—it was not easy. Imagine me, if you will, leaning far out over the bridge rail, straining to catch my reflection in the rushing waters in a futile effort to confirm an image conjured up in my mind—the image of a courageous, moral, good man!—Laughable!

How I Left the Kirchenfeld

You have noticed, no doubt, that I seem to have left the Kirchenfeld at this time, and that I sort of slurred over the incident in a hurry. Well, I am a little stronger now than I was then, so I will tell you all. I left the Kirchenfeld ignominiously, in a cowering frenzy of desperation.

"Sorry . . . sorry . . . ," my landlord and lady sadly declared, "But . . ."

And I did not know where to turn. The problem was, of course, to find a cheap room, which was complicated by the fact that I had no money and no job on the basis of which I might otherwise have guaranteed my prospective landlord the rent, in a month or even two months. My only asset was a rather vague connection with Radio Bern and my friendship with the C——s. Mrs. C—— searched untiringly for a room for me, while Mr. C——"loaned me money," knowing that his chances of getting it back were purely hypothetical. At this time I was taking practically all of my meals at his home.

Weeks passed in this way! My landlord and lady became more agitated and I understood their situation very well. I was vexed because I could do nothing about it. The food bill was piling up. The menu became progressively scantier, and when I sat down to the table I felt not only like a poor, unwanted relative, but like a criminal, stealing food from the mouths of two helpless old people.

Under this strain I wrote furiously and desperately. I even sent my manuscripts to Swiss editors now. They were kind, courteous and very careful. They sent me long letters of rejection in an apologetic vein, explaining that they appreciated the "fineness" of my work, its "literary quality," and that they wished to assure me that, though they had rejected my stories, it did not necessarily mean that they were bad stories, but merely that they were not suitable to the needs of their publications. They further explained that the Swiss public was small, and that the publication of unknown writers was dangerous as well as expensive. My stories were too long. I should shorten them, and give the "plots" a little more "action," for my stories were rather too "philosophical" for the general public. They opined that the German market would be better for me, and better still would be the American market. Why did I not try America! they advised. And lastly, they wondered if I had ever considered the "race problem" in America as a theme for my stories. European readers would be very interested to know, for example, why, since America claimed to be a democracy, the government did not put a stop to racial discrimination? I should tell, they thought, what the Negro thinks about life in America.

Now frustrated as I was, I actually tried to satisfy these editors. I momentarily closed my eyes to the virtue of the spider, cursing him for flaunting it in my face, as I tried to pin the nigger down. But each time passionate anger, an overpowering confusion and a sense of my ridiculousness clotted my pen. And I smudged many an immaculate page with bitter accusations, apologies and enraged exclamations. The writing was so bad that it even disgusted me. I tore up those pages and threw them into the wastebasket. And when the trashman came and took them away I watched from my window. I thought with ironic satisfaction that perhaps some contented old man would stick a flaming match to them and that perhaps they would make a pretty fire. I hoped, especially since it was turning cold, that the flame might be a brilliant one, and that the old man might warm his hands or light his pipe.

During this time, when I left my little room to go into the

city in order to look for my life, I tiptoed past the landlord's
door and was grateful that he did not expose my stealth in the
presence of the barking dog!

The New Room

ABOUT THIS TIME I made the acquaintance of a young Turkish dancer through Mrs. C—— one evening at the Stadt Theatre, where I had been invited to see a dance recital. Mrs. C—— had spoken to me of the young lady before, and upon this occasion took the liberty of inviting me, commenting as she did so, that we two "artists" should get along very well. As it turned out Mrs. C—— was absolutely right because I found the young lady to be very pleasant. I saw her frequently after that and discovered that she was not only Turkish but Jewish as well, which fact, I often thought, accounted for a certain rapport between us from the very first. We had much in common. We responded to similar rhythms, as it were, and though our languages were different (however, she also spoke English very well) and the places of our birth were different, in spite of the fact that the details of our childhood experiences were as unalike as possible, the qualities which we perceived from all of our "differences" had rendered our sensibilities flexible enough to enable us to imagine how we each felt about life in Switzerland. We were both members of minority groups away from home whose experiences in Switzerland had been similar enough to enable us to share them without pathos, and what was more important, without boring each other. In a short while we became friends.

It was very fortunate for me because when she learned that I would soon have to leave my room in the Kirchenfeld and that I would have no place to go because I had no money, she asked

her father if I could stay in their apartment, in a quarter of the
city known as the Weissenbühl. And her father, whom I had
never seen, said yes, and apologized to me because they were a
little crowded due to the presence in the apartment of his wife
and son.

Needless to say, I was grateful for his generosity, but at the
same time I was embarrassed by the situation which I had created. This embarrassment was in turn reinforced by the eternal
irony of my being in no position to refuse. I pictured myself as
a shipwrecked man in midocean, clambering to get into the last
lifeboat, which was already full to capacity. That is to say, the
compassion of my new friends prevailed over my embarrassment
and I accepted their invitation to stay with them until I could
afford a room of my own. Then another unexpected bit of luck
came my way.

My friend, upon remembering that there was an old storage
room next to her attic room, inquired of one of the neighbors,
a very charming Madam P——, as to its availability, explaining
without exaggeration the sorry condition I was in. Madam P——
agreed to prepare the room for me, charging the modest sum
of twenty-five francs a month (a little more than five American
dollars) for the rent. Soon after I learned of the lady's generosity I met her and thanked her and assured her that I could not
possibly complain simply because the attic would be very hot in
summer and very cold in winter because the walls were not insu-
lated. "A room in a cold winter or a hot summer is better than
no room!" I said. So she scrubbed the room clean and white-
washed it and covered the floor with a rug and made a bright
little curtain for the wall, in order to at least divert the wind. She
furnished the little room with a small bed, a table upon which
was a small lamp and a brand-new blotter (since I was a writer),
a *Schrank* (clothes closet) and a chair. After the furniture was
crowded in there was about two square feet of floor space left,
so you can see that there was no place for my luggage, nor for
my trunk, which I had to store in the hall.

But it was sort of cute. I felt like a little bird in a nest. The toilet was out in the hall, and the water which ran into the metal washbasin was almost as cold as the water which runs from the blue-white Alpine peaks into the clear mountain streams for which Switzerland is famous!

A tear trickled down my face on the first night I slept there when, upon laying my head upon the icy pillow, I saw through the little skylight window, about a foot square and directly over my head, a star. And I was later pleased to observe that when the moon shone my head lay upon a pillow of silver framed in velvet darkness!

I was happy not to have to impose upon the Turkish family by living in their apartment, but I had to accept their offer of food because I simply could not feed myself. Nor could I adequately express my gratitude for their generosity. They did not know me and yet they gave me food to eat without question, and in spite of the fact that I did not work. They seemed to have understood all that I might have explained without my uttering a word. I fancied it was because their daughter was a serious dancer.

However, with all their understanding they wondered if it would not be well for me to look for some work to do that would not take all of my time, in order to earn money, "Because eventually," the mother opined, "you'll have to face the reality of an empty stomach." Knowing that she was right, even though she said it in French, and that everyone was right, I clamped my eyes tighter together, as I strained out over the bridge rail, so far that I heard the swirling current. So near the sound! For weeks I trembled above it, afraid to look and afraid to jump.

Why I Did Not Work

I WAS AFRAID, that is the straight and simple of it. I was afraid for my writing and I was even more afraid for myself. Why I was afraid for my writing I have explained, now I must explain my fear for myself:

Firstly, *The People Looked at Me All the Time!* On top of that they pointed with extended forefingers and laughed at me when they looked. They mocked me, I thought. It happened in the streets and in public places. I was referred to as *"Der Neger,"* which sounded so much like the word nigger. And you know how I felt about that. It had sounded so much the way it had sounded back home that I could not always make the necessary allowance for the different mentality of the people who uttered it, or for the different context in which it was used. The fact that the context was different overwhelmed me with a sense of irony which was grotesque, to say the least. Acceptance of this word necessitated the readjustment of my whole emotional life. In rare perceptive moments I would say:

"What matter if the people look and point at me? Am I not the only black man in this place!" But then, in the very next instant, my reasonableness would vanish and I would reply to my own question, thinking of America, no doubt, "Yes . . . but the result is the same, I am isolated from the people."

I was a queer fish whose every move was noticed and commented upon. I was the only American Negro in a city of over one hundred thousand people. A few Negroes, African and

American, passed through from time to time, but after a day or two, or a month or two, they usually went away. When I walked into the Mövenpick knives and forks dropped on plates, heads turned and chins dropped; babies cried hysterically and women exclaimed, "Jesus!" Some courageous mothers held their little tots up in their arms in order that they might see the black man. Near accidents have occurred in the streets because drivers were too busy watching me. I do not exaggerate, my position in this town was so singular that anyone—just anyone at all!—who wished to find me could do so by simply asking the first or the third person he met on the street. Take this example:

"Hi, Vince! I've got a ticket for the movie, too!" my friend Harry said to me one day, as he sat down beside me in the Mövenpick and ordered a beer. I was astonished by the fact that he knew not that I *had* gone, but that I *intended* to go to the movies.

"But—but how did you know?"

"The waitress at the Rendez-vous saw you looking at the *reclam* [by which he meant advertisement] in the *Anzeiger*. The paper man on the corner—you know, the one by the statue of Bubenberg—saw you walking in the direction of the Mövenpick. Then I met Uli Schmidt and he said he had just seen you buying a ticket at the Jura, and then going into the Mövenpick. So I bought one, too."

"How long did it take you to discover all that?"

"About ten minutes—after I stepped out on the street, of course."

"Oh—of course!"

My working in Bern was further complicated by a circumstance over which I had little control, the fact that a foreigner can only do work for which there is an excessive demand and in which he will not compete with Swiss citizens in need of jobs. From what I have heard good places are hard to find and difficult to maintain because the requirements are so strenuous. The average secretary speaks four languages. To sell bread in a bakery one must have a school certification stating that one has successfully completed two years of training! When the citizens get through picking there is little left for the foreigner except menial jobs, such as dish-washing, portering, delivery-boying and occasional buffet-servicing in restaurants. Women usually find ready employment in households.

I might have found a job in an office translating something had I known German well enough. I could have, on one occasion, taught English in a school but for the same requirement. The only immediate possibility left to me was to take a menial job until something better came along.

Now I am not proud about working. "A man should never be too proud to do honest work," my father used to say, and I believed him. I could have done such jobs as those which were open to me in Bern in America, though I would not have liked it there any more than I would have liked it in Bern, the difference being that in America I might have to work in some menial capacity in spite of my qualifications for other types of work. Some Negro waiters in restaurants have Ph.D.s. But, at least, in America my presence would be accepted as normal by most people because Negroes in their accustomed roles are taken for granted, whereas in Bern the situation was entirely different. Could I have gotten a private job, in an office, for example, everything would have gone well, indeed, but I have told you how the people gasped—almost strangled!—with excitement when I merely passed them in the street or in a restaurant. I ask you, what would they have done had I worked among them, in some public, full-view capacity!

I could not even think of it. I was a writer and a writer, with or without a full stomach, I would remain. All that one could say to the contrary was of absolutely no avail. Mine was a curious state of mind. I knew my attitude to be a silly one because I felt silly—all the time. I felt like a Grade-A fool when my friends asked me, and with reason: "Why mind the people? You know who you are. Besides, you've got to eat!"

"Yes yes yes, you're right!" I would reply, admitting that I was a weak and insecure person. "I know that my trouble is all of my own making. I know, as well, that work in your country is no crime, it's almost a religion! It's not the work that I fear anyway, it's the conditions under which I would have to work.

"How often have I envied the dignity enjoyed by those venerable old men who clean the streets with their immaculate blue uniforms and well-polished shoes, smoking their Brissagos as they sweep in fair weather and foul without looking back. They feel by no means debased because they have the good fortune to be accepted by the whole society. No one pays them any attention.

"It's true, they don't frequent the wealthy families in the Kirchenfeld, nor the aristocratic families in the Junkerngasse, which may be a blessing! but they just might as well play jass with a member of one of those families if they chance to belong to one of the many choirs in the city. They may if they live in the same canton see or sit next to the Bundespräsident on the bus on the way to work, which though possible, is highly improbable, I'll admit, inasmuch as the street cleaners begin work a little earlier, at five-thirty or six—for I have seen those gentlemen sweeping the stones in the dark of the morning—while the Bundespräsident begins his work a little later. But there is no doubt that they ride on the same bus, and that they both probably have an *abonnement* [monthly pass].

"So you see, I understand very well that, though the people would look at me and point and exclaim and things like that, my actions would bring no social disgrace upon my head because of their attitudes toward work."

And then, choking with emotion soaked in pathos, I attempted to explain my deepest feelings, the very source of my dilemma, which had accidentally enveloped me in the guise of work.

"I will not work in a menial capacity in public because the only conception which the Bernese have of the Negro is the one which is presented in American movies and newspapers, the 'noble savage,' the 'ignoble savage' or a member of a suppressed, suffering, passive minority. Now these are stereotypes which I feel that I cannot exemplify. And although I realize that no stereotype is completely false, and that I undoubtedly possess attributes which set me apart from my countrymen, I am so hypersensitive about racial distinctions that even the beautiful, desirable attributes of my Negroid character are taboo to me. I am almost ashamed to admit it, but I no longer dare to sing in the streets at the top of my better than average second tenor voice, as I did every day of my life in Kansas City. My attitude concerning my disposition in your country reminds me of a little incident which was supposed to have happened when the great Pavlova first toured America. She is alleged to have said to her troupe before a performance in some obscure far western town: 'This evening we will have to dance better than ever because these people have never seen ballet before!'"

All the while, as I apologized for my behavior in this manner, I suffered from chronic embarrassment, which resulted from an acute awareness of the disparity between what one knows intellectually and what one feels. I felt dizzy, like a drunken man whose reflexes defy his reason. How does one reeducate his feelings? I kept asking myself. For that is perhaps the greatest problem which you and I will ever have. Brains are not enough. Once I naively thought that if I could just understand myself and my neighbor everything would work itself out in good order. But by now it was clear to me that what I had understood by the word "understanding" was also not enough, and that Real Understanding involved elements of thought which have little to do with reason. The "understanding" of my previous thoughts I now perceived as merely an intermediate phase of Thought, the end of which must be a cosmically comprehensive synthesis known, since time immemorial, as love.

But I will have to come back to this later. Before I go any further I must point out a new element of consideration, which now sprang up from even deeper areas of my consciousness. It places my former state of mind in a new perspective and serves to illustrate how various are the ways in which the mind plays tricks upon us, and how illusory are the apparent boundary lines which "separate" such seemingly opposed values as "good" and "bad," "right" and "wrong," "wisdom" and "folly," or any so-called "opposites" whatsoever.

The truth is that aside from all the reasons I have given for my not having been willing to go to "work" there was still another. It had to do with the spiders which I had seen on the Kirchenfeld bridge. I could not conceive of a spider playing a violin. That is out of his line. Such an occupation would disrupt his whole pattern and thrust him back into the world. I could not imagine the spider, because flies were scarce on a particular day, deciding to take up fishing! In so doing he would lose his identity, he would become an anomaly, neither a spider nor a fisherman, again he would be thrust back into the world of unrealities.

Let me give you an extreme but actual example of what I mean from an account of a spider which I read in Rachel Carson's marvelous book *The Sea Around Us*. She refers to an island which had pushed up from the floor of the sea. Its crest, because the volcanic impulse had played out, had been worn away by the waves, so that its surface was now almost level with the sea. Scientists visiting this forsaken spot found no sign of life, with the exception of one lonely spider: he was building a web amid the wet, wave-washed rocks! What could he have been thinking, way out there in the middle of nothing, building a web! But isn't that just beautiful, the fact that he did it? He was a spider—come hell or high water! He was God, as sure as God Is!

Now all of you reasonable people, wipe your hands across your mouths and laugh at me, imperfect creature that I was (and am!) for having dared to "disturb the universe," for having dared to "presume." I R O N Y has been the plague of all my life!—to misquote a celebrated enigma.

A Portrait of Irony As a Part-Time Job

ONE DAY I encountered a young man upon the street who approached me in a very familiar manner, addressing me by my first name, which I found a little uncomfortable because I did not recall ever having made the gentleman's acquaintance. He presented his card and asked me if he might speak to me. "Oh, I guess so," I replied, and we went into a rather pleasant café, which was near at hand, where he ordered coffee, over which he suggested that we might speak more comfortably. And when he made it clear to me that he was paying for the coffee I relaxed in my chair and gave the young man my undivided attention, for, as you can well imagine, I was a little curious as to the nature of his business. After a quarter of an hour I gathered the following information:

This gentleman, a Mr. Z——, was an ambitious, well-meaning, alert promoter for one of the largest chain supermarkets in Switzerland. His company had just finished the construction of a new one. The grand opening was scheduled to take place in a matter of weeks, with press coverage, a general open house period of public inspection and some special feature, which they hoped would attract the customers.

"Now, I have seen you several times—in the town and so on," said he, "and I had—I told my wife!—such a favorable impression of you that I thought you would be the very person for what we have in mind!"

Mr. Z——'s eyes blazed with ecstasy!

"You would give color—atmosphere!—to the whole thing!"
Then he drew nearer to me, his mouth watering with enthusiasm,
and spoke in a secret, confidential tone:

"We're having a run on bananas!" He paused significantly.
"You"—he grasped my arm—"you would conduct the selling
. . . Up front . . . In a colorful uniform!" Again he paused and
looked wildly into the space above the curtained window. And
then: "You would be just the thing!"

I took a long, quiet look at Mr. Z——. He was a bright young
man with a cheerful face. He was dressed in a handsome gray
suit, and in very good taste. His mother or his wife ironed his
shirt, I thought. And I observed that his expression was serious
and that he was completely innocent of the crime for which I
was silently hating him. Although I strove to control my anger, I
could not help taking the measure of his chin. My fingers balled
into fists and the knuckles shone pale against the skin.

But wait! I thought. He's married . . . He has a baby; his first
. . . He wants to make a good impression upon the boss . . . My
fists relaxed into fingers, as my mind quickened to his proposition: It's really not a bad idea. It certainly has the Hollywoodian
flavor. With music! There should be music. Drums . . . And how
should I dress? Leopard skins? Grass skirt? Naked! With a little
brass, a little copper, here and there. With perhaps a missionary
bone or two in my hair—I wonder what stature is the mode
this year . . . My lips white, perhaps baby-pink. And, of course,
a toothy smile . . . Sensational I would surely be. I could have
pictures made and send them home to my mother and friends.
Oh yes! I would surely be a sensation. And a financial success. I
would sell seventy-seven tons of bananas and even make a little
money for myself. Heaven knows I could use a little money! Just
like this poor young man so newly married whose charming wife
has just given him a baby, probably a girl whose name is probably
Guinivere . . . And his poor little old mother who slaves all day
over his shirts. Or does his wife do them?

All this I thought, and more, as he sat there waiting for my
answer. I tried very hard and half succeeded in controlling the

quaver in my voice as I refused him, keeping my fingers occupied with the spoon and the handle of the coffee cup. I even managed to thank him for going to all the trouble to find me, which expression of gratitude was my gesture to his wife, his daughter, Guinivere, and his poor mother.

"I deeply regret that I am very much occupied at the moment," I said. "I am composing an epic poem, which I couldn't possibly—out of loving consideration for generations to come—interrupt . . ."

Sadly I watched him walk out of the café. When I stepped into the street perhaps thirty minutes later I did not hear the screeching brakes of the car which almost ran me down. I caught a vague image of a man with his head stuck out of a car window, making violent gesticulations and shouting curses. I wondered what I had done to make the man so mad.

In the weeks that followed I settled down to my new way of life. I lived as the birds lived. I awoke from my cold bed and looked upon the day with only one question in my mind: how and when will I eat today? I had to get used to eating less and stop doing many things which I had previously thought absolutely necessary to my "way of life," sometimes enjoying and sometimes hating the sympathy and money given to me by my friends. When they asked me if I had found work, I answered no, but that I was looking for work and that I welcomed any suggestions they had to make, which suggestions, however, I always managed to divest of their applicability to me. One friend from the radio gave me over four hundred francs, little by little, in the form of rent or a meal or a splurge at the Chikito. And he has never asked for it back, nor was he ever angry when he needed money desperately himself and could not collect it. So constant was this friend that he never spoke badly of me to his colleagues behind my back because of it, though he was at times quite a talker.

Confronted by life in a vital way every minute of the day, I grew thoughtful. Much of my fear of survival wore away because I came to learn that though matter is displaced, it is never destroyed. This idea sort of took the sting out of the thought of dying. I also discovered that because I feared death less I could afford the luxury of taking a closer look at myself and at my neighbor. Most of all I found that I could better afford the luxury of honest work. And since the work happened in "time," it also happened in "place." The place was a tearoom called the Rendez-vous.

The Rendez-Vous

I NEVER COULD work in absolute silence, I have always needed a little noise, some general sound like that of many people talking, no one voice rising above the others, like the sound of traffic or of the sea. I have read somewhere recently that Schiller needed the scent of rotten apples in the table drawer just beneath his nose in order to produce his best work. For Freud it was a certain degree of misery that served as the necessary obstacle to concentration, which, in order to overcome it, required an even stronger effort of concentration, the certain degree of misery being just enough to "ground" the excess tension and enable his thoughts to flow freely. I sought and found my ideal working atmosphere in the tearoom.

I first went to the Rendez-vous because most of my early acquaintances from the radio took me there; no doubt, because it was very convenient, just across the street from the radio building. In time I came to like it because the people who went there were pleasant and friendly. Most of them were small business and professional men from nearby office buildings and from the French Legation around the corner. And there were always stragglers, passersby and discreet couples from other parts of the city who sat in quiet corners and whispered. Women with babies came to the Rendez-vous on shopping days and free afternoons. Middle-aged women's groups met for tea, coffee, creams, canapés and talk every Thursday between four and five-thirty. Young people who had no parlors or difficult parents whiled away the evenings with their friends, some of whom played chess after dinner. Even those who bought merely a glass of Henniez-water for thirty centimes or a coffee also played chess often until closing time.

It was nice to sit in a warm, attractive place, which was full of friendly, familiar faces, and talk or read or write, while the streetcars shifted up and down the line, causing the pattern of eyes, noses, legs and elbows to wax and wane in a rhythm, which was almost but not quite, never quite, predictable—especially since my little attic room was so cold that my fingers froze when I tried to write there, and since the only thing between me and the howling wind was a tiled roof! By the time winter really set in the Rendez-vous became for me a welcome asylum, a place where writing was possible.

However, sometimes I could not write there because I had forgotten to fill my pen before I left home—they gave me ink with a smile. Sometimes I forgot to bring money with which to pay for the coffee which I had drunk or the dinner which I had eaten— they gave me coffee and food until I remembered to pay, with a smile. Occasionally I needed money for tobacco or the price of a movie or a franc or two or ten for this and that— smilingly they gave all, the five wonderful girls who waited tables there.

Nor could I easily explain why they did it. Of course, they were very kind, but I often thought that aside from mere kindness they perhaps knew—I am sure they knew—that I sometimes wrote for the radio, and seeing me with various members of the staff, with Herr Dr. this and Herr Dr. that, they felt themselves to be in no danger of losing the money which they had loaned me. But still the pleasant fact remained that they did not have to do it. So when I paid them back I always tried to tip them as generously as I could.

Our relationship was ideal, friendly and yet formal without condescension from either side. I was simply grateful for their friendliness, while they no doubt appreciated the fact that I treated them with gentlemanly respect. For there exists in Switzerland a tacit class distinction between client and waitress which does not exist in America. It was our ability to ignore it and still keep our dignities intact, which made possible the pleasant relationship which we enjoyed. Then too, I was an outsider, and not only that, a *Neger*, which was something quite novel and which placed me beyond the ordinary social conception, for no Swiss man would dare admit that he was hungry and borrow money from the waitress with which to pay for the food which he had eaten, writer or not; at least, very few would.

I remember the mild scandal it caused at the radio when it was learned that I owed money to the waitresses at the Rendezvous. "It's a disgrace to the radio!" I heard they said. I heard that they even considered paying the debt (I owed one girl fifty francs, which I have long since paid) out of sheer embarrassment, but I forbade that. When one of the directors asked me about it (it was his duty, he felt) I tried to insinuate as subtly as I could that what I did was none of his damned business. But the gentleman did not agree. "One who works for Radio Bern is as much an employee in as out of the office," he said. "You see, it is all a question of form," by which I took him to mean that it was not the condition of being hungry or the act of borrowing money for which he was "censuring" me, but for the indiscretion of allowing myself to be found out.

Speaking with this gentleman made me sad. A previous, but until this moment unarticulated, observation came to mind, that the radio employees worked in an atmosphere which was charged with fears and anxieties. They felt obliged to think, look, act, even walk in a certain way, lest they be observed by the invisible eye, which was always just over their shoulders. These good ladies and gentlemen, their husbands and wives, their children and their children's cats, dogs and parakeets watched the extremely sensitive barometer of opinion, which rose and fell according to the immediate administrative humor, exclaiming, "Oh!" and "Ah!" from behind false faces with an ardor which was no less than religious.

My sadness deepened and I vowed secretly to be more discreet in the future, sympathizing with their unfortunate plight in having to suffer the indignity of witnessing my poverty.

I looked up at the gentleman who was just then disinterestedly looking out the window and had an idea, which, it occurred to me, might possibly solve both his problem and mine.

"Sir, you say that you like my programs. The listeners have written in and said that they liked them. I could use a job."

"There is nothing available," he said. "You don't speak German and the volume of English material which flows over the domestic wire is very small."

I understood him to mean that as a novel Negro I could be amusing only once or twice, maybe three times, a year at best. The 150 francs they would pay me for a program would be too much because they would have to translate my material. The Bernese radio could not afford the four or five hundred francs (about a hundred dollars!) which it would cost to produce my programs. So when the gentleman stopped talking I rose to my feet and said, "Good day."

The Rendez-vous was the seat of many discussions of such problems, of, for instance, why so few Bernese writers were able to work for the Bernese radio.

"Because they don't pay enough!" one of my friends, who is no longer with the radio, used to exclaim heatedly, though a little too discreetly, I thought—he would almost whisper. "They're not willing to give the local writers a chance—"

"Are they worth it? I don't know many."

"There are not very many and most of them are not especially good, I admit, but the ones that are good go to Germany, where they can earn a decent living. The Swiss are willing to pay enormous sums—enormous!—you know what I mean for German writers and actors, while the Swiss have to take what they can get."

"Why is that?" I asked.

My companion became quite confused. "Well now it's not that! I mean . . ."

"Yes?"

"Well, the Swiss are so—so . . ."

That was as far as he could go, so great was his emotional

involvement with the question of Swiss-German relations. But after a few seconds he looked at me rather aggressively and said:

"I see that you have an opinion. Let's hear it! It often happens that people on the outside can see things that the one who is in direct contact with the thing could never see—or, at least, from another point of view. Do you know what I mean?"

"Yes," I said, adding, "and I do have an opinion. My own problems with the radio have caused me to think about it very much. Then, too, I've heard Swiss people expressing themselves about the German people ever since I've been here. I thought it strange at first that they don't like to speak German and that very few persons whom you meet are able to speak it correctly. And yet, though they speak their own Swiss-German, they always feel that they have to apologize for it."

"Is that your answer, then?"

"Oh no. As I have observed it, the Swiss attitude toward the Germans is composed of many elements. Their attitude is one of fear mixed with contempt and a very profound respect. Fear because Germany represents a powerful military force just over the border. Contempt because of a peculiar species of barbarism which is peculiar to the German character because of his feelings of inferiority in the community of nations which is Europe. Germany has an extremely energetic driving force, which is in our times rendered desperate by a satiated sensibility due to the economic, social, political and religious development of Europe, which drive has been steadily increasing in intensity since the day Martin Luther posted his ninety-five theses on the churchhouse door. And these are precisely the same tensions which are frustrating the rest of the western world, but in other ways.

"The Swiss have a deep respect, however, for the cultural tradition of Germany, especially since the eighteenth and nineteenth centuries. I refer to world leaders in philosophical thought and to poets—you know their names—and to writers, the crown prince of which hierarchy is, of course, Goethe. Nor do I wish to slight Nietzsche, Kant or Hegel, nor fail to pay due respect to Schiller and Rilke and to Mr. Einstein, the Shakespeare of the modern world. And I must apologize for failing to mention the score of prominent others who will not suffer, I trust, because of the omission.

"Swiss culture is not independent of the German culture, and yet these two peoples are disparate—"

Now at this point I interrupted my discourse in order to survey my thought and discover a way of crystallizing the feelings which I had had as a result of contact with and observation of the Swiss people because now that I was discussing the Swiss people's relations to the German people my former feelings came to mind, and I was surprised by the similarity in their qualities. I thought of the size of Switzerland as compared to the size of Germany, and of how I had always been impressed, from the very first, by the smallness of Switzerland in many subtle ways. As my reflections accumulated, a strong impression stirred within my consciousness. Suddenly I was forced to smile at the simplicity of what I believed I saw. Recklessly I opened my mouth in a welter of confusion and said:

"To the Swiss the German symbolizes a 'majority' group. He is to the Swiss what the 'majority' group is to the 'minority' group in America. They, the Germans, are to the Swiss what white Americans are to black Americans!"

Confusion and embarrassment completely overwhelmed me. My mind went blank for an instant and I was not able to follow the idea.

"Do you mean to say that the Swiss are an inferior-feeling people—as a whole—who have a mentality which is similar to your own!" asked my companion in a slightly hysterical voice.

"Yes!" I declared blindly.

Just then the door of the tearoom flew open and a gust of chilly air burst in upon us, followed by an astonishingly beautiful girl, wearing a yellow raincoat. At the sight of her I was astounded by the following apparition: I saw my face sharply and clearly reflected in the water flowing beneath the bridge. At the same time I perceived that the face which I saw was not my face. Could that be! I wondered.

"What have we here!" I exclaimed aloud just as the pretty girl was passing my chair, to the amazement of my companion and the people who sat at the table nearest us. "Is Switzerland—could it be?—another nigger in Europe! A Jew metamorphosed into a state!"

The sound of rushing water hissed in the channels of my ears. It sounded like ironic laughter.

"Are you having a fit?" my companion asked, but I paid no attention to him.

"This is absurd!" I said vacantly, as calmness gradually returned. My companion simply looked at me in wonderment.

"There's nothing to say," he said. "What you're saying is so personal that—"

"No! I'm not being entirely absurd," I interrupted. "The intuition merely illuminates—in a flash!—the area in which the strongest tension exists. It lacks precision. It is like a lightning streak in the dark. Observation and analysis—science—provides the details, the "facts," which when evaluated and generalized upon, yield the precious little aspect of truth in a form which is comprehensible to the intellect."

"You go too far," he said.

"How? In what way?"

He simply looked at me with an expression of unbelief upon his face and said nothing, perhaps because he had no reply to make or because he wished to spare my feelings. In either case I was in no position to hear what he might have said because I was completely lost in the powerful process of synthesis, a synthesis which crystalized many heretofore disconnected feelings. I felt as though I were about to be born still another time. A new world with new horizons opened up before me.

For a year and a half now, through summer, autumn and winter (Christmas had come and gone in a mysterious frenzy of frustration and loneliness) and now spring, I had suffered what had seemed to me the ironies of my position in Bernese society. I had flinched at every shadow and read disaster in the expression of every face. I had clashed head-on like a stubborn goat into the numberless little ways in which they did it differently over here, as compared to how they did it at home. Subjected to hunger, reduced to my essential self by the necessity of existing, I now began to see (forgive me if I offend thee) that the Bernese people were just like me!

Absurd, my conclusion about the relation of the Swiss people to the German people? Perhaps. But the "facts" could be modified by the historians and anthropologists. It was significant for me that the quality of my intuitive experience was valid. Truth appeared to me as a thing which could emerge only as a result of personal experience. So I might say the following:

The Rendez-vous phase of my life in Bern marked the period of the dawning of right understanding. My spirit became toughened somewhat. I was less easily wounded by each trifling experience. I was getting used to the town and the town was getting used to me. I had a small coterie of sympathetic friends with whom I could talk and who appreciated my ambitions, as well as my resulting poverty. Therefore, the synthesis which my personality was undergoing became manifest in an aura of friendliness and sympathy which I found at the Rendez-vous.

From this period on there would be fewer incomprehensible experiences with the people which would befuddle me. For I had discovered, I felt, not only the pattern of Swiss society, but the key to the pattern. From now on I would merely fit in the pieces. As this activity began in earnest, my personality dwindled in importance.

And the old feelings continued to return whenever I was attacked by morbid moods of self-pity: the feeling of being a little ridiculous and absurd, as the "nigger" problem faded into the "human" problem, and the "human" problem, as a species of particularized, isolated phenomena, became lost in the multitude of such problems, which yielded to the ever-relative circumstances which created them.

I was like the woman from Benares who held up her dead child to the eyes of the Great Teacher who was then passing through her village. "Why did this have to happen to me!" she cried out in despair, feeling herself to be the most cursed of all human beings. And the Great Teacher (I believe it was Siddhartha Buddha) told the woman to return to her village and knock upon the door of a house in which no loved ones had ever died.

"When you find one you will have the answer to your question."

The woman departed, taking her child with her, and searched for such a house. When she finally returned to the spot upon which she had first encountered the Buddha the sun had set, the stars were out and the fires burned brightly. She complained to Him that in all the villages she had not found a single house in which no loved ones had died.

"Woman, do not all things die and pass from one life to the next?"

"Yes," replied the woman in a sudden illumination of understanding.

"Well then," said the great one, "why do you weep?"

The singular image now forever filled my thoughts, that of a man, leaning far out over the rail of a bridge. He stared at his reflection in the waters of the river below. Only now he was constantly astonished by the fact that the longer he looked into the water the more numerous the faces grew. In spite of the fact that their shapes and sizes and colors and sexes were various, they all appeared to him as one face, his face and yet many. With indescribable alarm he looked into the waters one day and saw the faces of all humanity streaming under the bridge!

In order to distinguish my face among the faces of the multitude I began to peer into every eye with the aim of discovering the many facets of existence which reflected my being. In that multifarious reflection I discovered movement, the mode of its movement was its rhythm, and the rhythm of its movement was its pattern.

Now the bridge from which I looked out and down into the waters had become the Rendez-vous tearoom. I suffered from the illusion (or was it an illusion!) that the people who came in and out of it were but reflections of myself! Not only that, this complex feeling waxed and waned like night and day, like the moon. As a result, I experienced alternating periods of clarity and confusion.

The periods of clarity were distinguished by a depressive heaviness of heart, which caused a certain venomous tone to creep into my voice, accompanied by dizziness and an intense throbbing within my head, which finally resulted in a peculiar modification of visual perspective, which tended to heighten the distinction between "You" and "I," and "This" and "That" and "Good" and "Bad"—"Right" and "Wrong" rendered my thoughts perverse and burdened me with disquieting feelings of guilt and absurdity.

On the other hand, when I was possessed by the—illusion? —of water containing myriad eyes staring back at me, I was not burdened with conflicts which derived from perceiving experience in terms of opposites. Since such values constantly fluctuated, I occasionally found myself to be in doubt as to their existence at all! But there was a disquieting note.

I was often troubled by the suspicion that I was attempting to avoid the truth about myself by avoiding the truth about others, that I was attempting to do this through the medium of some ridiculous, abstract symbolism, which had no real meaning whatsoever. In attempting to define my existence in the existence of others I was further inhibited by the perception of the fact that my thoughts were relative, since the values upon which I based them were relative, since my humors waxed and waned like night and day and the moon, causing me to vacillate so between periods of profound depression and a state resembling visionary bliss.

To combat this danger, I determined that if I would consider the phenomenon which was myself, I would have to, in all respect for the truth, as I vaguely perceived it, approach myself differently, in some way which would be comprehensive enough to allow for all the errors I would make, and for the dangerous observations which I may lack the courage to articulate into thought. I would have to approach myself as some species of poetry, romantic fiction, or as farce.

My determination was further strengthened when I made a

special trip to the bridge in order to observe the spider. Quietly, modestly, he built his web. I tried to apply the terms "Good" and "Bad" and "Right" and "Wrong" to him, and was overwhelmed by my former feelings of absurdity. On the other hand, I observed that his web, the product of all his effort, was in essence a poetic—at least—fantastic and at the same time a natural expression. To build a web seemed the only thing for him to do. I relaxed a little. I thought: Beneath all the confusion conjured up in my mind is something constant, something *real.* I experienced a great joy! But that joy was tempered by the realization that the thing which I was trying to bring within the grasp of my vital consciousness was as illusive as air.

In pondering my position in space and time, then, my thoughts were devoted to defining the position and the nature of the place which housed my being—at the moment. So I considered the role of the tearoom in Swiss (Bernese) society, in which connection I would like to clear up a little matter:

The tearoom is not really a tearoom, but a coffee room because relatively few of the people who patronize it buy tea, while in any tearoom in Bern one may buy at least five varieties of coffee, which is prepared with very elaborate machines and with the utmost care, tea being merely the result of a plastic bag filled with tea leaves plopped into a glass of hot water! On the other hand, it would not be accurate to call the tearooms coffee rooms either because most of those rooms in which tea and coffee are served also function as restaurants, in which a more or less complete dinner may be had, some with and some without alcohol. And yet they can no more be called bars or restaurants than they can be considered as social clubs, in spite of the fact that most all of the tearooms are clean, pleasant (sometimes beautiful), well-managed places, which function as a home away from home for eighty-three percent of the population.

The Bernese, even many of the wealthy ones, do not entertain at home very often. Except to the intimate members of families and a few very old friends, invitations home are avoided because they are socially inconvenient and demand formal attention.

They must be returned within a prescribed period of time, one must bring flowers, etc., and the counter-invitation sets the subsequent invitation in motion. If the standards of the Bernese man's pretensions are adhered to, his social life will be expensive. The Bernese is close with his money, and seldom gives something away without getting something in return. Then again, social intercourse disturbs his privacy. Because his country is small privacy is a rare thing, and it is, therefore, insisted upon with a will. Outsiders, even when they are Swiss, seldom—or with difficulty—enter a Bernese home, or are able to establish friendship on more than a superficial level.

The place of meeting is the tearoom, where the formalities are relaxed, where the family secrets can remain intact and where each person can pay his own way, irrespective of his class, age or sex. The Bernese girl is prepared to pay for her own coffee and walk or ride the streetcar home alone without so much as blinking a complaining eye, though the young man with a car is as welcome to her as he is to the American, English or Ainu girl.

The tearoom in Switzerland is a national institution, the function of which is as various as it is far-reaching. Its guardian is the waitress, whose role is unique, though not without parallel in other famous parts of the world, as will be seen by the following passage which I happened to read in a book by Frederic F. Garis and Atsuharu Sakai entitled *We Japanese*—who are also known to be great lovers of tea and to be great frequenters of tearooms:

"Geisha (Gei—art, sha—person; pron. Gayshah) . . . are highly specialized types of women entertainers—mistresses of song and dance. A foreign writer describes them as 'the perfect arrangement for tired Japanese businessmen.' Fascinating and mysterious, geisha are like brilliant butterflies floating from flower to flower. Few ask what becomes of the joyous creatures when the winter winds blow. The geisha's glossy, jet-black hair, wonderfully arranged, her gay kimono and gorgeously-brocaded obi, her airs and graces make her unlike any woman in the world. She forms a conspicuous feature of the life of Japan's chief cities. She sings, dances, and plays Japanese melodies on the samisen.

When banquets or gatherings of merrymakers are held, she is hired to drive dull care away. She is a mistress of etiquette, and in her profession is usually an accomplished artist—and an expensive one. Also she is most trustworthy and loyal to her patrons. In the past, and even today, many important conferences of politicians and big business men are held in the machiai, or head geisha-houses—but whatever the geisha overhears seldom leaks out. A budding geisha (called han-gyoku or maiko) embarks early on her career. From her 10th year to 16 or 18 years of age she is trained in singing, dancing, music, etiquette, deportment, writing, flower arrangement, the tea ceremony and other accomplishments. When proficient she takes on the duties of her profession in earnest. In her mature years she may become the mistress of a geisha establishment, or be fortunate enough to be chosen as the wife and preside over a house and family. Many are not so fortunate, and the butterfly wings are broken and soiled in the mire of a great city. Some of the geisha find wealthy patrons who buy them out of bondage. The majority are not so lucky, and the butterfly existence of the geisha does not always end so happily.

"A geisha is engaged for a period from five to ten years, a certain sum of money is paid for her to her parents, the highest prices being paid for the most beautiful. Her earnings go to her mistress, to whom she is always in debt for her training and resplendent clothing.

"There are thousands of these professional women in Tokyo, Kyoto, and Osaka, while every provincial town has its quota, as well as all resorts . . .

"The vogue of western dancing and entertainment means the eventual doom of the geisha, and to meet this competition many geisha are taking up the western style of dancing—but like other old-established customs in Japan the end of the geisha system is far in the future."

The Girls Who Work in the Tearooms

COME, FOR THE most part, from modest families outside of Bern. They come to the city because they wish to escape the dullness of village life, and because there is a shortage of suitable men to marry. They want husbands and babies, a modern apartment, or a big house, or a villa in the Kirchenfeld, like the ones Madam Schmidt and Madam von Gluck have. Since girls are attracted to the tearoom because (if they are pretty) they may earn more money—more quickly—than a secretary, a window designer, or, say, a dentist's assistant, with which they may increase the family fortunes, or their own. And then there are those who drift into the tearoom for no known reason, except, perhaps, in obeyance to some subtle but nonetheless radical, nonetheless destructive, impulse inspired by the naive passionate love of truth which torments the breast of youth . . .

Unlike the geisha, they have, as a rule, no specialized training, nor are they especially gifted in arts commercial or fine. On the other hand, and very much like the geisha, they are encouraged by the society to exemplify an attitude of humble feminine solicitude.

Although there is no overt racial prejudice in Switzerland—as we know it in America—there is a tacit class distinction, a semi-senile aristocratic tradition which derives its influence from bygone days when the *Bürger* were more or less masters of the state. I do not understand this too well, but one of the results is that there are certain attitudes, which have grown out of this distinction by class, among others, which makes the tearoom girls usually taboo as wives for the nice young men who are beginning to make their way into the world. As for the older, established gentlemen, the reason that the tearoom girls are taboo is fairly obvious, the gentlemen are married. It is for this very reason that the tearoom girl, like the geisha, may be aptly described as "the ideal solution for the tired businessman . . ."

The gentlemen visit the tearooms at all hours of the day for business conferences, or perhaps for a moment's reflection over a cup of coffee immediately before or after working hours. Therefore, they are usually without their wives. Because they are friendly, warm-blooded gentlemen with eyes for beauty they are particularly attentive to the young waitresses who are eager to please, who must be eager to please and please if they wish to be successful.

The gentlemen are highly appreciative of this pleasant convenience, of this neutral domestic efficiency, which alleviates the tedium of their workaday hours. Appreciatively the moist corners of their parted lips give poignancy to the dilated glow in their eyes, as they plumb the depths of the fleshy vortexes of proffered breasts—when the waitress bows low, left palm extended and picks out the change with a lacquered fingertip. And as the gentleman presses the coin into the palm of her right hand, he fixes her with a glance. It is just this glance, I reflected, which has had such far-reaching effects upon the pattern of society at large, especially when one considered the question:

Why the Gentlemen Are Appreciative

THE GENTLEMEN ARE appreciative because they are married, for the most part, and not only that, they were married under peculiar circumstances. The peculiar circumstances under which they were married are as follows:

When they were young they struggled night and day, in and out of every type of technical and professional school available, in order to qualify for a "place" in their "chosen" business or professions. For various reasons they would not always choose (or felt that they could not choose) their preferred occupations and, therefore, often had to compromise by rejecting their preferences in favor of those occupations, which, though less desirable because less sympathetic to their interests, promised the greater *security*, by which was meant a job with a steady income with graded advancement until the age of sixty-five and then retirement, the popular opinion being that one can rarely occupy himself with work which one also likes.

Meanwhile, while the gentlemen looked forward to the day when "security" would be assured, and as they were young, intelligent and extremely curious about the vital issues of life, they came to learn about the movies. It was there that they stepped out into the street, blinked their innocent eyes and looked at the pretty girls, the many many pretty girls, and fell completely, romantically, Lancelot- and Guinivere-like in love with them. The pretty girls, having attended the same movies, loved the boys back. As a result, sometimes babies were born and sometimes they were merely conceived. However, as a rule, they did not marry.

Why the Pretty Boys and Girls Did Not Marry

I LOOKED INTO the multitudes of faces, bubbling upon the surface of the waters from the rail of the bridge. I listened to the water's roaring din and heard it articulate the following answer:

They did not marry because he had a plan, which would require five more years of study and then an apprenticeship at half-salary or less before he would have his "secure" place in his "chosen" occupation and earn the six or seven hundred francs, minimum starting salary, with which, in addition to the dowry his prospective wife would contribute, he could rent the modern apartment and furnish it with all the equipment necessary for a safe, comfortable life. He would have to wait until he had a position in which his future was theoretically foreseeable, in which he would know that at thirty-five and forty-five and fifty-five he would earn so much and so much, after which he would retire, after which retirement he would die.

The reason why he did not marry his first, his truest love was because he believed with all his heart that marriage without "security" was a terrible risk. No woman would agree to work and help her man for long—and respect him. Besides, it wasn't done, except by a few crazy artists, "perverts" and "existentialists." What would his family say and what would her family say? What would his neighbors think of him if he did such a thing?

The pretty girl who loved him and who was going to have his baby (which she would have to get rid of, she saw that with

Spartan courage) understood his point of view and agreed with it. For she was no less a child of her time and place than he.

So after the abortion they parted. With a hurting wrench they turned away from each other and down different avenues, which, however, led to the same destination, the ideal situation, which would bring "security" and, therefore, "happiness," until the age of sixty-five, and then death. They walked and watched on the parallel avenues, walked and watched for the right opportunity.

She had to be careful when night fell and she stood too near the gaudy lights, under which all the gay young men passed, especially those who were coming from the movies, because discretion was more important for her than for her lover on the parallel avenue, walking under the gaudy lights, which glowed like glow-worms.

While she waited as she walked, she was forced to lead a bachelor's existence. She had read the papers, the movie magazines, the fashion magazines and had been to see the latest movie, so she knew a thing or two of life. After finishing her secretarial course (her plan was much simpler and required less specialized training than his) she took a job in an office with dozens of secretaries, or only one or two, all of whom smiled hopefully at the boss who reigned like the proverbial cock in the barnyard. There were rules which she had to follow because there were about two and a half Bernese women to every Bernese man.

She had to be as pretty as possible. She had to be discreet. She could not say, "No," too slowly, or say, "Yes," when she should have said, "Oh, I don't know . . ." She could not afford to make a mistake in judgment because if she made a mistake everyone, just anyone at all, would know about it because the town, though larger than the village, is small. The word would circulate among the young men in the bars and around the counter and over foamy glasses of beer in the Mövenpick with a titter, as she passed through the doors. She would acquire an unwelcome popularity. The respectable man with the secure position with graded advancement and a pension at sixty-five might slip from her grasp, and she would be condemned to a life of bachelorhood.

Our prospective husband had his problems, too. He had to work like a dog to get a start. Almost all of the young men do because they are young, and a young man, in order to be accepted by his superiors, has first to prove that he is "serious," and that takes time. Switzerland venerates the aged, even when they are mediocre or decadent. While our happy-to-be young man was working like a dog to get a start, he got lonely very often. Nor had he any too much money to spend for diversions. His plan was advancing slowly, but the end was still enshrouded by a nebulous future, for any radical change anywhere in the world would bring disaster. All this he explained to the bachelor girls whom he met on the parallel streets, which led to "happiness." He explained it under the gaudy lights, which glowed like glow-worms in the darkness.

Meanwhile, she was lonely, too. Besides, he sort of looked like the boy on the avenue parallel to hers. Was his name Lancelot? she wondered just an instant before she asked him what his name was, and he replied, "Herman," and she said:

"Oh . . ." an hour or two, or a week and a night before she said, "Yes."

(The baby could be aborted without too much—yes, some, but not too much—trouble, and they knew by now things which one could take without consulting the doctor.)

But after much hard work and much patient waiting the great day came, that is, he got his precious place, though he still had to be careful, he had to be vigilant because They were watching. He had more money now, and he could afford to dress better. He walked down the street and regarded the prettiest women with the assurance of a man who knew his purchasing power and with the shrewdness of a Missouri horse trader he chose one of them.

The woman of his choice had to be pretty, if not pretty, then respectable with, say, education or money or family. If she had none of these virtues, perhaps she simply had to remind him a little of the first girl whom he met one night when leaving a movie and who now walks the avenue parallel to his.

(He saw *her* quite by accident the other day. She appeared

older than he had remembered her to be and she had grown a little stout. But her eyes were the same, as their glances met when they spoke their incoherent greeting and passed on. He had the memory locked in the dark chamber where he kept his secret thoughts.)

But now he had chosen a bride, and he was in possession of all the equipment which he needed in order to begin being happy. He had a secure position garnished with the standard insurances against all the hazards of life, with graded advancement, a pension at sixty-five, an apartment, house or villa in the Kirchenfeld and social respectability.

While the bride, with the memory of her first (she, too, had a first) love burning in her breast, takes up the post, which duty (it is her duty to be safe and secure, she feels) demands.

One night in the dark, while imagining the embrace of the lovers they should be, occupying parallel beds in strong houses at the end of the avenue, in the quarter known as "happiness," they conceive a child. And while they wait for the second one to arrive they pray that it will be of the right sex, upon which to lavish their secretly cherished first names.

Meanwhile, the plan is fulfilling itself. The moons wax and wane. The family grows. She is a mother now—with a baby carriage for two—who has embarked upon a career, one among thousands of dutiful wives who scramble to the market twice a week with baby carriage, babies and a bag in each arm, one of leather (imitation or plastic and one of net, plastic or cord-string) overflowing with stores for the pantry:

While the gentlemen sit in the tearooms, taking their morning coffee, highly appreciative of the neutral domestic efficiency which is afforded by the presence of the tearoom girls because it alleviates the tedium of their workaday hours. This appreciativeness has far-reaching effects upon the pattern of the society at large because, for the gentlemen who are established and married, the pattern of life is set. The novelty of connubial bliss has worn off and been replaced by habit. For the society into which the couples enter who reside in the happiness quarter at the end of the parallel avenues is a rigid and highly formalized one. It is a society clearly written down in the books of custom and its pages are clearly numbered. One empties his garbage pail every Wednesday and Saturday, and that is all there is to it!

Then too, because they do not love, because they do not hope to love, because they do not hope, having insurances at reasonable premiums to take care of that, the creative sympathy, which true lovers possess, is denied them. They live in several secret worlds, the world of the profession which they preferred but had not the courage to enter, the world of one street with its remembered dead, the world of two streets, which connect—embarrassingly now and then—at hurting intersections, at subversive, secret conjunctions, which degrade the spirit and rob married life of its sanctity. In the dark the women conceive and contrive to remember the cherished first names to which tedious last names must be quietly, covertly conjoined.

I have seen her on the bridge at three and four and five o'clock in the afternoon and evening, this passionate one who suffers from the lack of attention. The matter-of-fact performance of her mate has left her as cold as April with no fire. Mocked by the irony of possessing children with false names, she secretly hates (or pities) him and herself for being parties to a situation, which she thoroughly believes they cannot avoid, but which, nonetheless, makes her unhappy (though secure!), the full import of which unhappiness she may or may not consciously realize, in which latter case she will only notice, wearily, that she has trouble sleeping at night. If the pain fails to swell the flesh under her eyes, she may buy a bright ribbon for her hair, and smile with a desperate insistence, as she points her pretty toe, while crossing her shapely leg, lifting it oh so subtly over the other one, as she seeks the most comfortable position from which to squeeze a new perspective from the teased wine glass: at a center table in the Mövenpick, between the children and the children's father, at eight-thirty of a foggy evening when a heavy curtain hides the stars from view.

If she is still single and her décolletage is low enough and her

Italian shoes are trim enough, she will not notice until much later the young man who has not yet found his place and who smiles at her over the rim of the empty beerglass. However, later, eventually, she will drop her eyes, rise from her table and leave—and pause at the intersection of a parallel street, under fog or lamplight, and smile into the eyes within the eyes of the young man for years, or only briefly, intermittently or sporadically, to the hurting extent to which that which is done cannot be undone.

She may try, as did Lady Macbeth, to scrub the pain away. She may smooth it over, over and over again with innumerable coats of Johnson's wax, and then scrub it smooth again until her insinuating nerves are worn away. Indeed, varicose veins and nerve infections, especially in the fingers, arms and legs, are so frequent as to constitute one of the nation's major occupational diseases, though they have made Switzerland one of the cleanest countries I have ever seen. This pain within the world of body, mind and spirit in which she lives is a heritage which is very old, a heritage for which the pattern was established long before Napoleon swung his gray green cape over his shoulders, mounted his big white horse and rode away.

As the years advanced, the children began to shoulder the burden of excessive parental affection. For they bore the hope that was thwarted when love first dawned upon the consciousness of the lady and the gentleman. They were the personifications of love preserved in the names of the honored dead. Their eyes, lips, words and smiles gave expression to the ineffable memories of lives which had passed beyond the pale of reason and into the realm of fantasy, only to mock the loves which begot them and distort the relations between lovers, mothers, fathers, sons and daughters in ten thousand ways, until the mothers and the fathers died at the legal age of sixty-five and retirement, bequeathing their legacy of "security" to the "happy" sons and daughters-to-be, which they in turn begot.

However, the pattern is not without variation. Sometimes the emotions were not always able to blind reason, and reason, frustrated because rendered helpless, went mad and destroyed them.

The Swiss people resort to suicide more than any other people in the world, occasionally dropping to second or third place in favor of America or one of the Scandinavian countries whose problems are similar. Then again, our unhappy people often resort to another solution to their problem, which is divorce, in spite of its being frowned upon to the extent that it often places the woman without the protective influence of the law of the state.

Meanwhile, the gentlemen are pressing the coins into the extended palms of the girls who came into the city in order to escape the dullness of village life, to find husbands and homes and to satisfy dangerous impulses. As the gentlemen's glances swell and multiply into propositions, which advance file on file and falter before the armor of innocence and virtue once, twice, or perhaps a dozen times before the fall, the tearoom girls learn the difference between a proposition and a proposal. They learn that, having accepted the proposition (in a moment of weakness or loneliness), the proposal goes the way of all good intentions.

Once their position is clear, many of the girls live only to save enough money to buy tearooms and coffee rooms of their own. With tearooms and coffee rooms of their own they can, like the daughters of the rich peasants from the surrounding villages, buy a pretty husband with which to decorate their ménage and enjoy the rest of their lives in an aura of higher social respectability. Many of the girls actually accomplish this Herculean feat! Many of them, like the many daring women since time immemorial, stake their fortunes upon their bellies—and win a kind of satisfaction. Society, neither yours nor mine, seldom ask where the money comes from, and neither do the lucky husbands.

But many of the tearoom girls are not so fortunate. As with the geisha, their butterfly wings are often spoiled in the mire of a great city. Some petrify into eccentric curiosities, wither like flowers and become quite beautiful and strange. Others, the rare ones (here there and everywhere), are able to make a successful adjustment. They marry a simple man whom they love and bear their children and thrive, like grass, finding peace and a sort of contentment in the ever-interesting spectacle inspired by those human rhythms, which articulate the rising and the setting of the sun. I know of one such case, maybe three, but not seven.

"But Why Do Not More of the Men and Women Who Marry Under Such Unhappy Circumstances Learn to Love Each Other and Make an Adjustment—Together?"

I EXCLAIMED, ADDRESSING the multifarious image of myself, which bubbled upon the surface of the waters, flowing under the bridge. There followed a great uproar. All of the mouths in all the faces seemed to protest at once:

Because the habits of the present way of life are deeply ingrained in the religious, moral and social consciousness of the people. The German part of Switzerland is predominantly of Protestant persuasion. The Protestant Reformation in Germany had its independent counterpart in Switzerland through the leadership of Zwingli and Calvin. At first tolerant and humanistic (especially Zwingli), championing freedom of worship and freedom to earn one's personal salvation, they later became (especially Calvinism) sternly dogmatic, suppressing the freedoms for which they had so ardently fought, as well as the pleasurable aspects of life.

It was one of the characteristics of the early Puritans that they were unable to reconcile romantic (pleasurable) love to connubial (dutiful, functional) love in one and the same person. They burned with the conviction that man was born in sin, and that the way to deliverance from sin was one of faith and penance. Accordingly, Mr. Calvin established in the city of Geneva a theistic society based upon the Word as written in the Divine Book.

Sex was a bad thing. Life on this earth was to be suffered, not enjoyed. Joy was the reward of those who one day enter the kingdom of heaven. Therefore, it was the duty of the chosen few who were elected by God to impose moral order upon the sinful majority. As a consequence, the lives of the Calvinists were regulated in the minutest detail by the guardian of the Word.

However, the number of sinners who were burned "by a slow fire," as was Michael Servetus, soon indicated to the faithful that they had much work to do. Many quarrels broke out between the Protestants over doctrinal differences as Calvinism spread throughout Europe, conquering much of Luther's territory. Much faithful as well as sinful blood was shed. Protestantism fought for its life. It fought Catholicism and in some cases it fought for the state. Power politics (sometimes the Protestants fought with the Catholics) modified the original practices of the Puritans, as well as the economic and political developments during those stormy years. In time the life of the Puritans was to lose its purely religious emphasis. Political, material and religious practices were separated into different areas of moral concern. This separation consequently developed into a categorical system of ethical, as differentiated from religious, behavior. That is, religion became for many a Sunday attitude, while business (and politics) was business all the time.

After many years had passed a general confusion developed. A fascinating case of mistaken identity on the part of those among the faithful who had become rich and powerful was brought to light. It appeared that they mistook the obeisance paid to them by the weak, the humble and the powerless (the Un-God-Graced) for adoration. Blinded by their power to control the lives of their less fortunate neighbors, as well as the fate of governments, some of these pious gentlemen mistook themselves for the very generous God to Whom they owed their state of Grace. Could they not make the meek bow down to the golden calf? And was not the Church their Chief Lieutenant? and the Artist the Chief Jester of their court, or at best, in the case of a few men of genius, court magicians who wrote from dictation upon the stars and dotted their *i*'s with atoms!

Now that God was dethroned, the spiritual agencies of the society became merely social agencies whose apparent purpose was to reconcile us to the cold, abstract, conscienceless power, which only a few centuries ago was thought necessary merely to secure the produce, which provided the proof of the preference of the lucky few by the Good God!

Now—because the religious life became separate from the social life, the distinction between women as mothers and mistresses of the home and as the objects of romantic love could be made more easily. The former simply belonged to the category of religion, while the latter belonged to the category of business, which by now was a far more potent force in the daily life of the society than the Church, its senile parent. On the other hand, sex was looked down upon as merely a beastly necessity, a loathsome reminder to man that, though he was just a step lower than the angels, he was often obliged to act like a dog; on the other hand, sex, sinful as it may be, was found to be pleasurable, and since the wife was merely the medium through which the race was propagated (preferably male members), two types of women emerged from the consciousness of the people of western Europe, the modest, sacrificing forbearing mother (who, like the American buffalo, has long since disappeared from many parts of the western world), and the "bad" woman, by which was meant the "radical" woman who did not conform to the accepted pattern of social behavior (how could she!), who divorced, or tried, as only a woman can, to undermine the monogamous system. Wives became a sort of glorified domestic servant who bred stock for the master . . .

In spite of the innumerable exceptions to the gross generalizations I am making, one of the results was that the gentlemen left their wives at home after the children were born. Pursuing the needs of business—appointments, meetings and so forth they frequented a society of men. A good wife, as in Elizabethan times, should be seen and not too often. To escape the tedium of business and loneliness (it goes without saying that often merely financial considerations had been of uppermost importance in the choice of a wife) the gentlemen often resorted to "bad" women, upon whom they lavished the romantic affection which their wives (at home with the children) languished for. And since the "bad" woman was taboo, the gentlemen needed not to feel responsible for her. Needless to say, many of those "butterflies" broke their wings, which were trodden upon "in the mire" of great cities. Nor would the betrayed wife who suffered from being too good to be bad say a good word for the harlots upon whom their respectability depended.

Thus, a precedent, as old as man, was reinstituted in European Protestant society. Traces of it remain till this very day, practically unaltered. How it affected the Germans in particular one may read in any history book; my concern here is with the fact that Germany is the conduit through which European culture was infused into Switzerland, hence, the institution, in the canton of Bern, of the tearoom . . .

"This Explanation of Yours Cannot Apply to All the Bernese!"

I HISSED AT the faces in the water. The faces seemed to wince with pain. Flecks of foam burst from their mouths as they replied:

No, it does not. Many of the young people who are waiting for "economic security" and who suffer from cumulative anxieties, which have been nurtured down through the centuries of emotional suppression, have evolved a greater variety of complex character than the mind can conceive. However, one other prominent manifestation of this pervasive anxiety is homosexuality. I have seen many homosexuals in Bern, many more in proportion to the population than I have seen in many other places. In fact, I have rather strong feelings about it because I remember the great numbers of homosexual men who used to follow me home during my first three or four months in Bern. I would encounter them almost any night, especially in the Bundesterrasse, standing in the shadows of the trees or walking in front of the park near the Catholic church, and in certain bars which they frequented. I would often accidentally stumble into one of the bars and stumble out half an hour later, regretting a little that some of the pretty men whom I had seen were not their sisters, or that I was not also of a homosexual state of mind.

I had cause for regret because I had found many of the men I encountered to be intelligent, sensitive and quite interesting persons. Many were cultivated, and were able to speak with authority on a variety of subjects—once we were able to dispense with the basic questions and their monosyllabic answers.

I had cause for regret because I often felt that some of the young men whom I met were—how shall I say?—misplaced. I have had the same feeling when I have seen a man driving a truck who should have been a doctor, or waiting tables on a train when he should have been practicing law or doctoring, or practicing law when he should have been driving a truck! However, realizing that the cure of this neurosis requires knowledge, courage and much willpower, I can admire a man who possesses these virtues to the degree to which he can help himself, but on the other hand, I cannot condemn a man who cannot. I lament the fate of those who enter this difficult way of life "needlessly," simply because their fathers and mothers did not love each other when they were married, or because they were divorced and compensated for the lack of affection in their lives by overloving their children, or because they have so long been conditioned by fear, which permeates the society as a whole, that they choose this means of escape, or simply because they do not have a job and the "necessary furniture" with which to set up housekeeping with a man or woman.

Nor am I overlooking the psychological reasons for homosexuality. On the contrary, it is my consideration of them which leads me to believe, as Freud says, that most homosexual manifestations do not evolve from those deep neuroses which happen to the mind in earliest childhood, but are superimposed from without the basic personality; that is to say, they emerge from the general tendency to homosexuality, which is an aspect of the composite character of every man. They can be cured by psycho-analytic treatment, which, in some cases, may merely consist of one's removal to a healthier environment. I have seen, as a soldier, young men who became homosexual for no other reason than that the environment was stronger than their powers of resistance. When the camp was situated near a town in which women were available, the homosexual state of mind yielded to the bisexual one!

I wish to suggest that the reason for my sadness, while reflecting upon the problem of homosexuality in Bern, was the fact that I found Bern to be, like the army camp, a breeding place for artificial homosexuality. Where the "legitimate" neurosis appears it often seems to me to be the best possible solution to a man's or woman's problems—provided the persons can live with it, and contrive to transcend it (in which case there is no problem!) and thereby win their own self-respect as well as that of their neighbors. Indeed, in many happy cases, this bivalent aspect of the personality may be of vital benefit to mankind, as the world of art will show to anyone who cares to look. The "problem" is always the same, though its form and content be as various as that of a cloud!

Though I am willing to admit that the Bernese did not invent homosexuality, it is clear that the status of women—at least in the German part of Switzerland (I have seldom ventured outside of it), as a result of the pattern of the socio-economic development of Europe, previously mentioned—places that premium upon male society which inhibits many a more or less "normal" bisexual adjustment: there are too many doctors and lawyers who should be driving trucks, and too many truck drivers who should be doctors and lawyers. Homosexuality should germinate between the ages of, say, six months and five years of age; if it appears later it possibly could have been avoided.

Lastly, I had cause to regret the baseness and vulgarity in the personality which comes to light when young people resort to this or some other expression simply because they wish to rebel against society at large, simply because the love which they bear for themselves and their fellowman, for truth and for life, is so strong that they throw themselves—upon the cross, as it were, of some raucous despair . . .

Now I Hear You Telling Me

THAT I HAVE painted a rather gloomy picture of Switzerland. Am I not letting my subjective fancy run away with me? you wonder.

You are right about the first point, I answer, with greater sympathy than seems apparent, which sympathy may be obscured by the state of mind under which these thoughts were conceived. For I was a man suspended upon a bridge—a very high place!—looking down into the waters which rushed beneath it. In the waters I fancied, at times, that I saw my reflection in the reflection of the faces of all humanity, bubbling upon its surface. Therefore, what I found to be true of myself I found to be true of others. The fact that the bridge was a Swiss bridge (which was actually built by an Englishman!) in a Swiss town was merely incidental. In time the vantage point from which my conceptions were perceived changed, the "bridge" became the Rendez-vous tearoom, and the multitude of faces which flowed beneath it became the neighbors who drifted in and out at various times of the day and night. I was they and they were I—the fact that the tearoom was a Swiss tearoom in a Swiss town being merely a matter of chance.

In such an atmosphere terms like "good" and "bad," "right" and "wrong"—most of the "opposite" states of human consciousness—faded from view. However, my perceptions were not constant, they waxed and waned, and were distinguished by alternate moods of depression and peacefulness. Gradually the peaceful humor, no doubt because of the pleasure it brought, and because its validity was confirmed by my perception of the spider, which symbolized perfection, prevailed for longer periods of time.

Until finally another remarkable thing happened, an experience which overwhelmed me with wonder, and for which I was not wholly prepared. I began to experience the sensation of not being the man on the Kirchenfeld bridge, nor the man in the Rendez-vous tearoom, nor the multitudes of persons reflected in either "place," but someone or something totally—or almost totally—beyond, outside of both. The complex images which I had formerly seen now broke up into myriad particles of perception, and partook (at least, it seemed so) of the nature of All Things, "human" and "inhuman," "animate" and "inanimate" alike. Seeing, feeling and thinking became a more integrated process. Space and time became diffused functions of dynamic and less dynamic movement, pause and rest—in short, rhythm . . .

But, as I was formerly disturbed by the pretty girls in tight sweaters and skirts who walked over the bridge, and by the feeling of being ridiculous in the presence of the spider—wondrous creature!—and of fluctuating moods of profound depression followed by correspondingly profound moods of peaceful elation, I again experienced these feelings, however, in a more subtle way, in a new sense of irony which was as poignant as a flicker of sunlight in a woman's eyes! I was aware of a farcical element in myself, and consequently in all the events which I perceived around me. I found myself thinking aloud that *All sense is nonsense!* And the mere reflection upon the thoughts which I had—in all seriousness—conceived in the past was enough to sink me into profoundest despair, which despair appeared, in the same instant, laughable because "ironical." Alternately, like the waxing and waning of day and night, and of the moon, the "ironic" humor held me in its grip. It was the desire to transcend even this refined "illusory" "pain" which encouraged me to fix my thoughts upon an even more "objective" view of the dynamic "life" around and within me. The result of that effort I will mention shortly; however, now I must deal with the second objection which I imagine you to raise: that I am allowing my subjective fancy to run away with me.

Since, as I have admitted that I had lost the capacity to distinguish between what was fanciful and what was not, and as I have described in detail how it came about, you must judge the matter for yourself. But allow me to declare the position as well as I can. And this may involve, I fear, what may seem to you a digression:

An Essay on Human Understanding

Now, WHETHER YOU are "right" or "wrong" about me, one thing is evident: I must have really looked at myself and at the Bernese people, I must have lived with them and *tried* to understand them, in order to arrive at "conclusions" about them. More than that, I must have *tried* to imagine how they felt and to put myself in their places, and, therefore, to have *sympathized* with them, in order to give expression to my thoughts. Now it is just this attitude of sympathy, which is based upon intimate experience with the object of one's interest, which I call love. Love is the ability to experience another individual not in terms of his positive attributes, nor in terms of his negative attributes, but in terms of both, which takes us to a higher, more general level of human consideration.

But wait . . . There is something in the attitude of the lover which brings to mind the attitude of the scientist toward the subject of his inquiry: he is not concerned with "good" and "bad," with ethical values, they are relative, created by man for his convenience; they are values which do not exist in Nature (of which man is a part) when perceived as a "whole"—dynamic—phenomenon. Nature is positive, by which I mean that Nature is *creative*—even when it is apparently (negative) "destructive." What we call "positive" and "negative" are but states of tension which hold this world and all the worlds together.

I claim merely to have looked deeply into myself, and there I have found you. You, *my Switzerland!*—pardon me if I offend thee—have emerged from the depths of my consciousness as an entity which is none other than myself, a member of a minority nation—which, after all, only means a part of a whole, in which sense who is *not* the member of a minority!—in the society of nations on this little spot of dust which we pompously call "the World!"

When I look into the skies which shelter this land (it took a long long time before I dared to consider such profound abstractions as the "sky" and "night" and "day"), when I glance toward the tall borders which close it in, when I, without straining my ears, hear the not too distant thunderings and lightnings from discontented corners of the world (for I know that at this moment the Russians are slaughtering Hungarians and the English are slaughtering the Egyptians and a friend of mine is being cremated tomorrow! . . .) my fears are your fears. Your fears weave wrinkles in my brow and vein my spirit with stinging fires and cause my heart to shrivel up like the leaves in the fall. I look for a way to escape. Exhausted in my search, I raise my voice to the heavens and cry, "Lord, I went to the rock to hide my face, but the rock cried out, 'no hiding place! There's no hiding place —down here! . . .'"

But surely you must have something positive to say about us, I hear you insist. Yes, I reply, all that I have said, if understood as I have intended, is positive, to the highest degree conceivable by me. If the picture of the Swiss (the German-Swiss) who live in the canton of Bern, which I have *tried* to describe, appears "gloomy" (and I have to say that it is so, too, because it impresses me that way) it is because the way for the Swiss (and for you and me) is extremely difficult. Our pilgrims, our happiness-seeking, unhappy pilgrims, the "conveniently" married, the lonely bachelors, male and female, our "synthetic" homosexuals, the clinging aged and the vicariously born, the God-Graced rich and the damned poor, the lame, the dying and the hopeful wearily cup their palms over their brows and look toward the sky, ubiquitous, simple, inscrutable . . . The sun is rising over the mountains. It is dawn. Let us see what the day brings . . .

What the Day Brings

The day—and the night—brings the Weather!

Enter *Weather*

I HAVE HEARD that the weather four or five years ago (when you were a little girl and you were a little boy, long before I ever thought of Bern) was more agreeable than it is now. They say that there were long hot summers and cold snowy winters. It is no longer so. The weather, under the guise of winter, summer or autumn, may descend upon the city without the slightest warning at any moment. Spring may arrive at eleven thirty-two on a Monday morning in November and astound you with its beauty, doing perverse, out-of-season things to the landscape . . . I've felt the cold hand of October in June and seen its icy fingers strangle a budding rose until the petals fall . . . Summer, so unrelenting in Texas, Kansas City and Cannes, is such a capricious imp in Bern, waxing hot in one moment and cold in the next, or just lukewarm—without provocation. And winter!—it is hard to tell where winter resides, she wanders so, dragging her heavy wardrobe of clouds with her, as though she were afraid of running out of something to wear!

However, the seasons occasionally behave. But then comes the *Föhn*, like an ominous-looking stranger (as I must have come, looking savage!), that terrible African wind, decked in luminous garlands of radiating heat, which sweeps down over the Sahara, overleaps a continent and winds its way up the rugged mountain channels in a warlike attitude, only to be repelled by the high, steel-blue wall of the Alps (the same which yielded to Hannibal), mushroom and press down upon Bernese heads with a powerful intensity, creating a sometimes unbearable but most certainly disturbing atmospheric pressure. It is a mysterious wind, and it has mysterious effects.

During my moods of despair I came to think of it as some evil metaphysical force sent by the devil to undermine the happy spirits, which are inspired to joyous exaltation by untroubled sunshine. I was led to this dark conclusion because the *Föhn* usually came on the beautiful, sunny days, stretching the clouds into sugary banks, which hovered helplessly above the mountains' sharp peaks, which stood awesome in the sky. So breathtaking was the beauty of the scene that it was hard to pity the clouds and hate the devil and wonder at the patience of God, in allowing the beautiful torment to continue!

And, as though that were not enough, the sky on such days was not only azure but burning, aflame with efflorescent filaments of light which attacked the retina with what I felt to be demonic subtlety. With that same subtlety it attacked the nerves, and caused them to tingle through the body like whip stings, lashing one's mood into an explosive condition. But even when I was not sunken in a mood of profound despair I had to admit that the *Föhn* caused one's head to ache, that it made one feel as though one's brains were baking, as though one's breath were being cut off, and at times, as though one were being quietly roasted by infra-red rays on an aluminum spit—without having had a fair trial.

I could never feel satisfied with my thoughts on *Föhn* days, and my writing was almost always certain to be bad. I have heard from others that nothing pleases when the mountains stand out so clearly that you feel as though you could touch them. You may have met a beautiful girl, or have received a raise, or bought a new suit, but no matter. Not even the excellent meal you may have ordered at the Café du Théâtre or at Andre's will taste really good. And they said (I felt it, too) that the terrible thing about it all is that you can't fight back. You can't, for example, quit your job, or write a letter to your congressman, or fire your secretary, or beat your wife. It were as though some sinister devil!—there's no other word for it—held you dangling by a nerve—just for the hell of it! Painfully tantalized by the beauty of such a day one is reduced to an impotent speculation, as to why a little sunshine —so rare!—should cost so dearly.

But the effect of the *Föhn* is not merely pathetic, it is often tragic, for I have heard (Gotthelf, Switzerland's most famous writer, whom I have not read, speaks of it) that whole villages have burst into flames as a result of the dryness of a *Föhn* atmosphere!

When one considers the weather in German-Switzerland one sees many of the characteristics of the people and its institutions in new ways. For example, I had often wondered why the Protestants in Bern were so gloomy and severe in their religious practices; why Calvin and Zwingli had found Switzerland (aside from the apparent need which gave rise to the Reformation, and the element of truth which the new doctrine contained) such fertile ground for Puritanism. After experiencing the weather it became clear to me that I had hit the "mark" harder than I knew when I, upon entering Bern by train, had observed that "The people make the land and the land makes the people." Sunny people, I reflected, have sunny dispositions. The wrath of God is ominously imminent when a mysterious wind blows from another continent and subtly undermines the morale of a nation! Who under such circumstances can forget the misery of this world? Who can forget long enough to revel wantonly in the bliss of a "pure" pleasure? It took no great oratory to convince the Bernese that this world is not to be enjoyed but suffered. This point of view had such far-reaching effects upon the western world at large that those stalwart Swiss who fled to the New World were able to help to build a new nation from the constrained passions which they could not fully express in the Old World. It was the hot zeal of Puritanism, catalyzed by the *Föhn* which, perhaps, roasted the adamant Quakers alive in Massachusetts! That was not so long ago. Perhaps the pious trouble is not over yet, for the *Föhn* is by the Grace of the same terrible God Who demanded proof of the Grace He had bestowed upon the Chosen here to stay.

Topography

THE LAND MAKES the people and the people make the land—a momentous first impression as I rode into Switzerland on the train and watched its carefully nurtured landscape unwind before my eyes. *Carefully*, I reflected, was just the word needed to indicate the degree to which the rich fields were cultivated and surrounded with orchards, offset by quaint little fairylike houses, which were very new (washed and polished and arranged in picturesque detail) though they looked very old, like the neat, patched quilt your grandmother made. *Carefully* was the right word because nothing was wasted. No field which was capable of producing a crop lay fallow. It was quite different from the American landscape, in which one may see uncultivated land for miles and miles, between clacking telephone posts supporting as many miles of copper wire, from the window of a very fast train . . .

. . . I remember once . . . while traveling by train through America's great northwest, having marveled at the sparseness of the population in this region, as compared to the teeming, pigeon-holed throngs which inhabit the great—especially—eastern cities, so vast and wild was the landscape! And while I was occupied with this observation I suddenly became aware that the scene had changed, and that we had been running beside a plowed field for quite some time. There seemed to be endless acres of it; and suddenly—quite mysteriously—a little road no bigger than a wagon trail, worming its way parallel to the railroad tracks. I watched it for what seemed like hours in total amazement. And finally I came to the conclusion that—obviously!—the road led somewhere, but where? When would we reach there! I gazed on and the little ribbon of a mud road continued to unwind without giving so much as a hint of where it was going. As I continued to look at it it appeared to take on the animate form of two skinny snakes with horizontal stripes across the back. How lonely it all is, I thought, trying to imagine how people—like you and me—could find fulfillment in such a wilderness.

I was lost in my speculations, when suddenly I noticed (with a great throbbing within my breast) that the road was turning. Anxiously, I followed the curving snakes up a gentle grade, which straightened out for about a mile, it seemed, and stopped, quite matter-of-factly, before a little tin house with two small windows with four square panes in each, curtained immaculately white, and centered by a little door with a shiny brass knob—it shone so brightly! On one side of the house (from the chimney a thin stream of smoke trailed into the sky, which was azure) stood a funny-looking little T-model Ford. On the other side of the house, extending from the wall to the upper branch of a tender young tree, was a long thin clothesline. From the clothesline hung about twenty gleaming white diapers, flapping merrily in the breeze. In the exact center of the line hung a bright pair of men's long red underwear, and by its side, a woman's white nightgown with a flowered pattern.

"Civilization!" I cried, throwing up both arms, poking my dozing neighbor in the ribs in order to bring the wondrous scene to his attention; feeling good; thinking, that though New York was crowded up to the skies (and Chicago—and Philadelphia), though Kansas City was getting bigger all the time, a man could still find someplace to go and be alone, where he could still stretch out his arms, full length under heaven, and plow his fields, husband his woman and father his children!

In Switzerland such a wild, untamed landscape, with its solitary dwelling, could not exist, because the land—all of it—is occupied. It has been occupied for centuries. The young man or woman who has to make his way in the world is very much troubled by the problem of finding a place, a little foot of earth upon which to solidly plant his feet, and be . . .

I remember once—it was in Zürich, not in Bern, but still in Switzerland—a friend telling me with justifiable pride and pathos that he had recently seen, upon entering the railroad yards of Zürich, amid the crazy work of twisted steel rails, a little patch of earth about a foot square. It was set off by a little fence of new copper wire. From the soil within the enclosure, in several neat little rows, thin green shoots of onions could be seen sticking into the air!

The land in Switzerland is fast disappearing. With every new house which is being erected, with a front lawn and a little garden out back, the land is going away. Therefore, every arable strip is cultivated with a careful, pathetic interest which commands my deepest sympathy, as well as my greatest admiration. Even the largest farms are nurtured to such an extent that they look like gardens . . .

The rich green woods stand tall against the mountains, which rise to eerie whiteness on fair days, and when the days are dull they are obscured by a sort of "oriental mist" of varying hues, from hoar to musk-blue, while the fields slope sharply, and then gently down from the trunks of tall birch, walnut, oak and pine trees. Then they level off and follow the serpentine gyrations of the emerald river, Aare, which sparkles with the freezing waters of the Alp and Ural mountains, its banks lined with silver birch and hanging birch and willow. A little to the right or left of either shore a fat dray horse hauls a long flat wagon, groaning under a burden of golden hay; while men, women and children toss the fresh-cut bunches and spread them upon the ground to dry . . .

From the valley floor the music of ten thousand bells, strapped around the stout necks of immaculate cows, echoes throughout the mountainside. The Bernese houses, with their low-swinging roofs of tile and thatch, repose quietly, warily, upon the hillsides, surrounded by thickets of roses, gladiolas, petunias and a host of other flowers, domestic and wild, of which I have never heard and would be at a loss to describe. Chickens peck into corded manure stacks as immaculate as a widow's guest bed. Plump red tomatoes burden the vines, while musk-colored onions sprout and curve gracefully into the air like fine green rabbit's ears. All the vegetables flower in their season and display their prosaic beauty before the curtain of subtle greens which deck the hills behind them—supported by the rocks of ages, the Alps. Sweet fruit swells on the trees, and fat birds dawdle on their boughs. Neat, clearly marked roads, carefully strewn with washed gravel-rock design the intricate ways from house to house, and from house to main highway. Every wire and every screw upon every fence is in its proper place, and every raw surface which needs or might need paint is painted, and all the questionable ones are under observation. All the wild grasses are clipped. And nature is hard put to improvise.

The peasant folk who "work" these idyllic farms are strong and ruddy, and many are rich. Their fathers and their fathers' fathers before them worked these same fields. Only they were much larger then than they are now, so much rain has fallen and so many winds have blown, so hard. And all the land is taken.

Flora and Fauna

I WAS AMAZED when I first encountered the indigenous inhabitants of the Jura and Alp mountains, the mountain flowers!
They were so small, so perfect in every disquieting detail. Sharp
cold winds, like skillful knives, seemed to have shaped them
into weird, intricately beautiful patterns, with colors that were
extraordinarily bright and intense.

Imagine, on a peak of one of the tallest mountains in the
world, little patches of solitary flowers, each of which is about
the size of a fly, bursting with subtle beauty, as though forces
from without, as well as forces from within, had restrained them
to miniature size; perfect in every sophisticated detail, with all
the subtle nuances of structure, which are typical of those large
leafy plants that linger languorously amid the luscious foliage in
those low, hot southern countries!

The eerie contrast was startling, to say the least: you pick these
flowers and touch the petals, they are dry! they rattle! Put them
into a vase and leave them, for a month, a year, and they look as
fresh as they did the day you picked them.

How wondrous is the work of God! I thought, not clearly
understanding why I had been moved until much later, when
I reflected more earnestly upon the Swiss landscape and upon
the Swiss people, especially when I remembered the people as I
had seen them on the day of the great pageant, during which I
had observed how contemporary the historical characterizations

had seemed; this and the prevailing consciousness of smallness, which I perceived the first moment I entered the railroad station!

My mind was still full of such impressions, as I made my way down the mountains and into the city.

The City

THE OLD SECTION of the city of Bern presented to my consciousness a feeling of patient, fearful watchfulness. It was so gray and
heavy and low and close together, like a crowd of old men huddled around a secret. Upon viewing the town from a high place,
the grayness and the heaviness seemed to spiral into varying
shades from the center of town toward its periphery. The age of
the town, it seemed, should have been determinable from the
concentric rings, which traced its movement in time and space
from one level to another, as it ascended the gentle grade, rising
from the banks of the emerald river, Aare.

The little knot in the center I imagined to have been the original seed—planted by the powerful Duke of Zähringen—from
which Bern grew, and the successive rings to have indicated the
movement of the farmers from the surrounding villages to various convenient places, where they gathered in order to trade with
their city neighbors and where the need for tradesmen and shops
soon after arose, which place synthesized and grew in population
and importance until it became the capital of the nation, and
the capital of the nation became the host to the community of
nations known as Europe, housing the embassies and legations
not only of Europe, but of every major power in the world.

Although Bern is surrounded by green fields and orchards
(drive fifteen minutes in any direction from the center of the
city and you are in the country) it is a city which is principally
inhabited by the *Beamter*, or civil servant, who comes from every

canton in the nation and is a part of the diplomatic complements of visiting nations.

The land and the houses were (and are now) the property of the wealthy burgher who rose to power as the city, and consequently the federation, grew. However, Zürich became the center of the nation's economic interests, while Bern's major role became ultimately political.

The capital of Switzerland and the diplomatic center for world mediation, in order to meet the needs of the ever-growing bureaucracy, had to have houses and shops and produce, in order to sustain its role in the western community of nations. As a result, the city has developed in a peculiar way, for because of its peculiar position in relation to its neighbors (Switzerland does not have enough natural resources to exist independently) it must depend upon quiet, peaceful, profitable relations with its neighbors, all of whom are more powerful than it is.

Bern, therefore, has the air of a brightly polished shop with a full stock of goods on display with which to satisfy her own needs and attract the fearsome but necessary strangers. Its thick gray stones house the stores, which are supplied by the peasant farmers and by trade procurement, and thick bars on the bank windows protect the currencies of the entire world, and the banks are in turn backed by an economic-political policy of careful conservatism, which is inspired by the awesome view of the mountains on clear *Föhn* days.

Contrary to the city citizen's life, the peasant's life is relatively secure. He has the house (with many improvements, of course) which his grandfather had. He rises at dawn, just like farmers everywhere, and goes to bed with the chickens. Because he works very hard his hands are gnarled like the trees in his thickets and his face is rough and leathery from relentless wind-lashings. Though his eyes are bleary, he wears no glasses.

He has a stout wife and sturdy children. They are over there, tossing hay in the field. He has cows. They are tinkling on the hillside above. He can read, write and figure, and there is a man in town on market days, in front of the Metropole cinema, to explain the new machines. He has several. There is a thick silver watch with a heavy chain in his trousers pocket, but he seldom looks at it because he is used to reading the time by gazing beneath a down-cupped palm at the sun. His daughter, however, has a shiny new gold wristwatch. The boys can take care of themselves; the oldest, if he will only settle down, will have the farm, but it is the girl who worries him. He dresses her up in fine city clothes and buys her a big new American car, in which to ride to town on market days. A good dowry will get her a respectable city man, a doctor maybe.

In the city the land is all taken. The young man or woman who wishes to make his way in life is perforce confronted with the problem of finding a "place," a little piece of earth, upon which to plant his feet solidly and be.

The secure man has a job with a living salary, graded advancement and retirement at the age of sixty-five. He lives at the end of a parallel avenue with a wife who bears his children and keeps his apartment in order. The children go to elementary and commercial school, in order to become tradesmen, businessmen (the story of Horatio Alger is very well known in Switzerland) or they go to the gymnasium and to the university, in order to become doctors of medicine, national economics or engineers.

To make his way in life easier the buildings and streets, as well as the patina on all imposing statues, are thoroughly scrubbed and polished, and the street signs are freshly painted. Every turn to the right and to the left, every curve and curving tendency is clearly indicated. He can make no mistake, whether on foot or on wheels. Nor can he err in matters of form. All of the standards by which he lives are prescribed so clearly that there can be no room for doubt. The heel of every respectable citizen's shoe is level, nor does the rust thereon embarrass the foot of his knitted sock, though, in spite of the vigilant needle and thread, a hole frequently appears in her hose. But by and large, all the wild threads are dutifully snipped away and the mere outward signs of poverty are hard put to improvise.

Unlike his grandfather in the country, the city citizen is apt to be a little soft and round from a lack of regular exercise and from overeating. His hands feel boneless when you shake them. Upon the fourth finger of his left hand he wears a ring made of a precious metal, offset by a precious stone. Upon his left wrist he wears a Swiss wristwatch, which protrudes proudly from an immaculately starched cuff. The watch he checks daily at six, twelve and six o'clock when he listens to the news. He often wears glasses and he has a slightly ailing heart, a troublesome liver and the nerves of his arms and legs are often inflamed.

The city differs from the country only in degree, which degree, however, imposes a greater variety of ethical situations upon the inhabitants of the city than are imposed upon the inhabitants of the country. This means that the simple, clear, almost instinctive conservatism, which constrains the thoughts and actions of the country folk (who are protected from foreign influences by the mere fact of their isolation and their work) manifests itself in the city in ways which are as various as its function.

In the city the emphasis is upon form. To belong to the society means to conform to its norms. And there is no escape because, though the city is larger and more complex than the country, it is very small as compared to the capital cities of the world. Relatively speaking, the society of the city, like that of the country, is very intimate. One lives a public life simply because one cannot avoid being observed by one's neighbors. One result is that any radical or nonconformist element in the city, like the well-nurtured "wild life" surrounding the countryside, is hard put to improvise.

Therefore, one walks wearily down the straight, narrow avenue, looking neither to the left nor to the right (in the day-time) because the ubiquitous eyes of the dangerous strangers from the powerful nations beyond the mountains are upon you, because of the imposing stares of the strangers from the next canton, because of the accusing eyes of the lovers who occupy the parallel beds who gave birth to strange children, now dead, except for the memory of projected first names and finally because of the empty stares in the eyes of the strangers who face each other over coffee in brightly illuminated kitchens at half-past seven in the morning.

Nervous tensions carve deep intricate patterns into the secret places of the city citizen's consciousness and dilate the pupils of his eyes with subversive desperation—as he registers surprise at the crowded intersection when the stoplight flashes Go! Centuries of accumulated anxiety augments fears, in order to silence which, he eats, drinks, insulates his body with stout pairs of long woolen underwear and covets his wife and his secretary not merely in order to satisfy his appetite, but in order to store up provisions, as it were, in the event of an eminently novel catastrophe.

The Tendency to Overdress, For Example,

BRINGS TO MIND an experience, which was passed on to me by an American acquaintance whom I met by chance one morning at the Mövenpick. After we had ordered our beer we began to indulge in the favorite pastime of the Americans, criticizing the Swiss. And as we were American men, relatively young and energetic, we naturally spoke of Bernese women. We agreed that they were often strikingly handsome, and then proceeded to exchange appraisals of their manner of dress. This turn in the conversation caused me to mention my amazement over the fact that they managed to look so well, in spite of the abundance of clothes they wore. My friend was delighted that I had mentioned this fact because, said he, "I have had an experience in this very connection, which made a very deep impression upon me!"

"What is that deep impression?" said I, and he obliged me by relating the following incident.

"Well," said he, "shortly after I began the third week of term I met a very charming Bernese girl who was really a—I mean really—pretty little thing. She kindly agreed to help me out with a few problems which I had encountered in the difficult subject of anatomy. In order that we might work more conveniently, I invited her up to the apartment one agreeable evening, during the course of which, among other things, we had an excellent supper, which was garnished with a bottle of excellent French wine."

"Don't editorialize!" I exclaimed. "Get to the story!"

"Well," said he, "the fine food—she was a very good cook—
and the wine mellowed our humors, and soon we were exchang-
ing confidences. Shortly after that music was added and we
danced. We both enjoyed it thoroughly.

"These preliminaries were necessary, you see, in order to
induce the proper scientific attitude."

"I am aware of the fact," said I, "having acquired since the
days of my childhood not a little experience in the fascinating
subject of anatomy!"

"Anyway," he said, "finally the tensions rose and the experiment was in readiness.

'Take off your clothes!' I whispered huskily, whisking off my
own in good military style. Then I flung myself upon the bed and
tittered with gleeful expectation as the cool sheets crinkled. But
as my body relaxed I was mildly shocked by a feeling of dreamy
uneasiness, which I was powerless to shake off because, relaxed, I
almost fell apart. Until this moment I had not realized just how
strong the wine was! But now I could feel it, a perverse heaviness
creeping into my bones. It overwhelmed me with the desire to
sink deeper into the bed.

'If she would only come now!' I thought.

"Through heavy eyelids I watched her take the pins out of her
luxurious red hair, one by one, and place them upon the little
glass shelf under the mirror, which hung over the washbasin. My
senses rallied a little. And when her hair fell in a huge coil down
her back, unable to bear it, I tried but failed to fix my gaze upon
the webs of frost that chilled the windowpanes. And I screwed
up my determination not to fall asleep.

"She wore a sort of sweater over her blouse. It stood out in
two soft mounds in front of her chest. She took that off next.
And then she carefully removed her skirt—it was as thick as a
small rug—and laid it out upon the back of the chair beside the
bed, so as not to wrinkle it!

"As though it could wrinkle!" he exclaimed angrily, adding:

"Finally, she gave up the blouse." He paused with a significant smile.

"And then what?" I asked.

"And *then?*—then—she was merely down to her underskirt! It was almost as thick as that tent, which she had just leaned against the chair! Off it came, with a heroic struggle, to be folded and laid away in the same manner as the other articles of her apparel.

"At this point I made room in the bed, giving expression to my happiness due to her apparent willingness, at last, to join me. But she wasn't ready yet. Not only was she not ready—she chided *me* for being impatient—while she rubbed her pink satin arms and complained: 'Brrr—it's cold!'

"I smiled indulgently at her and tried to imagine what there might be left hidden under the rest of her clothing. And while I did that fatigue weighed me down again and I tried but failed to suppress a yawn. Huge drops of water swelled over the brims of my eyes. It's getting late, I thought, sensing vaguely that my strength was waning.

"Meanwhile, she tugged at her cotton half-slip, which she had worn as an extra precaution against the cold night air. And though this phase of her work was only half finished, she stopped and sipped her wine. She shivered sensuously as the warmth crept through her body and her eyes flashed with an animate sparkle. Hurriedly now she proceeded to unfasten the strong black halter, under which was still another scantier, more delicate one, which was also black but transparent with fine lace trimming, through which the soft flesh of her breasts appeared a bewitching pink.

"And all this was heightened by the roundness of her shapely shoulders. I tell you those shoulders extended in a long sweeping line upwards and continued her neck, which was crowned with spangles of devilish red curls! I grew quite excited because I hadn't expected so much loveliness and—

"Finish the story!" I cried.

"Well," he paused reflectively, "now came the delicate moment. The thick cotton panties, which the women of our mothers' time called 'snuggies' started to come down. When they were practically off I discovered to my utter amazement that she was wearing another pair. Black satin ones, fine, transparent and trimmed in lace to match the upper part! There was nothing else to do but wait—until *all* the pants were off. And when they were off I thought, Now—at last!

"But not really—the contraption which held the stockings up had to be unstrapped and unhooked, hook by hook, and the stockings peeled off carefully.

"'A good pair of nylons cost six francs [about $1.50] a pair!' she protested when she chanced to observe the expression upon my face, laying them upon the chair as though they were tender children.

"By now I was biting my fingernails in order to keep from falling asleep. As each nail sliver fell my head plummeted upon my chest and my elbows sank deeper into the bed's pillowy ooze. However, the long-awaited moment did actually arrive when she, realizing that there was nothing else to remove, suffering from a sudden attack of shyness, clasped her arms about her naked body, blushed to the roots of her crimson hair and switched out the light.

"The darkness struck me right between the eyes like a huge soft fist and I fell back into the bed, almost unconscious with sleep. I tried to blink my eyes but they were too heavy. It was then that I realized that my sight had forsaken me and that my other senses were abandoning me one by one. My sense of hearing dissolved in the darkness. I felt as though I were dying or slipping into a coma. Next it was my sense of touch that left. I felt as though I swam in a river of warm flesh—except for an instant when a cold shivering mass of flesh crashed against me with a deadening thud. But the effect of the shock was negligible because I was just passing over into the world of dream!

"I dreamed a peculiar dream. I dreamed that I fell into a river of black freezing water, which stiffened my body into a block of ice. And that presently I looked out and saw that the little berg, which was myself, was floating dangerously near the edge of a deep fall. Suddenly I fell. The ice block dashed against a bright pink rock.

"I awoke and discovered that the door was ajar. Half-consciously I got out of bed and closed it and then crawled back into the bed, where I dreamed once more that I was a block of ice. After a time I began to melt slowly at the base of the big pink rock that turned out to be the sun. But, of course you shouldn't take this too seriously because one's accounts of his dreams can never be depended upon. But of the sun, at least, I feel fairly certain because I awoke a little after eleven the next morning due to the insistent ray of sunlight, which shone through my frosty window!"

With the end of his story we laughed heartily, though somewhat sadly—I believe I mentioned that we were both bachelors! In the silence that followed we stared thoughtfully at our empty beer glasses. The waitress appeared just then and wished to know if we would order more, but we declined and paid for the glasses which we had drunk.

And then my friend excused himself because he had an appointment for lunch in this very restaurant. "I expect to meet a young lady," he said, and I told him that I understood very well.

"And thank you for the enjoyable story. I must excuse myself as well, today being one of those rare days when I am invited to Mrs. C—— who is preparing one of her famous fondues. I, too, have to hurry because Mrs. C—— is very distressed when one is late for one of her fondues because when one is late, when one fails to eat it just as it reaches its point of perfection, it becomes very gummy and, therefore, very difficult to chew."

As I was saying all this I noticed that his eyes brightened and that he looked happily toward the door. I instinctively looked toward the door, too. Just a little inside the room stood, indeed, a "pretty little thing" with flaming hair, apparently searching for someone. At the sight of her I felt a rush of excitement stir within me. Something about the girl seemed familiar, though I did not remember having seen her before. And yet I was embarrassed by the fact that I seemed to know—or felt that I knew—her intimately! Extremely delicate details flashed through my mind as she rushed toward my friend now, having caught his eyes, with a smile of fond recognition.

My friend looked strangely at the girl and then at me—just in time to catch my expression. He blushed scarlet, while I blushed a sort of dusky plum color. We both burst into a laugh just as she reached us. He greeted her and introduced her to me as Guinivere something which I do not remember because when I heard her first name I forgot all else. From the shock of hearing that name superimposed upon the excitement from which I was already pleasurably suffering, I cried out, "*What* did you say your name was!"

"Guinivere," she replied, looking at me with an open expression of impersonal friendliness.

"How—how do you do," I muttered confusedly. "Excuse me for—I mean—I am just leaving. I have to go somewhere just—just now. You see, I am invited to have a fondue at the home of friends, a Mr. and Mrs. C——. Which means, of course, that, that I shall have to hurry because Mrs. C——," and so on . . .

The point of that little experience is, I reflected some days later over a cup of coffee for which I could not pay A——, one of the waitresses at the Rendez-vous, while evening darkened under rain clouds and people streamed in from work and settled down to their vegetable soup, picata milanese, salad and coffee, that the desire to be *safe* is ingrained in the Swiss consciousness many layers deep and that it expresses itself in those characteristic ways which are determined by the landscape.

In the country the peasant personalities burst into flower like the miniature blossoms which cover the mountain peaks. And in the city the personalities of the city citizens function like the precision parts of a Swiss watch, the most precise watch in the world, and to the silent, insistent rhythms of an all-pervading fear; which fear would also be your fear and mine—if Russia were as close to you and to me as New York is to Kansas, and America were as close to us as Kansas is to California, and if we were caught between these two great aggressive powers.

The Swiss "Movement"

IS, THEREFORE, THE mode of existence of Switzerland's highly organized business, political, and social life.

Switzerland is *besetzt* (occupied, taken, sold out), like all the seats in the movie on Saturday night. There is standing room only. In spite of the beautiful, bountiful little farms and villages surrounding Bern and other cities, Switzerland is, on the whole, far from being self-sufficient. She has neither enough natural resources nor space with which to accommodate her increasing population. She must live upon produce imported from the rest of the world, principally America, England, Italy and France. The coffee which one drinks in the tearooms comes from South America. The famous Swiss cow, who gives the finest chocolate and the most famous cheese of its kind in the world, is an immigrant from Yugoslavia. Timber comes from Scandinavia and woolen fabrics come from England, and so on.

Switzerland lives upon her exports, watches and precision instruments of all kinds, which she must make smaller and finer than her competitors in order to survive. She lives on her export chocolate and as a result of her fine sense of business organization. She is banking house for the world and a center of political mediation. Switzerland lives upon her tourist trade, for she is a nation of hotels, pensions and conference halls. She plays hostess to the nations during times of political strife and of war.

William Faulkner said—and rightly, it occurred to me—in some book or in an interview, which I read or heard of some time ago, that Switzerland appeared to him to be a neat little business, a sort of supermarket.

For Switzerland lives upon its mountain snows and scenic grandeur. There is no doubt about it, her landscape is one of the most imposing to be found anywhere! In short, Switzerland survives and prospers because of her ability to accommodate a luxury market, which means that she produces things, which are, for the most part, not really necessary for the maintenance of life, but which she makes so appealing that the nations of the world cannot resist them. She must excel in this ability in order to "justify" her existence!

Now this is a very difficult thing to do. It requires art, if not witchcraft! Certainly it requires a sensitive ear, an ear which must be attuned to the rise and fall of every gold and silver note, and to the loud blasts of war—as the tempo of world affairs accelerates and retards, augments and diminishes. She must observe all the pauses, rests and full stops. She must be watchful and patient, and know how to wait. She must not wait too long. She must not, for example, say, Yes, when she should say, No, or No, when she should say, Maybe so. And what is most difficult of all, she cannot afford to make a vital mistake!

Therefore, because she must have good business relations with her neighbors (good business relations mean good political relations) she must have economic efficiency and *order* at home. Every man must work (prove that he is "serious") and assume the financial responsibility for himself and for his family. He must live quietly and inconspicuously and do the required thing at the required time. But most of all, *he must be quiet!* and nice to strangers because strangers bring business and business means prosperity and prosperity means economic security for everybody. On the other hand, strangers are dangerous, they bring new ideas and arouse disturbing impulses, which can be destructive, so they are to be watched. One must stand a little apart from them.

The Most Important Words in the Swiss Vocabulary

ARE "INSURANCE" AND "control." In my youth I wondered at an article which I had possibly read or heard of in which the writer revealed the fact that the universally admired legs of a certain movie queen were insured for, I believe, three million dollars. Others were said to have insured their noses, breast nipples and toenails—any and all of those parts upon which their success as film stars depended—for equally fabulous amounts. Now, I have often thought that Switzerland must be teeming with film luminaries, because the average Swiss citizen is insured from the soles of his feet to the tips of his head-hairs. The major insurances, for fire, against theft, etc., especially for shops and other business establishments, are required by law; and all the others are encouraged.

One good result of this precaution is that no Swiss citizen need worry about hospitalization should he become ill, or should his wife or girlfriend have a baby. I myself have visited the very efficient polyclinic, and was grateful not to have to pay the normal fees required by a personal physician; especially since I have often heard of doctors in America and elsewhere who inquire into the patient's financial circumstances *before* they administer aid!

In the Swiss household glasses are insured against breakage, and water pipes are insured against leakage, bread is insured against "moldage," soufflés against "fallage," and roses against "cankerage." I'm sure there must be, though I have not actually seen them, insurances against "dish-pan handage" and "tattle-tale-grayage" of underlinen. There appears to be nothing that anyone can do about the weather!

I have suggested that absolute order prevails; everything is clean, polished and shipshape. The "control" and maintenance of that order is the responsibility of the police. The police function in Switzerland is primarily a civil-service, bureaucratic extension of the body politic, rather than that of a law-enforcement institution, as it is in America. They do not beat you over the head and drag you to jail in a semi-conscious state for talking back to an officer, as they do in Kansas City, because the Swiss do not talk back, they are very law-abiding. Crime is rare, as it is known in Paris and London and New York, even when considered in ratio to the population: so pervasive and powerful is the inculcated admonition to be quiet.

And the law is clear. The traffic directions, for example, are clear enough for a blind man to read, but as a precaution, in case they might not be, I have heard, though I cannot consider my source reliable, they are considering writing them in braille. Bicyclists stop at crossings at three o'clock in the morning and look both ways—I have seen them!—when no car or pedestrian is within sight or sound. And how many times have I seen, not a policeman, but a pedestrian, a citizen, reprimanding one who has failed to observe some minor regulation. The police are quiet, soft-spoken servants of the people who walk their beats in pairs more for company (a man needs someone to talk to on quiet lonely nights) than for protection. They are nice young men who are apt to remind the stranger who comes from a more dangerous land of friendly boy scouts who are, as their motto encourages them to be, always ready to serve. Order prevails, and the authority of the state is unquestioned; not out of fear of the police as agents of social discipline, but out of the generally felt need to be quiet, because the whole nation must be quiet, which quietude is absolutely essential for the very survival of all.

I was amazed once, when I heard of a man who called the police because his wife's lover, whom he discovered in the act of seducing her, refused to leave his house! Now according to the unwritten law of every land on earth the husband had the right to kill them both, on the spot, to spatter their entrails from the foot of the Jungfrau to the summit of the Matterhorn. But such a barbarous act never occurred to the husband, who was a soldier—as are all Swiss men—who had—as has every Swiss soldier—his army rifle, complete with bayonet and ammunition in his own house!

The police function as a sort of big or elder brother who is authorized by the aged father, the state, to maintain civil discipline, and to control the actions of the citizenry. For example, no businessman can lose money because a client refuses to pay his debts. When the payments are tardy he sends you three or four urgent letters, and when you do not respond he writes and tells you that if you do not pay by such and such a date he will place your account in the hands of the "Betreibung" office, a government agency whose function is to collect delinquent debts, plus administration charges. When the "dead-line" date comes and you do not pay, two uniformed gentlemen come to your home and seize not all of your possessions, but only the "luxury" items which exceed what the state considers absolutely necessary to maintain one's domestic life. Needless to say, that is very little, a bed, a table, a chair, and so on . . .

The state takes care of every situation which might result in violence—or even unrest—if handled privately by the private citizen. The police shoo you out of restaurants and bars if you stay too long—three minutes or more—after the legal closing hour; and they collect the tickets in dance halls on Saturday night when you are taxed for the privilege of dancing longer than usual, etc . . .

The police also control the activities of tourists and foreigners who pass through or live in Switzerland very carefully. The tenets of international law are followed to the letter; they have to be, in order to avoid complications with other governments, and to protect the interests of Swiss citizens. For Switzerland abounds with refugees and laborers from many nations, the most numerous of which latter group are the Italians.

The services mentioned above are by no means all which are

rendered by the police, there are many more, which to enumerate here would require much patience, strong finger muscles and, above all, a sense of humor. But before I end this chapter I must mention one over-all effect which police controls have upon the citizenry in general:

It makes them feel like fish in an aquarium. They are aware of being watched, and they are afraid to step out of line. Harassed by the tedium of constant observation, they harass others. I have to suffer this—you shall not escape, is the attitude which rises to the surface of the social consciousness. Petty jealousies arise as to the equal distribution of privilege. Fear and jealousy of one's neighbor are the most predominant attitudes which color working relationships. The workers do not cooperate with each other willingly, especially the experienced workers who have to supervise those who are new and are serving their apprenticeships. The newcomer is looked upon as a competitor and a potential threat to his colleague's existence. And there is strong, even crushing opposition to any kind of "radicalism," which really means to "new ideas."

As a result, most of the citizenry is attempting the impossible, it is trying to maintain a private social life where there is no possibility of doing so, and it is seeking "security," even at the expense of its neighbors, where there is none! But in spite of the internal competitive tensions the Swiss people are strongly united in their opposition to the outsider. The cohesiveness of the Swiss society is one—I would hazard to say—of the strongest in the modern world.

Swiss private life is perhaps the most public in the world, that is, among the nations which have a democratic form of government. If, for example, you want to locate any citizen, from any canton whatsoever, you can simply look in the telephone book; there you will find his name, from which you will possibly be able to determine the canton in which he was born, and naturally his address and telephone number, as well as his profession, from which you may determine his probable salary. But if he has no telephone, you may simply go to a police bureau, pay a small fee and read his personal history in detail. The status of no citizen need be in doubt.

A man is judged in Switzerland, as in most countries, by the bourgeoise standard—and Switzerland is, above all, a bourgeoise state—which is based upon his financial position, and by the age and, therefore, venerability, of his family name. In Switzerland I might even place family first, as the distinction between one man and his neighbor, as I have observed it, is one of class. The rich may, if they wish, buy aristocratic standing, as the Jews did during the Renaissance, and as many Americans are doing today. Class distinction in Switzerland is—I believe I have said this before—vertical rather than horizontal.

There is no place where a Swiss citizen may go and be alone in his own country. This is one of the reasons, no doubt, why privacy is so ardently insisted upon, and why strangers find it so difficult to enter Swiss society; why the people are so close-mouthed and fearful of hazarding opinions about new, uneval-uated happenings in the daily life of the community, and in the world at large. The tendency is to conceal one's personal feelings as much as possible until an official position is published.

Is it any wonder that their nerves are frayed? that their veins harden? that anxiety and fear dog their footsteps? To be free! Free from all of it! they seem to be crying; as they laugh and dance and overeat and overdress, and perspire in overheated apartments in which the walls are so thin that they can hear their neighbors' scratch; as they toss restlessly in their parallel beds, dreaming of Spain, Italy, Africa—all the hot countries—until the early morning, when they must tumble out of their beds, and stare blindly at the stranger over coffee, and thread the many-corded loom which designs the grim-petty pattern of "security."

However, I Can't Repeat This Too Many Times:

YOU AND I would probably be the same way (are we any different!) if just over the mountains lay several powerful nations, hungry nations, with big armies, navies and outlets to the sea; with planes affording outlets to the moon!—hungry nations, running out of colonies and trusts to exploit, in a world in which two thirds of the people are practically starving, or are politically enslaved. And that is why

Switzerland Is Neutral

SHE IS STRATEGICALLY unnecessary to the maintenance of the "balance of power" between the strong nations of the present world. She can have no other policy if she wishes to survive. A jet bomber can flit across Switzerland as swiftly as a young bird can hop across the river Aare. The principal value of Switzerland in international political affairs is one of convenience. She provides a parlor in which the nations can sit and discuss the fate of the world. She makes them comfortable, and performs those tedious little tasks—perfectly—which the larger countries do not find time to do, or which they can have done more cheaply by someone else.

That is why Switzerland's domestic life is so carefully controlled, and why in political matters the protocol is so religiously, almost fanatically, followed—to the letter, to the "i-dot," "t-cross," and the "end-stop."

This is a very difficult position to have to be in. Here are some of the reasons why they have to be in this very difficult position; or, why they *feel* they have to be in this very difficult position; and why, to a great extent, I agree with them:

A Little Sham History of Switzerland, Which Is Very Much to the Point, and Which the Incredulous or the Pedantic May Verify by Reading a Formal History of Switzerland, Which I Have Certainly Never Done, and Will Probably Never Do

... Once upon a time a few farmers in three different parts of the country which is now Switzerland, Uri, Schwyz and Unterwalden, got tired of being imposed upon by the decadent aristocracy of the Holy Roman Empire. They guessed, and rightly, that they could protest more strongly, longer and more effectively together than they could alone; so they got together with sticks and rakes and pitchforks and stones and much willpower and resolution, and beat off the decadent princes who had insisted that they pay exorbitant taxes, without granting that representation which made the rule of the British odious to the Americans, one of whom made quite a mess about it, as a result of which mess, a truly noble word was uttered, which I had to learn by heart, in order to pass my history examinations several hundred years later at the William Lloyd Garrison Elementary School in Kansas City. Nor were the reasons for the revolt limited to matters of taxation, the Swiss fought for freedom, the right to judge their own affairs without the interference of indifferent and usually avaricious petty princes and to defend their own land. The farmers knew the terrain well, I have heard; and they knew the mountains; they knew, for example, where the dangerous stones lay, and how to throw them profusely and accurately.

So when the dreaded enemy advanced they threw and threw. And the dreaded enemy fell down dead and fell down dead, and then he stopped falling down dead for a while.

The determined farmers won. And having won—together—they were afraid to separate after that, the woods were so dark; so they stayed together, and watched and listened all around. And when the time came, the enemy came, fresher and stronger than before . . .

The determined farmers waited quietly . . . And when the dreaded enemy was in the breach of their slingshots, just like an army of little Davids, they slung their shots and slung their shots, and shot their arrows, and threw and threw their stones . . . And the dreaded enemy fell down dead in the breach many times; until he stopped falling down dead; and then, of course, as before, the determined farmers won . . .

They thought that they had better stay together a very long time after that, just in case. And after that other farmers from other parts of the Holy Roman Empire which are now Switzerland, heard what the farmers from Uri, Schwyz and Unterwalden had done, how they had slung their shots, and shot, and how they had thrown their stones from secret parts of the mountains, causing the dreaded enemy to fall down dead and fall down dead in the breach, and joined them.

They all became Swiss.

The confederation which was Switzerland grew and grew, and became stronger and more effective.

This was the point at which the confederation began its second phase, in which the struggle for leadership took place, like the one which took place in America when there were only thirteen colonies, and then more colonies, until the north and south got into it and the United States became, more or less, a politically homogeneous entity—at least, on paper; a few stalwart spokesmen for the Ku Klux Klan have recently proposed, I have read somewhere, secession. The powerful, the rich and the most intelligent citizens of the Swiss Confederation, which happened to have been the titled class—I do not hold to the idea that the aristocracy *has* to be decadent, or that the system which they once maintained was necessarily a bad one—won. But there was no king, no tyrant. After the bloody civil war in 1848 everyone realized that internal unity must prevail if the national security were to be maintained.

When the aristocracy lost its power, it was because of old age; the times simply changed. The new era ushered in the burghers, some of whom tried to establish new aristocratic houses.

The confederation held its ground.

Then the burghers became not so much corrupt, as old-fashioned; nor did they necessarily die of old age, they—more or less—were modified into capitalists, some of whom also bought titles and tried to reestablish aristocratic traditions, but failed because the times, as the times will, had changed again . . .

Meanwhile, the confederation evolved naturally into a democratic form of government with a strong socialistic tendency, and with a very conservative conviction.

Emerson has said—and I believe him—that the history of mankind may be likened unto the history of one man. Switzerland, more than any other country I know anything about, may also be likened unto one man—and let me carry the thought a little further by suggesting that its brain is the absolute controlling authority to such an extent that the emotional part of the man suffers, to which suffering his organs and extremities have been conditioned for centuries by the "necessity" of living in a cramped condition: for he must always *think* to keep his head securely tucked down behind the mountains . . . Where he crouches, his heels dug in, his gun in hand, his rations secured, waiting . . .

An Interesting Effect Which This State of
Consciousness Has Upon Women

SWITZERLAND IS A man's world. Certainly because of the religious, economic and politic development of the nation, and possibly because of the necessary division of labor, due to the position in which I have hypothetically placed the nation (personified as one man), the Swiss woman is, politically speaking, a nonentity. Her major function is a domestic one. She has no effective voice in politics and she does not vote. Aside from the domestic life there are but few professional and semi-professional fields which she may enter. The dominant idea with regard to women in this country is that the woman's place is in the home. If she steps outside of it, into the world of the professions, for example, she is violating a deeply entrenched concept of woman, and she is threatening the stability of the social order. Furthermore, she will have to compete with men. Men control the society completely, therefore she has no protection, nor can she appeal to the state for protection, because the state is governed by men. Her possibilities are, therefore, limited.

As far as I have observed, women are prominent but not by any means conspicuous in the fields of medicine (child medicine, internal female diseases, obstetrics), social welfare fields and teaching, mainly in the elementary and secondary schools.

One result is the existence of a woman who is seldom "intellectual," which many men, especially Americans, consider a good thing, though she is intelligent, abounding in a rich variety of those subtle wiles which men are pleased to call "feminine," and which have made the "weaker" sex—the Swiss woman included —masters of men from time immemorial.

She is usually more sensitive than her man, not because she is a woman, but for the same reasons that minority groups are usually more sensitive than majority groups, because their sensitivity is their principal means of survival. The Swiss woman thoroughly understands her role in the society and she generally appears to be satisfied with it, though she suffers from its short-comings perhaps more than the men. She submits with resig-nation, apparently because she feels the life in Switzerland to be inevitable. She, like her man, is fearful of change, the change in her life which independence and political responsibility would bring about. She strongly suspects that changing the attitudes of men, as well as her own, would be very much—too much—trouble and that most certainly it would require a phenomenally long time. Besides that, she, too, is convinced that her place is in the home, that she should cook, sew, clean and mother her chil-dren in peaceful respectability and leave the complicated matters of government to men. If she is unhappy it is because she cannot achieve the maximal status which is idealized by her society.

Both men and women in Switzerland seem to want what men and women from every land want, though I will not attempt to name it. As I walk among them by night and by day, I can see that they feel (some more vaguely than others, of course) that their problems are much bigger than themselves. I think that they feel, as we all feel at one time or another, that their particular troubles, the shapes of their personal pains, have to do with the "times" in which they live and with their peculiar position in "space." With all their hearts they pray for change—do we all not pray for change? for something different from that which we have? for peace? And do we not cringe with fear at the dreadful sound of the rumble of its wheels! However, meanwhile, whether we like it or not, whether we understand it or not, we (the worlds) are changing all the time—like the light deflected by the snow, gleaming white on the mountains: now you see the flakes, each of which is a world, complete, now you do not. But they are there, they are always there, golden in sunrise, spectral in mist, a mysterious icy spectrum of blue as the evening falls, a thick jagged wall of darkness when there is no moon: and behind them teems the frothing surge of disaster . . .

An Interesting Effect Which This State of
Consciousness Has Upon the Concept of Charity

"I ACCEPT THIS ten francs [about $2.50] in the same spirit in which you offer it," I said to the gentleman, and continued with a statement, the significance and full import of which was, because I saw, I believed, a condescending glint in his eyes: that I am just as good as you are, even if I can't eat tonight without your money; which sentiment I expressed more subtly, of course, and with philosophy; to which he replied:

"I believe it, but do you?"

The gentleman's reply disturbed me very much, and all the more because I was not sure as to just why I was so disturbed, except that his reply had made me feel even more deeply that he was condescending to lend me the money, and that he could be so effective only because my state of mind gave him some justification. I hemmed and hawed a little in order to gain time with which I could review my position. Then a thought came to mind, which resulted in the following long, if not edifying discussion on the subject of Charity in Switzerland.

He was very laudatory about the generosity of his country-men and spoke in glowing terms of the many international ser-vices which they rendered to the poor and needy. "Take, for example, the present emergency," he said, by which he apparently referred to the Hungarians, but by which I had reason to believe he really meant me. I tried to guess how many barrels of grease one would get if one melted down the fat hanging from his thick chin, as I lit a match, and then lit my pipe, and said:

"Have you ever heard of Max Frisch?"

"Of course I have," he said.

"Well," I said, "he wrote a play—I don't remember the name of it. A friend to whom I give English lessons twice a week, and who feeds me, and who allows me to take a bath in his tub every week, and who accepts me as practically a member of the family for all that, told me about it. In fact, he said it seemed to him quite strange and wondered if I would give him my opinion of it. And because I find it apropos our discussion, I would like to relate the incidents in the play to you and perhaps have your opinion, as I also found the play very interesting."

The gentleman looked at his watch and consented.

"Now, this is the plot, as far as I can remember. It seemed that two strangers were for some adequate reason hungry and destitute in Switzerland on a cold winter night. They knocked upon the door of the first house they came to and described their unfortunate condition with much pathos to the master and mistress, who were just about to sit down to supper. After hearing the strangers' complaints, they took them into their house, fed them well and entertained them after the custom of the land. After supper was over their host offered them a bed for the night in their immaculately clean, well-aired attic room, which the 'poor devils' gratefully accepted, and went to bed.

"Shortly after that the master and mistress of the house also climbed into bed and finally put out the light. Presently they were counting their eighty-seventh lamb, at least, he was counting lambs, his spouse counted rams, her eighty-eighth was, in fact, suspended in midair, when she perceived the faint but persistent odor of something burning. It was so persistent that it wouldn't let her count her rams. And the longer she perceived the odor the more it smelled, she thought, like the odor of burning rams, but at the same time suspected that her dream was running away with her.

"But it was the host who cried out first:

"'Smoking lambs! I believe something's burning.' With that, still half asleep, he jumped out of bed and ran to the stove in the kitchen in order to see if the lambs were really burning. Of course, there were no lambs burning in the oven, and as he became more wideawake, he soon discovered, after running first to this room and then to that, that the smoke seemed to be coming from upstairs because the whole staircase was filled with it.

"'Something's burning!' the hostess cried with a terrified shriek, finally convinced that, though her dream was not running away with her and her rams were not burning, though the eighty-eighth was still suspended in midair, *something was burning!*

"Meanwhile, the host rushed fearlessly up the smoking staircase, warning his wife as he went to stay behind. When he reached the top floor he perceived that streaks of fire were sucking through the cracks of the attic door. 'The strangers!' he cried anxiously, and dashed into the hissing inferno.

"The strangers were standing naked in one corner of the room with sticks of broken furniture in their hands. They looked upon the host calmly, as he exclaimed, more to himself than to them: 'Thank goodness they were not suffocated in their beds!' He rushed toward them in order to inquire as to their condition, when suddenly he froze in his tracks because he now perceived their attitudes to be rather odd under the circumstances, for they were not trying to escape, nor were they attempting to extinguish the flames, which were now licking the paint off the ceiling. In fact, they stood leering at him, breaking forth into bursts of frenzied laughter. Then presently he saw that they were breaking up his furniture with the heavy sticks, which they had wrenched from the bed, and throwing the broken pieces into the fire.

"Now, the host, upon observing this strange behavior, upon beholding the fire as it consumed his furniture and his house, torn between the desire to save his possessions and the desire to be a hospitable host, succumbed to the latter and more powerful of the two, and joined the guests in their work. He was fascinated by the beauty of the destructive flames. He worked at his own

destruction even more feverishly than they, laughing as he flung
this treasured piece and that treasured piece into the fire, feeling
a cool airy sensation of release course through his body—as the
flames grew and grew and grew.

"I forgot what happened in the play after that," I interrupted
my narrative to say, "but I think it ended soon. Now, how's that
for a story?" I asked my benefactor.

"I don't get it!" he replied, looking down at me curiously.
Even while seated he was very tall, and he spoke American very
well, so well, in fact, that he even spoke his own language with
an American accent.

"Well, I didn't read Mr. Frisch's play," I said, "but I gather
that he wished to convey the strangers' rage because of the inhumanity of the charity which they had received at the hands of
their benefactor. I say 'rage' because they perceived that they had
not been aided as a result of love or compassion, but as a result
of fear, which was inspired by the mere sight of suffering in the
world; and of guilt for having bought their 'security' at the price
of their souls; a tendency which is pervasive enough to warrant
a generalization, or rather, in this case, representation as a comi-
tragic theme for a work of art."

"A guilty conscience!" he exclaimed.

"The whole western world is guilty," I said. "You've no special
cause to be ashamed of that. We are guilty because of the thing
which Adam and Eve did, especially since they were not married.
And we also feel guilty because of what Oedipus did, and for just
the opposite reason, because his mother *was* married.

"Now I personally have felt guilty for years, not only for the
standard reason which I have just mentioned, but also for the
mere fact that I exist. I find that very interesting, to say the least.
My society taught me from the first moment I entered it, in ten
thousand different ways, that to be black was to be bad, or at
least, not to be as good as other persons who were not black. My
kinky hair was ugly, my thick lips and flat nose and big round
eyes were laughable. Even when I stuck my hair to my skull with
heavy pomades and changed the shape of my nose, in order to

make it look 'Caucasian'—just to please them!—they laughed at me just the same.

"Why, I came to believe myself that I was ugly; and I was deeply sorry because of it. And not only was I sorry for myself, but for the beautiful nonblack persons who had to tolerate the ugly sight which I imposed upon them.

"I remember as a child I—I used to try to make myself smaller when I walked down the street, so that I wouldn't look so big and black and bad.

"I felt inferior, as well, because my society taught me that all nonblack persons were much more intelligent than I. Learned, celebrated professors descanted upon this theme. Therefore, every time I thought a thought or had an idea, or was obliged to utter a word in their presence, I stammered and scratched my kinky hair very comically.

"It took a long time for me to learn the truth about myself in relation to nonblack persons. And even when I did learn the truth it was very hard for me to accept. Men who are in prison often grow accustomed to it, they even learn to love the pris-oner's life, and are at a total loss when they are once again confronted with the world, which had been the object of so many futile dreams. And some men even find freedom behind prison bars when it would have been impossible for them to do so had they remained a part of the society at large. My life was very confusing when I discovered that nonblack persons were not innately more intelligent than I. I had to learn to act a new way and under very discouraging circumstances. The problem was to keep the secret which I discovered and yet act as though I didn't know it. I wanted to stay alive, you see, just as you do. Needless to say, I had much trouble because I forgot sometimes, and then I became more confused again, and frightened, and so on . . . You may read the story in the American papers most any day . . .

"But now, the Swiss, my friend, are guilty for the standard reasons and because they want to stay alive so badly that they're frightened to death every time there is a mere hint of poverty or suffering—it is against the law to beg in Switzerland—Gypsies can tell no fortunes here—or war, every time a diplomat from a major power raises his voice. They look at their bountiful fields and well-stocked storehouses and say, 'Thank God that we have been spared the fate of our neighbors!' But they have not been spared because they die every time an ill wind blows in the world. They suffer from guilt for not having shared the world's suffering. They are quite beautiful because they *can* suffer, because they are ashamed to eat their buttered bread in the presence of the hungry stranger. What is not beautiful is the fact that they feed the 'poor devil' not for his sake, but for their own, and with hatred in their hearts, the way . . .

The Way I Used to Give Willis James My Candy When I Was a Little Boy . . .

".. . WHEN I WAS a little boy, another little boy, but much smaller than I, lived next door. Neither of us ever knew who his father was, and his mother worked all day, here and there. He had three sisters who were older than he and who had different fathers; the youngest of them was Annie, who used to follow us all the time, but we chased her away because she was only a girl. Willis James and I were boys, but I didn't like him because he was only a little boy; only four when I was seven, and seven when I was ten. His nose was always snotty, and his eyes were so sad and dark. He was as dirty as a little root, and went barefooted all the time; he could not climb the big walnut tree in the lot behind Aunt Nancy's house and climb onto the porch roof, or run from the top of the alley to the lamppost in front of my house as fast as I could. He was very little.

"He followed me all the time . . . Especially when I had a piece of candy or a bag of corn. We used to buy a little cello-phane bag of red candies with yellow tips made in the shape of kernels of corn for a nickel. Willis James would follow me and watch me eat them. He would watch me plunk them in and swallow them. His eyes would droop, the corners of his mouth would sag, and his head would sink between his shoulder blades, as we sat on the old stone wall of the old condemned house that used to stand next to our house. It was filled with trash and ashes,

and we used to play ghost and cops-and-robbers and Indian in
it. As we sat on that old wall, he would watch me plop them in
and finally he would say what he always said on such occasions:

"'Vin-sun . . . gimmie sum . . .'

"I wouldn't answer. Just plop them in and swallow them. He
would watch me. And then:

"'Vin-sun . . . gimmie sum. . .'"

"'Here!' I would cry at last, practically throwing the package
at him. And then I would feel ashamed. He was so little; too
little to climb the big walnut tree in the lot behind Aunt Nancy's
house and climb onto the porch roof, and he couldn't run very
fast yet. I would gently, perhaps even tenderly, divide my corn
with him and walk away. He would stuff the whole handful into
his mouth and smile, and follow me up the steps of our house,
where I would sit on the porch in front of the kitchen door. I
could hear Mom moving around inside; sometimes she would
hum quietly and sometimes only move around. Willis James
would sit noiselessly beside me, snot running from his nose, his
lips clean where he had licked them so that all of the sugar taste
was gone, while I would eat my corn. He would watch me as I
plopped them in and swallowed them. He would sniff or lick
the snot from his nose or wipe it away with the back of his dirty
little hand. Then his big eyes would droop, and the corners of his
mouth would sag, and he would say in a pathetic voice:

"'Vin-sun . . . gimmie sum . . .'

"'I gave you some, Willis James!' I would cry angrily. He
would sit very still for a minute. And then:

"'Vin-sun . . . gimmie sum . . .' he would repeat, a little
louder and in a tone so sad and appealing that my mother would
hear him and come to the door and look at the dirty little mutt
and say to me:

"'Vincent! Give him some. How can you be so selfish!'

"In a rage I would give him the rest of the candy and watch
my little cellophane bag become smaller and smaller as the corn
color went out. He plunked them into his mouth, one by one,
and sometimes two or three at a time, and swallowed them.

When they were gone I would run into the house and slam the door.

"'What's the matter with you?' my mother would ask, but I wouldn't answer. I would go into the toilet and sit on the stool and stare at the wall. A little later I would hear Willis James's voice through the door. As I stared at the wall in front of me I could imagine him standing there on our porch, his little snotty nose pressed against the screen, looking at my mother with his big sad eyes, the corners of his mouth dropping, saying:

"'Mrs. Carter?'

"'What is it, honey?'

"'Kin Vin-sun cum out an play?' . . .

"It is no accident," I said to the gentleman, after a short pause, "that the Red Cross is a Swiss invention—the Lord works in mysterious ways: its conception was inspired, in part, by a desire to compensate for a national sense of guilt. Isn't it interesting that 'good' qualities may often issue from 'bad' effects! However, sometimes the quality of this experience is obscured by the fact that charity which is condescending or which exacts gratitude or subjects the recipient to the will or authority of the donor is apt to be embarrassing and ofttimes vulgar. It sometimes enrages one to the degree that he might wish to burn his benefactor's house down. And the benefactor may suffer from his position in his society to such a degree that he might take great joy in his own destruction, through his desire to express his love, to communicate with the world at large and with himself. Now, that's what I think Mr. Frisch was trying to say, and I am proud of him for having the courage to say it, especially because he is a Swiss citizen!"

"Wait a minute!" he cried, flushing angrily, but I waved aside his unvoiced objection, believing that I had anticipated it.

"Oh, I don't say that the Red Cross, or other Swiss-inspired charities are bad or negligible, I simply mean that it would not make me particularly happy to be the recipient of a charitable act which was not expressed out of a personal, human concern for me, as an individual; not simply because my poverty made my benefactor miserable or fearful for himself. Here is another example of what I mean:

"A lady I know said to me one day, 'I've felt miserable all day. I've had terrible headaches, and I've been very nervous . . .'

"'Why?' I asked.

"'Because of the earthquake in India,' she replied.

"'Oh, yes, I saw the pictures in the movies,' I said. 'But why don't you feel well?'

"'Why don't I feel *well!* Just think—of all those poor people!'

"'It doesn't break me up,' I said. 'Oh, I can feel miserable enough about a Bernese man I happen to see being run down by a car, but as for people I don't even know, I can feel only a certain abstract sorrow, and that is all.'

"'You're an egoist. You have no feelings!' the lady declared, with much more passion than the situation seemed to warrant.

"On the contrary,' I replied. 'But the world is full of suffering. Man's mind cannot stand the tension of sustained suffering. In order to survive he must see suffering in perspective. That is why the mind is able to forget, though it knows all . . . But if you are so worried about them, *do* something for them; that is, if you can start *without* pausing to help the needy multitudes whom you will meet on the way; the ones who are much nearer to you, and whom you might better serve than those who are beyond your reach.

"'You know, the Mississippi River valley is flooded almost every year. Yearly I used to watch my own Missouri River rise and wash away the houses and lands of the farmers on the North Kansas City side where the land is low. People volunteered and built levees to stop the water. And when it finally went down they built their houses and tilled their land again. There was simply no time for headaches and fits of nervousness.

"'The whole world suffers all the time. I said that the mind of man cannot accommodate that suffering; well, I meant no ordinary mind, such as yours and mine. But the world has had its Buddhas and Jesuses: they have always advised us to *cast down our buckets where we are!*: to pluck the arrow from the wounded man's breast, and ask not from whence it came, *and go on your way!* Suffer for the Indians if you must; if, upon perceiving the needs of your next door neighbor, you can find the time.'

"That's what I said to her, my friend," I said to the man who had loaned me the ten francs on which I would eat that night. And then I said:

"Now, I wish to suggest that this lady's 'suffering' was caused by none other than a hypersensitivity to the mere idea of suffering, and of death, which is shared by the entire Swiss nation —before and since the Napoleonic invasion, and that it is the spirit behind its proverbial neutrality in the modern world.

"And on top of that they want gratitude for it, they want you to sit up on your hind legs and open your mouth and catch the little morsel which they plop in—like so many American congressmen who are spreading the good old American way of life! Swiss children and dogs are well fed, are fat even, but they have to eat 'humble pie' in order to remain so. I myself have often been the recipient of such generosity. When I published my story in *Annabelle*, many well-meaning people, who associated me with the character in my story, sent packages in order to cheer up the 'poor devil.' Many people are nice to me now because they have just laid aside their copy of *Uncle Tom's Cabin*: but not out of friendship, or love for me, a man, with a name and a personality, who is also a human being. Your Mr. Frisch was right; one's rage can become so strong as to inspire one with highly inflammable desires!"

"Do you mean to tell me that *all* of the Swiss people whom you have met are like *that!*" he asked.

"I certainly do not," I said, "but enough to comprise a type which is numerous enough in your country to inspire one of your major writers to write a play about it. But it is not so bad as you seem to think," I tried to comfort him, because I now suspected that he was sorry that he had loaned me the ten francs. "No one acts out of what one might call 'pure motives.' Life is in a sense the act of relieving the tensions most irksome to us. I ask you, what would have been the fate of Europe had Napoleon

been a tall blond man instead of a short black-headed one? or
of Switzerland, had she a land area as vast and as rich in natural
resources as America? or Russia? or any one of the large South
American countries? or if she had been England, a little green
rock sticking up out of the sea!

"I do not belittle or even underestimate the Swiss," I told
him; "I merely tell you what I see. I wish to cast no aspersions
upon the virtue or the valor of your people—Swiss soldiers have
fought valiantly in almost every major historical period. Her
mercenary armies were a terror to her enemies. How does it go?
. . . 'No flower stands where a Swiss boot has trod?' Geographical
accident has produced peculiar and highly understandable effects
in the mentality of a people. Staying alive has been its major
concern. The price which it has paid, which it pays every day, is
a dear one: the slow atrophy of its spirit. In your country we may
see an example of that extreme condition, in which the domestic policy mirrors the international policy in a socio-political
composition which, if it is altered in any detail, will destroy
the whole. In few other countries can it be said with so much
truth that its destiny is the destiny of the world at large. A larger
country might absorb the shocks of civil and international conflicts, but not Switzerland. Yet, even as I say it, what I have said
about the relative stability of the major power, I realize that it is
much less true, in view of present world conflicts, than I have
asserted and that the world's condition is not likely to improve
by tomorrow night . . ."

"What would you do about it?" my benefactor asked with a
satirical grin.

"Oh, probably the same as you have done, the Swiss people
have done, if I were Swiss. I have often thought about the problem and I admit that it is very easy to merely find fault with
one's neighbors, and that to offer a solution to their problems is
another matter; if for no other reason than that our neighbor's
problems are usually the same as our own. There are no perfect
states of man, and there are no perfectly practicable answers, nor
can there ever be; there can be merely more or less temporary

reliefs from the most immediate and the most destructive tensions in the dynamic phenomenon which is life. But when I platitudinize, as I am now doing," I said, a little weary now, and a little hungry, "I am obliged to define my terms more clearly . . ." My mind hovered around the tension which radiated my state of awareness, like a world hovering around a sun; and I thought, quite audibly:

"For what is government anyway, but an imperfect attempt to create a form, which will serve as well as possible the needs of the majority of its citizens? The existence of a minority in any society is inevitable; and it is necessarily radical because it strives to come either within the protective influence of the law, or creates a new order in which it will have a place. Its attempts to equalize matters is the history of the human personality on the individual level, and when it manifests itself in the dispositions of nations, why then it is the history of the world.

"And what is the rule which governs us as nations? Dog eat dog! I can hardly—"

At this moment I noticed that my benefactor yawned, and that he tapped nervously upon the table. A waitress, hearing the noise, came to our table, and he paid for the coffee.

"It's getting late," I said.

"Yes, very late," he cut in hastily. "I am sorry to say that I have an appointment." And so we left the Figaro tearoom, which had been the scene of our little discourse. I was glad to get away, suddenly agitated by an excitement which stirred within me.

We shook hands. He turned into his building and I walked toward the corner and crossed in front of the station and headed toward Monbijoustrasse and the Rendez-vous.

It was six o'clock. The sky was an intense blue. The Bahnhofplatz was filled with people. I looked at the sky and at the people, and listened to the noises of feet falling and motors running and trams rumbling into the station. A jackhammer rattled like a machine gun somewhere down the street, and suddenly my senses were overpowered by the flux of sound and color and movement which assailed them:

What will you and I do? asked the voice, which was neither his nor mine, again and again. And I felt the answer stirring within me, but I could not articulate it. Then, presently, I lost sight of the question, I lost sight of the thought, I *became*. I felt as though I had become an experiencing consciousness, without arms, without legs, without eyes; that floated, without weight, along the currents of air, which wafted the street; like a breeze rippling over the surface of the waters, like a breeze rippling over the troubled waters; leaving, however, in its wake a question:

What would you do? You and I? . . .

(But first):

An Interesting Effect Which This State
of Consciousness Has Upon Art

WHEN LOOKING AT the skies over Swiss cities and at the expressions upon the faces of many Swiss people, I sometimes feel that I can perceive the reason why Ferdinand Hodler is one of the greatest modern painters and why much of his work does not make me happy.

The light in the Swiss sky is different from the light in the skies of other places which I have seen. When most vital it is diffused with a sort of wet, raw, pastel intensity, fired brilliant by exploding filaments of sunlight in a highly volatile atmosphere. It is the light of a *Föhn* sky. Capturing its quality was a challenge which Mr. Hodler met successfully, thereby paving the way for perhaps an even greater successor, Vincent Van Gogh, who was able to diffuse the light of the South of France into many canvases which you and I have seen.

But while Van Gogh's canvases are—yes—violent, they are also serene, free and somewhat naive in spirit. Mr. Hodler's canvases sometimes have a tendency—it seems to me—to be too strong and too tense. They are cramped and much too wary— too fearful—to be free. As a result I cannot disengage my attention from his work, or avoid becoming intimately involved in the artist's personal problems, which are none of my business. The sensibility—at least, my sensibility—cannot take the agonizing frustration, which like the *Föhn* itself, struggles beneath the pale washes of yellow and blue, which blend into the deep "tortured" greens, blues and blue-greens that fill his masterfully painted (to be sure!) skies . . . It were as though he had painted what he saw and felt too well, that he had painted pure feeling untempered by reflection, as though he had suffered in color, without the relief of irony or satire. It embarrasses me. Nor can my sensibility take, without a shudder, the agonizing tensions (in his portraits) in the faces of his Dostoevskian men and women.

In spite of the fact that painting and writing are different art media, I cannot help drawing parallels between Hodler and Dostoevski, because Hodler's portraits bring Dostoevski more strongly to my mind than perhaps the work of any other painter. And after all, it is the quality evinced by the work of art which determines its value. Therefore, though he is perhaps as powerful an artist as Dostoevski, he lacks the naive largeness, which prevents the weighty, psychological aspect of his "characterizations" from offending one's (my) sense of moral discretion. Dostoevski only partially succeeds in this respect, nor does he fail without a heroic struggle, while Hodler, master painter, innovator, pioneer that he is, who also struggles with his devils, lacks the naivety and the hopefulness with which great painters often—even when the subject is an unpleasant one—perceive the freedom—or the possibility of the freedom of the human spirit.

Though he saw the problems of his society very clearly, the mountains were apparently too high and ominous for him to rise above them. He would have had to transcend them were he to have placed them in a "universal" perspective. As a painter he could not, as could Dostoevski (or Paul Klee), sustain the shocking vitality of human experience without overpowering our sensibilities, by restraining his intensity and thereby achieving an even greater intensity, as well as a human warmness, and allow our imaginations and sympathies to develop what he had vitally suggested. Many of his paintings seem to me to be explosions rather than works of art.

This man, Hodler, is like Plato's wise man who, upon returning from the mystic heights of a great vision, was at a loss to articulate in simple language what he had seen to men of lesser sensibility, who, instead, merely frightened them (one of them) with intimate, highly subjective exhortations and violent descriptions of Heaven and Hell. Be that as it may, the prophet spoke and there were many who followed him.

What I wish to suggest is that a social atmosphere, which results when a society is organized along the lines which I have tried to describe, inhibits creative activity of its members because it greatly constrains not only their actions but their thoughts. Their spirits are, therefore, not free. Regardless of the fact that freedom of the spirit is not a condition which depends upon a place, there can be little creative activity where new and creative ideas are not easily tolerated.

One's ability to acquire a free spirit can be stimulated by the development of one's sensibility, but that sensibility must come originally from one's parents, and mature in an atmosphere which is conducive to its expression: the land makes the people and the people make the land in some dynamic way. The conditions in one's society do not provide necessary but adequate possibilities for the encouragement—or discouragement—of the creative attitudes of its members.

There are perhaps a dozen outstanding Swiss artists on the contemporary scene. The fact that any exist at all is to me just a little short of miraculous.

One is Mr. Max Erni, who is a graphic artist. His posters are excellent, while his drawing, though his draftsmanship is undoubtedly competent, is cold. His figures lack animation. There is no blood in their veins. I do not believe them. His bodies twist and turn wondrously but they appear to be made of wood. His animals recline in attitudes of powerful and graceful repose or recoil for an upward spring, but I perceive it because he has told me of it (illustrated his idea) rather than because I feel (experience) the movement—vitally—in his line. And whereas Mr. Hodler's work suffers from an excess of heart, Mr. Erni's work suffers from an excess of head. He seems not to be able to express his feelings—in the sense in which both Mr. Hodler and Mr. Van Gogh are able to express their feelings.

Mr. Giacometti, on the other hand, has managed to break through the emotional barriers of his own personality and has found a "line" which communicates a warm rhythmic movement. One is unquestionably moved by the vital intensity of his tall wiry figures.

Mr. Arp's concentrated fluidity in stone the world has admired for years, nor have I superlatives to add, while Mr. Honegger remains a masterful Swiss composer whose stature is imposing upon the musical landscape of our times.

And after I have mentioned Ramuz, Frisch and Dürrenmatt, I have exhausted the contemporary Swiss writers of whom I have heard during my four years' sojourn in Switzerland.

But, in all fairness, I must admit that this fact may well reflect my own deficiency rather than the paucity of contemporary Swiss writers, for I am told by my friends that they are more numerous than I suppose. However, I do not believe that the world knows them, at least, not the English-speaking world. Nor would I suggest that recognition by the English-speaking peoples is any criterion of the quality of an artist's work, but merely this uninformed writer's sole means (in this case) of determining "who's who," so to speak, in the world of contemporary letters.

The inadequacy of this criterion has been strongly brought to my attention when, upon several recent occasions, I have dared to lament (in the presence of my Swiss friends) the scarcity of Swiss artists. They seemed embarrassed, and either hung their heads in shame (as I have done when I have been reminded how few Negro presidents there have been!) or they have lauded those few Swiss artists who have made a noise in the world with a little more than generous praise. In retaliation they would ask me to name not the Negro presidents but some of the outstanding American artists. Big names would come to mind.

"Why, we have Giacometti—and so-and-so—and so. And in France there's Arp and Le Corbusier and Honegger and—"

"But they are Swiss!" my companions would protest with triumphant mimes.

"American! French!" I would counterprotest.

"Swiss—living in America and France!" they would insist in loud confident voices. And while I reluctantly drank to the victor's health, I would be astounded by this observation:

That Most of the Swiss Artists Who Become Famous Leave Switzerland in Order to Do So

OF COURSE, I would not have been astounded had I paused to reflect that artists have been running away from home for a long time. Dante left home, Hemingway left America, Joyce left Dublin, and Dostoevski, Gogol and Stravinsky not to mention Chagall and many others left Russia.

During my reflective pause I might have looked into my own little experience in order to determine why even the aspirant artist leaves his native country. I would have found, no doubt, that he leaves because his homeland is too much with him "late and soon," and that he must get away from it if he would really see it and "find" himself—if he cannot come to grips with himself at close range, as could Bach and Shakespeare but not Byron.

In a strange land, compelled by loneliness, the exiled artist creates not only himself, but that vital aspect of truth, which his existence personifies, as a product of the most formative environmental influence of his life, his own country. It was there that his mother and father begot him and propagated the tensions which he strives to objectify.

Swiss artists also leave Switzerland to become world famous in other countries because a new or radical idea is not tolerated, because of the justifiable fear that it would modify the prevailing pattern of the society and disturb the tranquility which is so necessary to its survival. In artistic matters, as well as in political matters, the paternal humor prevails. The fatherly state determines what is good or bad for its children. Creative ideas are, therefore, limited to certain accepted channels which are conducive to the maintenance of domestic quietude. Switzerland is governed by an attitude of accretive conservatism, that is to say, its political tendency on both national and international levels is passive. Active measures, be they hair styles or laws, are adopted only after they have become universally accepted and their official acceptance is merely a matter of ratifying the general practice.

Accordingly, the general artistic taste is determined by a puritanical moral standard, which I have already described. It is the general consensus of opinion that a work of art must exemplify the cultural tradition in a literal way. What the contemporary artist produces must not be radically different from what his predecessors produced. A tree must look like a tree, like *the* tree that stands in one's garden. Nor should any unfamiliar birds sit upon its boughs!

Even among the "traditional" painters seniority is more respected than (and given preference to) new painters, often in spite of the fact that the former are, though not necessarily, mediocre.

I am somewhat saddened by the fact that Switzerland need not suffer—one might say—from the lack of first-rate artists and works of art at home. For she is in the center of Europe and is virtually surrounded by great artists, any of whom could be commissioned to create works for public installations, or tutor and, thereby, inspire Swiss youth to invigorate Swiss (world!) art. But apparently the guardians of the federation intend that the show be a private one—in spite of its mediocrity!

On the other hand, I cannot say that the gentlemen are entirely indifferent to the talented foreigner, because they are assiduous collectors. In the private galleries of Bern, for example, and in private noncirculating collections, one may discover untold fortunes in ancient as well as modern art, which, like any other commodity, is bought and sold, but not really enjoyed by the majority of the people. In Switzerland (Bern), at least, it would appear that the all-too-frequent attitude is, as it is in America, commercial rather than "cultural," and that Oscar Wilde's definition of the bourgeoise, as one ". . . who knows the price of everything and the value of nothing," is as piquant and as true as ever. It is apropos this discussion to remark that in Bern movies are interrupted in the middle—no matter how tense the moment!—in order to afford the manager an opportunity to peddle ice cream and chocolate . . .

The fact is that the atmosphere in Switzerland is not generally conducive to creative effort of the highest order, and that she shares this failing with many other countries in the modern world. We must go beyond her borders in order to meet Swiss artists during their formative periods, for we will meet them in Switzerland—occasionally—only after they have been virtually deified by the rest of the world.

Paul Klee—though he is usually considered a German painter—was famous in New York and Detroit, while, if not practically unknown, then certainly generally unappreciated four years ago when I first came to Bern. I expected to see the highways leading to Bern lined with barefooted pilgrims beating a bloody path to the little door of the old house in Münchenbuchsee where the great man was born. But instead, often when I mentioned his name to the citizens of the town they met my enthusiasm with supercilious sneers. Why, merely meeting his son, and seeing real live originals of his works (I had heretofore seen only reproductions) on the walls of private homes thrilled me! In the house of one friend I sat in a room in which there were no fewer than eight or ten Klees; and more!—there were original works of Braque and Marc and Nolde on the walls of an adjoining room; and, as if that were not enough, the house was built by none other than Brechbühler! I was beside myself. I could hardly taste the excellent French wine my hostess had poured into my glass . . .

Even now, when it is generally "agreed" that Klee is a genius (I say with many others, the greatest painter of our times) he is rendered only lip service by many of the persons who discuss him. And that is because there is an exposition of over six hundred of his paintings in Bern's excellent Kunst Museum. Privately they have their doubts about the master's works because his trees, you see, do not really look like trees, at least, not like *the* trees in one's front garden, and the little birds that sit upon their boughs little resemble, they feel, the little birds to which one throws crumbs on cold winter days . . .

But Why Am I Being So Passionate About It

WHEN I KNOW that popular attitudes in whatever land are usually aggressive to the "new" (which, ironically, is never new in essence, for true art is the expression of the newness within the oldness of human experience, hence the superficial, the insincere artist signs his own confession with every false work which issues from his consciousness!) and the beautiful in art? and what is more, that it should be so, because a creative force must have opposition if it is to really assert itself, if it is, in fact, *really* a creative force. The "opposition" (I would rather say, "cooperation") of "positive" and "negative" tensions is the mode of that "objective" and "positive" result, which is the dynamic phenomenon, life. The artist synthesizes them in order to reveal "eternal verities," the perennial qualities of human experience.

But who among us can reconcile himself to the present days, which are different from the good old days when . . . ? And who among the rare ones who are willing to accept the novelty of the idea of change in a vital way are willing to accept the truth! Did not the Dutch burghers let Rembrandt starve because he would not paint the way they wanted him to? Was the fate of old Hals any different? Make your own list!

Then why am I so passionate about the fate of the Swiss artist? Switzerland (Bern) is my theme, the form through which I am taking a look at myself and at the world at large. I am a little saddened by a condition, which makes all the difference, the *degree* of the waste of the greatest of human effort. For occasionally it appears to me that the condition of art in Switzerland might be different, and yet I know that I am being absurd because it can be no other way. The fault is not with Switzerland, then, it is with me, with the smallness of my viewpoint. Switzerland, the world, Is. It is a fact to be accepted! It is clear that, though I aspire to the condition of freedom, I have not achieved it!

Besides, in spite of the "condition of art," which I have described, there is a surprising amount of creative activity going on below the Zytglogge and even on the outskirts of town. And Bern affords an adequate opportunity (though not as great as in other Swiss cities) to enjoy some of the best modern and classical music and dance. Mr. Harold Kreutzberg has established a school here, and in the Casino one may hear many of the superior performers in the fields of classical, modern and jazz music. I shall be grateful to the Casino for the rest of my life for no other reason than the fact that it was there that I first heard the great Andrés Segovia.

At Whose Performance a Peculiar
Thing Happened

I HAD PREVIOUSLY heard of Segovia only once when a friend in the city of Detroit, after dinner, as she poured the coffee into a pea-green cup with a yellow handle, suggested that we listen to music, offering for my approval a choice between Segovia and Slam Stewart. And, of course, as I had never heard of Segovia, I chose the more familiar pleasure, was thoroughly satisfied, and had I died on the spot, never having heard Segovia, one of the greatest performers of our times, yet would I have died a happy man!

But in the city of Bern, two years later—it was on a dull evening—I was confronted with the choice of going to hear Segovia or staying at home. So, inasmuch as a friend offered to pay for my ticket—I could not have gone otherwise—I chose Segovia. But even on this second occasion I chose the familiar, for I had now heard the great gentleman's name—once.

The *kleine Saal* (small auditorium) of the Casino was full to the top balcony, and standing. The stage was empty, except for one plain, straight-backed mahogany chair (it seemed: any dark chair seen from a distance is mahogany to me) and a little black foot-rest, which I like to think was made of ebony. There was not even a Steinway piano hidden behind the curtains. The stage was bare and bright and uninteresting. A false window painted white was in the center of it. I could not help feeling that it seemed a little severe as a background for one lonely man and a guitar. I supposed he would be lonely.

At the appointed hour Segovia—he had to be Segovia, I thought, because he carried a guitar—a tall stout but not fat man of perhaps sixty? or seventy? but certainly not fifty or eighty, with long white hair in abundance and horn-rimmed glasses firmly set upon a plain, undistinguished nose walked quietly, modestly onto the stage and bowed to the audience.

His tails were large and comfortably tailored. There was something boyish yet aged, serious yet grave in his air. I do not believe he smiled when we applauded thunderously—I, too, embarrassed that I did so—or if he did, only very faintly. He sat down in the straight-backed mahogany chair and waited until we were quiet; then he placed his sizable foot lightly upon the ebony pedestal, the guitar upon his knee, and his right arm swung familiarly around the guitar's waist.

Oh, I know, but I fancied it was a waist, his movement was so loving and full of tenderness. And then he pressed the strings.

A Ten-Line Cadenza

"OH, WHAT LOVELY hands you have. So fine! Do you play the piano?" asks the young man of the blushing, "mature" young lady who lowers her shy eyes, fiddles the harp-strung air and replies:

"Eh . . . No . . ."

"They look," continues the young man, "as though you might . . . play the piano—or the violin . . . The gentleman moves closer, while the young lady secures her position and beams with a satisfaction, which could have been no less had she whisked out her little Mozart score, regretting, a little, however, that she had not practiced her exercises when she was wearing her braces . . .

Segovia's hands looked from where I sat like the hands of a soft rock breaker or a retired bear wrestler; they were fat and the fingers were short. Bach's hands, after a picture of him which I once saw in a curiosity shop, looked like hams; so did those of "Fats" Waller; Art Tatum's hands (he died last week . . .) were as fat as sweet potatoes . . .

He looked down at the floor or somewhere deep inside himself, and presently his fingers began to move; so easily and quietly that one might have thought that he was stroking a woman's hair. He *is* stroking a woman's hair, I thought, as the most wondrous sounds began to fill the air. I wondered who she was. It was a long time ago, I thought, when he was very young . . . I wondered if her name was Guinivere. I closed my eyes . . .

But then I had to open my eyes very soon after that because I thought I caught the sound of a violin. I looked at the man hard, and then I looked toward the wings in order to see if I could discover a violin or see the curtains move. But I saw no violin in either wing, nor did the curtains move. A cello! A clavichord! A piano! Was it possible that those fat old hands—that the sensibility of that quiet old man could induce those magical sounds to abandon their heaven? He conjured such a melancholy air from the thing, so restrained, carefully thought-out, and yet fresh and spontaneous; so closely was the thought wedded to the feeling, and the feeling woven into an organic whole, in which the whole man was involved, and yet not lost; the conscious artist was never out of control, but able, nonetheless, to indulge in that perfect freedom of expression, which is permitted only to those who have achieved a complete, unfaltering mastery of their instruments, and of themselves.

The music from this one little guitar filled the hall, transformed it into a universe and made it ring with the powerful harmonies of Bach and the soft dreamy phrases of Couperin. *It was during the Couperin that the thing happened:*

I was astounded by what I thought to be a trick of the senses, a sort of auditory illusion. For, not only did I have the impression that I heard an orchestra—a string quartet, let us say—but I also thought I heard, though I *had* the program in my hands, and saw that it could not possibly be, a Negro spiritual—or jazz! For the sounds which I heard penetrated, as jazz and the Negro spiritual penetrate, an atmosphere of pure music, a source of "undifferentiated musical experience," which lies at the bottom of every music-loving consciousness, where the distinction between forms and genres of musical expression fade away . . .

I am always a little skeptical of those musical "purists" who can find beauty in only one genre of musical experience, in jazz, say, or in classical music, when the best in one genre—especially in our times—exemplifies the best in the other. And I have reflected since my first encounter with disputants upon the meaninglessness of all discussions as to the "appropriate instrument" upon which this or that music should be played.

So complete was Segovia's interpretation of "classical" and Spanish "folk" masters that all discussion as to whether the guitar or the piano, or the bagpipe is appropriate to this or that genre of music flew out of mind; so natural and spontaneous was his expression that, at one point, during a rest—the windows of the hall were open and sounds filtered in from the street—a streetcar bell rang, after which the motor of a truck roared; it sounded as though the streetcar conductor and the truck driver and the spirit which animates the million noisy airs which break in upon the silence were master musicians who, eyes fastened upon the score, played as though inspired, in the background, thereby heightening the tensions brought to a thrilling climax by the brilliant soloist.

Every extraneous sound is a part of the "orchestration" when Segovia plays; cacophony is miraculously transmuted into wondrous music!

"Abend Dämmerung . . ."

How OFTEN I repeated this phrase in the Rendez-vous, as I felt
my body expanding and contracting into the myriad shapes
which my mind conjured from the dynamic, nebulous essence
of life. For now the image of the bridge and, subsequently, the
image of the Rendez-vous, which had previously occupied my
thoughts, gave way to an image of twilight. It overwhelmed me
with a feeling of profound wonder, as when we stand upon some
remote piece of earth and contemplate the passage of "day" (of
the thought of which we have grown quite accustomed) into the
unknown reaches of "night." One perceives a moment which
marks the "completion" of something, the completion of a
mere phase of something which has no end, and yet, which ends
upon the pulsation of every conceivable fragment of the instant:
a thought burning through space like a comet! And because the
slow, certain diffusion of light into darkness marks the completion
of a movement which a thought makes through space, or so it
seems, we must face the fact that we can never think that thought
again, and that wherever we have been we can never return:

> The curfew tolls the knell of parting day,
> The lowing herd winds slowly o'er the lea,
> The ploughman homeward plods his weary way,
> And leaves the world to darkness and to me . . .

The "where," to which I could never return now that I had

reached the Rendez-vous, from which I sprang through infinite reaches of human pain and love, was the state of mind from which I began, that of the hypersensitive nigger. From this state, since the process had gotten so well under way due to the strength of the propulsive thrust which catapulted me from my mother's womb, I passed through other states at a dizzying rate of acceleration. For, once I ceased being the nigger, I became the provincial American, crashing my head naively against the many ways in which they do it over here, as compared to the many ways in which they do it at home. But that passed. And then I met the spider on the Kirchenfeld bridge one sunny day when I was full of remorse because of the dim view I was taking of myself due to the irony imposed upon my consciousness by my feelings of high purpose, which was the result—let us say—of the sweetness of my mother's milk. As I exclaimed platitudes to the windless skies, I felt the nigger (I thought I had lost him) tug at my sleeve and mock me. I looked anxiously at the spider modestly building his masterpiece and blushed with shame. And because the bridge connected the way I had to go in order to get from the Kirchenfeld to the town, I passed that way very often, confronted by the spider and by the breath-taking perspective of the town.

One day, quite by accident, as a pretty girl passed in front of me, I happened to glance into the water, rushing beneath the bridge many feet below. I perceived, or thought I perceived, that the water was filled with animate sound. Then I saw, as I strained far out over the rail, what seemed to me to be the reflection of my face; and presently the reflection of many faces; and after that the reflection of the faces of all humanity reflected in my face!

I was confronted with the new problem of locating *my* face in all those faces, for I sensed that my perception was illusory. The sensation which resulted from perceiving myself in the faces of humanity was so pleasant! Even when I left the Kirchenfeld, the bridge, and moved to the little mansard in the Weissenbühl and the scene changed, the illusion merely modified itself, assimilated the conditions of the "new place," in the "new time," for I had now come to believe that time and space were also illusory. I continued the search for myself in the faces of the persons who drifted in and out of the tearoom.

Even then I was already beginning to sense the approach of the end of the state of mind to which I could never return. I perceived that I loved too deeply to merely remain in a "static" state of consciousness! The task which remained was to *broaden my perception of "self"*—whether it was illusory or not ceased to be important!—since I had come to grasp, though imperfectly, the relativity, and, therefore, illusoriness of *all* things.

At times I seemed to have accomplished this—the world appeared in a dynamic light, in which all ostensible oppositions were resolved into perfect harmony. Nor can I ever tell you just how sweet the music was! This state of mind brought to me a feeling of peace which I had never known before. But it was not to last, it waxed and waned, like night and day and like the moon, as a result of which I was alternately submerged into moods of profoundest despair or catapulted into a free sunlit air, in which I floated as peacefully as a cloud.

In order to attach "myself" to something which would sustain me as I oscillated between humors, I resolved to seek an "objective" way of experiencing myself, and, consequently, of communicating (to myself) what I perceived. And then I was "tickled by the rub" of the irony suggested by the word "objective," and was forced to laugh at myself and at the world, which was also myself, and to exclaim, to the amazement of the peaceful citizens who innocently sipped their coffee: "*All sense is nonsense!*" That irony—it has a history as ancient as human awareness—underwent one subtle refinement after another until it reached that pure condition, which I was forced to liken unto sunlight sparkling in a girl's eyes!

In order to "objectify" that aspect of myself which was Bern, I took stock of my position in the "time," which was the instant the new awareness began, and in the "place," which was the tearoom. The tearoom, I soon perceived, was a world in itself, a world that had far-reaching effects upon the worlds that comprise the society at large, the further pursuit of whose effects led

me to ponder the nation—via many disturbing digressions!—
and from the nation I flung myself into the world.

It was then that I perceived a stillness in the air. A calm
vagueness permeated the atmosphere, giving an eerie, spectral
sharpness to the myriad forms which had seemed to be so "real,"
so vital by day. The mountains glowed with an intense amber coloring, which was washed in whiteness, against an equally intense
vermilion sky; but only for an instant, because it deepened after
that, the amber softened into degrees of red and then pink and
blue, as the musky hoar-mists rose from the floor of the valley until the mountains appeared as a vast jagged range of blue
ice stained with frost; the blueness deepening all the while into
tones which obscured the entire view by slow certain degrees,
leaving—but only for a few indeterminate minutes—a violent
egg-yellow border rimming the horizon.

It was during this interval that I hazarded another look into
the disappearing faces, which drifted within—and without—
my visual range, from atop the high place from which I viewed
the universe. I looked with the attitude of a lover confronted
by a dangerous, because unknown, aspect of love, on the one
hand, and in the attitude of a lover who regrets, as a matter of
futile speculation, the time and the effort which was lost because
of the incalculable oppositions between himself and the object
of his love, on the other hand. And yet I looked with the full
knowledge that it makes no sense to look back, to reevaluate
that which is invaluable by the mere "fact" of its existence—or
nonexistence; sensing that *all was well just as it was, as it is and
as it will be, because all IS*; wishing, nevertheless, to take one last
leave of the cherished pain, which contained the highest pleasure
I was able to conceive: *the illusion of myself as an aspect of all; all
as an aspect of myself.*

As I sat in the Rendez-vous, I looked out over the rims of
my glasses, over cups of coffee at the people and into myself.
Curiously insignificant, banal fragments of perception dinned

ironically upon my consciousness. For no ostensible reason I perceived, for example, that not all of the women whose glance had met mine, here and there, had exclaimed as they had passed me out of purely negative feeling. Indeed, some of them had exclaimed with a passion commingled with desire and desperation, which was at times so embarrassing to me that I was forced to divert my eyes out of a sense of modesty. They made me feel— and you will think me ridiculous, no doubt, almost as ridiculous as I felt when it happened—like a beautiful, innocent virgin walking naked through a crowd of sailors!

Some of the women looked at me with a strange, apparently unwarranted defiance in their minds, often crossing the street and breasting the heavy traffic in order to meet me head-on, only to suddenly—and much too conspicuously—jerk their heads to the right or to the left, making some disparaging sound as they did so, causing me to regret the pains to which they were put, as a result of some necessity, which I was at a loss to understand, to dramatize their indignation that I should so disturb their tranquillity by merely walking down the street.

And there were others who regarded me with fear, with a vague reproach, or with shyness. The ones whom I loved most simply looked at me out of a "normal" animal curiosity, the way a cultivated cat looks at another cultivated cat.

The egg-yellow rim was paling upon the horizon, as I paused to reflect that there is no doubt that many white women are attracted to black men, just as there is no doubt that many black men are attracted to white women. Is it the reciprocal love between night and day which causes them to aspire each to the condition of the other? I wondered, as a tacit laughter rose and tickled my throat. As a tacit laughter rose and tickled my throat, I reflected that often when I had suffered from loneliness I did not have to be alone, but that it was more preferable to be alone than to be not alone under circumstances which seemed to me false, undignified and even insulting: for example, simply because I was black or because my hair is kinky or because my nose is flat. And yet I had been hotly pursued for none other than these very reasons. But such, I perceived very clearly now, are the very features which actually attract us, one and all. Whether or not her nose is flat or sharp, her earlobe pendulant or compact, her calf fleshy or slender, can make all the difference in the beginning. Sometimes Adam chooses Eve for the curve of her arch—whether of her foot or of her eyebrow, it makes no difference—for the angle of the elevation of her breasts and sometimes because of the sound of her voice. And does not Adam conquer Eve with no less than a broad sloping shoulder, a new sport jacket or a Spanish mustache!

At this point the laughter which trembled within my throat became so violent that I was forced to turn my eyes from the reflection of myself, which was that of the people. And:

I Took Another Look at the City

I KNEW THE city well by now. I knew the lowest level of the old town below the bear pits by heart. I had sat on the "little Nydegg bridge" at four o'clock on a moonlit morning and cast sandstones in the Aare. On clear days I had climbed the Schosshalde hill and looked down upon the red roofs of the medieval-looking houses and had been calmed by the tranquil beauty of the town, which rose in tiers from the shores of the Aare in a graceful slope upward toward the new town, past where the Münster tower stood proud and free amid cranes, stretching their silver necks in the volatile air.

What a beautiful sight, I have thought with a little sadness mixing with the gladness in my heart; for no joy is unmixed with sorrow . . .

Why Sorrow Upon Looking Upon the Town from Schosshalde Hill?

BECAUSE I, TOO, dreaded the sound of the wheels of change. They were tearing down the old old houses and building cheap replicas of "modern" ones in their places; leaving the old facades intact, to be sure, but so sandstony and funeral-looking; and so expensive. My friends would have neither the satisfaction of a good modern house (the city planning commission does not understand it) nor the aesthetic, though not the convenient, pleasure afforded by an old one, but a vulgar, tasteless anomaly between the two.

Heaven knows there are enough architects in Switzerland, I know six or seven personally. And she has produced at least two who now come to mind who are world famous, except in Switzerland. Le Corbusier is rarely if ever given a commission to build a public building in his own homeland, while Brechbühler was accidentally permitted to build the Gewerbeschule, one of the most beautiful buildings in Bern, if not in all Switzerland. But never again! "Too radical! Too modern!" say the ultraconservative town fathers, as they permit their greatest artists to suffer for the lack of work. Brechbühler's little laundry—you can see it when you look down, a little to the right, from the central balcony behind the Bundeshaus—is a delight to the eye, a perfect blending of intense aesthetic quality and easy functionability. I have peered through its large spacious windows and have seen the women working there: the free and easy harmony which greeted my eyes suggested poetry and dance rather than that tiresome, steamy process that is embodied in the term "laundry." The master who conceived and built it finally got a job, but only in the last few years, as a professor of architecture, not in Bern but at an architectural institute in Lausanne!

These new "modern" houses, which they are tearing down. lovely nineteenth- and early twentieth-century houses to build, are mediocre compromises. They are dull and tasteless and they all look alike. *Their walls are thin to the point of indecency.*

Now, you may say, and with some justification, that the judgment of the city planning committee is just as valid as my own; that is true, but many Bernese people have expressed their opinions on this subject even more strongly than I have. Many fine architects have submitted plans which have been rejected in favor of mediocre ones because those persons with whom the decisions rest have seniority, gray hairs, but little or no sensibility for architecture. It is universally agreed that the Bundeshaus is an ugly monstrosity. The old houses did have character because they represented the most vital impulse of their time, they were beautiful examples of gothic and baroque styles, and so on. But the shacks they are building to replace them are not anything!

Even before the construction mania started, granted that new houses are needed, the beauty of the town was constantly being scrubbed away. Buildings are beautiful because they provide the eye with a satisfying form, which is most manifest when they have a patina. Who relishes new wine! It takes wind and rain and sun—time—to finish the architect's work. A house can be beautiful only when it has been lived in, and it cannot be lived in if it is always in a state of repair. Now they tell me that they scrape the buildings clean every year because they are built with sandstone from the local quarries; that, as sandstone is very soft, its flaws must be carefully controlled, all the crevices, like teeth, must be dutifully filled once a year: now, is it possible that the proudly rich bankers of Bern could not run down to Italy one morning—only six hours away!—and barter for a few of those old stones, among the ones which Michelangelo found, and build a building or two that is really solid! Could not the city of Bern afford at least one or two of those old ruins which the Greeks are not using, which, from sheer boredom, are slipping into the sea each time an earthquake creates a diversion? Should Switzerland's greatest architects languish at home? or beautify other cities? It must be pretty expensive to scrape all those ugly buildings every year, not to mention the blood-curdling noise it makes!

However, it cannot be denied that Bern is a beautiful city, if one views it as if in a dream, passing through its thoroughfares noiselessly and effortlessly, without pausing to examine the symbolism embodied in the forms, which project themselves upon one's consciousness. Then, if one looks aslant upon the city from Schosshalde hill, or hazards a full view from the Gurten or from the Münster tower, one will see that it is well planned. From such a height it is the symmetry which pleases the eye, and the rich verdure, the soft greens tinged with silver, that warm the heart and the tensions straining to turgid roundness the fecund fruit, which excites one's sensibilities.

But the niceness and the dullness of its clean sandstone buildings gives the city a funereal air, transforms the Rathaus into a huge sepulchre and the Bundeshaus into a house of correction for wayward girls or an asylum for the mentally retarded. The "modern" houses, which skirt the city's outer rim, look pleasant enough, if one does not look too hard or too long. However, they have not that kind of beauty which grows with the years. Enter any one of them; they are all the same; not like the decaying houses of Paris, for example, which surprise you at every turn, bearing testimony of the lives which have waxed and waned like night and day and the moon within their confines.

But, the city is well planned; however, with a pedestrian clarity, which is void of that noble breath-taking grandeur that distinguishes a great city.

The pity is that it might well be otherwise. There is certainly money and technical skill enough—Swiss engineers and architects are among the greatest in the world . . .

Meanwhile, the eastern part of the sky was filled with a porous blue darkness, which tacitly demanded my attention, for I was like a man poised upon the farthest point of the highest place he could conceive, looking backwards in an attitude of reminiscence, and yet compelled to ponder the unknown horizons which lay ahead.

Looking into the mellow darkness of the eastern sky, this thought occurred to me: how intangible is the thought of the thought, which is color . . . For it had previously seemed to me to be an entity which one might touch or weigh or even carry around in one's pocket. But now that the hour of departure was at hand I found darkness to be as colorless as brightness, and much less tangible than the earth upon which I stood.

Bearing this thought in mind, my eyes swept westward in the hope of verifying the terrain. The egg-yellow bank, which rimmed the horizon, was still there, though a little pale, I imagined, as though some of the "blue" coloring from the upper reaches of sky had tinged it. Fearing that the descent of night would take place too quickly, and at the same time perceiving the futility of my fear, I strained my eyes once more toward the city, and was forced to smile as I remembered, for no particular reason, it seemed (though I was well aware that I did so for every reason in the world!) how seriously I had taken myself as I had sat in the Rendez-vous.

For I had thought of that period of my life as one of abject poverty, considering that but for the warm atmosphere provided by the tearoom and a few loyal friends, I might have starved, in which case it would have been impossible to continue my work.

My little mansard had been so cold! When I awoke on wintery mornings I had often found a soft blanket of snow upon the covers. Had there been earth beneath it, instead of me! I might have become rhapsodic about it—that is, had I possessed the gift—so beautiful and so novel! did it often appear. Often I lay in bed all day long in order to keep warm, dieting on cold sardines and a crust of bread when I could afford it; a little proud of myself, a little too proud, in fact, of the "suffering artist"; a little superficial because not quite sincere because I did not really have to "suffer" as much as I did, nor had I to complain as much, nor indulge in neurotic depressions, playing theater in order to win the sympathy of my friends and in order to deceive myself: the trembling Verdi in a frosty mansard, scribbling masterpieces upon hoarded scraps of toilet paper filched from public toilets— I even owe the Kunsthalle a bar of soap!

I fancied that I had experienced a period of vital realization of the many ridiculous aspects of human life. I was always afraid, afraid of being hungry and of not being able to pay the rent. I was afraid to admit it when I was a little comfortable, lest my friends think me better off than I was and stop helping me. I was indebted to a hundred people, I owed a franc or a hundred francs or twenty-five francs, here—and over there. However I had suffered mostly from a guilty conscience, which resulted from the suspicion that I was deceiving many nice people because I had failed to justify my existence under the conditions to which I had pretensions.

But then one sunny day, I would eat a good meal with meat and warm my imaginary body by somebody's fire. My belly full and my bottom warm, I would laugh at myself like a fool. I would laugh at the city and at the whole crazy world.

We're all acting! I would think, remembering the ironic impulse, which informed my earliest childhood, adolescence and youth:

It isn't real, this whole hurting vanity-ridden cockeyed world isn't really real. It's all in the mind . . . For a fragment of an instant my sensibility would become sharp and clear, new and dangerous perspectives would suddenly loom before my eyes, and fade again into obscurity. I would resolve to be better, to look deeper into the human heart, by which I meant my own heart. I resolved to discover the most basic experiences and feelings and to write about them in order to improve myself, as well as my stories. And I would become more humble:

I am proud and vain, much—much too proud and vain, I told myself.

My feelings of contrition mellowed into feelings of spiritual purity, which condition rendered me, so I imagined, invulnerable to the world of opposite values.

Words and looks cannot faze me now! I declared, as the nigger (I thought I had lost him . . .) tugged at my sleeve. And I cried out in guilty surprise:

Nigger? Why—what is *that?* Me?

Why, why *yes!* I *am* nigger, I admitted, choking upon the ironic humor bubbling in my throat: That's just what I am, a black nigger!

I would say this over and over to myself, aloud, wondrously, as I sang through the frozen streets—until I felt wonderful, or so I had imagined. I wondered why I had never thought of it before, of simply being myself completely, like a tree, like a tree root, like a rock, a spider or an Englishman.

For hours I would malinger in this "sublime" state of what I thought to be "self-realization," looking out at the world around me as though it were a quaint museum filled with wondrous objects, which had been freshly discovered by me. I saw colors, I fancied, which had never been seen before, and smelled smells which had never been perceived by another nose. I generously reputed the world to be beautiful-terrible, to say the least! For I fancied that I perceived my senses to be assailed by "overwhelming forces," under the spell of which I wandered between the Kirchenfeld bridge and the Rendez-vous tearoom like a drunken man.

Life is potent stuff! I would reflect during an eventful pause, in which I was (on more than one occasion!) distracted by an undulating hip, threatening the seams of a piece of silk; beginning to feel a little wary of my invulnerability; looking anxiously, quietly, a little to the left and a little to the right, as I proceeded down the street; singing as I went: the streets were so quiet, the children stared so hard and their parents smiled so deeply.

And then (oh yes, I had expected it, as though the golden irony flashing in the girl's eyes would let me forget it!) I felt the world tugging at my sleeve: the rent fell due, a venerated story was rejected by an American magazine, a projected program for the radio was refused, and so on. Evening would fall down upon my head and bludgeon me with its misty fist, and the cold air would creep into my bones. Night would occasionally find me looking wishfully into the Aare River from the center—the very center—of the Kirchenfeld bridge. Sometimes I would see the cursed spider there, building his damnable web, in the dark! quietly, between the bridge rail and one of the stanchions which support the lights. I would sneak away, feeling ashamed.

And After the "Negative" Event, a "Positive" Event:

THE DISCOVERY THAT I had achieved social respectability. How had I achieved it?

Many people had heard my radio programs and had liked them. Besides that, public association with Radio Bern and members of its staff—Herr Dr. this and Herr Dr. that—assured the people that I was actually somebody because the radio in Switzerland is a state-controlled institution, which acts as the spokesman for the nation, and Bern is its capital. So the people in or near the radio addressed me as "Herr Carter" and not merely as *"Der Neger."* At last I had a name!

Previously, when I was introduced to people they never seemed to be able to hear my name. But now, at least to a small group of persons, I had achieved the status of an individual who was distinguishable from the other sixteen million American Negroes and I do not know how many Africans and other black, brown and off-white persons all over the world. Needless to say, I was pleased with my new status. But now, as I reflect in the glow of the pale border of light thinning in the western sky, I perceive that I ought to have been a little more suspicious of that status, in view of the amazing fact that I was often taken by strangers to be Japanese or Chinese or Brazilian or Ethiopian—no offense to any of those good people!

When, during my second year in Switzerland, I sold a story to *Annabelle* (the *Ladies Home Journal* of Switzerland), which practically all Swiss ladies read, they read it and liked it, in spite of its limitations and the poor translation of it. Because my name had appeared in print I became almost universally, "Herr Carter." In almost any café I was likely to be addressed by name by persons whom I did not know and to whom I had never spoken. Many of these friendly strangers bought me coffee and cognac and toasted my health. Once a woman whom I encountered on the street (it was in front of the Café de la Paix) stopped suddenly in front of me and cried, "It's you!," dropping her packages all over the sidewalk in her excitement. While I, in my excitement, looked anxiously around me, dumbfounded by her exuberance, especially since I was sure that I had never made her acquaintance. As she collected her packages, I collected myself and walked away as quickly as possible, regretting—say, a hundred steps later—my confusion, which had prevented me from taking cognizance of pleasant titillating little details as to her appearance, which now came to mind.

This experience caused me to speculate as to what would happen if I ever wrote a really good story, which was published, say, in *Der Monat*? But then, I thought, that lady probably doesn't read *Der Monat*!

Once I entered a butcher shop in a little back street in a very unlikely part of town and was astounded when a voice said: "Herr Carter, do you have your things yet?" in clear, perfectly articulated English. I looked around and told the young man who was smiling at me that I had ordered my things and that I thanked him for his kindness. It was not fame, to be sure, but it was something which I cherished most at that time, the respect of my fellowman.

And Shortly After That, a "Posi-Negative" Event:

Mr. A—— S——and his colleagues from the Atelier-Théâtre began to call me Herr Carter because a Swiss architect who is also one of Switzerland's best contemporary writers (unfortunately I cannot judge, because I read German very poorly) wrote a play entitled *Santa Cruz*. It required a Negro who could sell oysters semi-musically, smiling pleasantly, and provoke the hero into strangling him, causing the hero, out of frustration at the turning point of the play to lose his head, as well as the heroine, because the oyster vendor, in his indignation due to the hero's attempt to strangle him, calls for the police, which call catapults the hero and the unfortunate heroine into the awaiting arms of destiny.

I had natural Negro coloring, and what I had to say was not much, nor did I have to say it particularly well because what was needed was an effect more than a piece of solid characterization, which would have necessitated a well-spoken dialogue. So, they offered me the part. I accepted it because I needed the money, though I was much too skeptical at first.

I was supposed to cry out, "Oysters! Oysters!" melodiously and smile ingenuously, happily, childishly, as Negroes are supposed to do. Then, after several lines, I was supposed to succumb to the overwhelming strength of the hero, fall away in panic and cry out for the police because he had upset my oysters. It was such a pity that it had to happen to the hero because the oysters were already dead. It was my habit to sell dead oysters because I was a mischievous little cheat, which (it was somehow implied

in the story) it was my right to be—as a protest, say—because
of my position in society.

I did not like it. I balked before the prospect of walking
across the stage, in spite of my previous resolves, because I was
convinced that they wanted me to play the Negro of their imaginations. I thought of him as he had appeared to my utter disgust
upon the American screen. I threw up my hands: "I can't laugh
like that!" I said angrily, in agony because I knew that my indignation seemed silly to them, almost as silly as it seemed to me,
for I knew that the mentalities of these men were different from
what I supposed them to be. I also knew that it did not matter
what I did, for people will think what they will think.

"You're all wrong," they said, especially Mr. S——, the director,
who was very patient and more understanding than I had expected.

"The Negro's laughter is a beautiful laughter," U—— A——,
one of the English-speaking members of the cast, assured me.
"We Europeans have lost the ability to laugh. The part doesn't
have to be a stereotype if you don't make it one."

It was his last phrase which convinced me: ". . . if you don't
make it one . . ."

I asked a friend who spoke English very well to read the role
to me very carefully, and to explain fully every word in it because
I did not know German and would have to speak the lines without really understanding the values and weights of the words.
She was able to convince me that there was nothing subversive
in it. In fact, I was sometimes delighted because the language
used by Max Frisch was quite beautiful. I further decided that
my mother and father would not be ashamed of me if I played
the part well. Besides, I needed the money.

"But if they laugh, if I hear one goddamned giggle—once!—
I'll throw the whole basket of artificial oysters in the bastards'
faces—and walk right off the stage." I swore it. "I'll gum up the
whole damned works," I threatened secretly, secretly delighted
with the idea, knowing that I would not do it, yet dangerously
tempted by the speculation as to what would happen if I actually did do it.

The play opened and I played thirty-two performances. There was not one peep from the audience, not a half a giggle, only surprise and delighted satisfaction. Thanks to the good taste of Mr. Spahlmger, the reassurances of Uli Althaus and the splendid cooperation of the cast, the part had been restrained to suit the dramatic need of the play as an integrated whole, which gave it that objectivity which was satisfying to the audience and to me.

I felt triumphant. I had walked across the boards with my dignity poised dangerously upon my shoulder and it had remained upon my shoulder, undisturbed—how many times I had, as a child, walked a high fence or swung from the upper branches of a tall tree in the same spirit! Now I was really proud to be *Der Neger*, as long as my name was also Herr Carter. And I reveled in the speculation that my mother and father would have been satisfied had they seen the performance.

Once again I found my "self"-assurance. I even learned to enter the Mövenpick without flickering an eyelid. More than that, I learned to resist the rage, which I had formerly experienced, at the sound of the word "nigger": a friend walked up to me one day, as I was ordering a beer, and ordered one, too, exclaiming that it had been a long time since he had seen me, concluding with the observation: "Wince, you're the only nigger in Bern, are you not? I was just thinking of it today." And I, without spilling a drop of beer from my glass or choking upon a hidden desire to throw it into my friend's face, replied:

"Why, yes—yes—I . . . believe I am," placing the glass quietly upon the counter. I had never felt better in my whole life.

And Then the Golden Irony Tugged
Once More at My Sleeve,

FOR I CAME to see that while I had shivered in my Weissenbühl mansard, and reflected over many cups of coffee in the Rendez-vous, much of my so-called suffering had been self-imposed because I had simply transferred my American "racial" mentality to Switzerland. I had superimposed one upon the other and they just did not fit. I had forgotten the popular saying of the folks back home in Kansas City: If it don't fit, don't force it; which, when I finally remembered it, caused me to recognize the fact that Bern was merely like any other provincial bourgeoise city.

I might live here a *kalpa*, I thought, and I would still never belong . . . And then I thought of a well-known writer of anec-dotes and humorous stories who told me once that after having lived twenty-five years as a Swiss citizen, the other Swiss mem-bers of his club still refused to address him in other than High German, though he knows the Swiss language as well as they do.

As for the word *Neger*, I saw clearly that it meant "black" in almost every language, and was the anthropological way of classifying the races of man: white, red, yellow, black. Why *not* "Neger"?

How much energy I had wasted, which I could have put to better use, so much sooner!

But then, not all of the Bernese people were innocent of racial prejudice, I reflected, as though the retrospective view, which I was taking in my twilight hour, were a necessary part of the process which was passing through me. Even dying has a beginning, a middle and an end. Every thought is necessary, still trying to unburden my spirit of the apparently superficial aspects of itself:

. . . Yes, there certainly is racial prejudice in Bern, just as there is also anti-Catholic feeling . . . If there were a thousand— even five hundred—Negroes in Bern, instead of one or two or three, the history of their lives would be similar to the history of the lives of Negroes in America.

For I had seen the expressions upon some of the men's faces when I walked through the streets with a woman, or when I entered a café with her. I had seen, in bars, for instance, that it took only a light amount of whisky and sometimes no whisky, to serve as an excuse for the expressing of prejudicial feeling. Whenever I went where people drank I was prepared for the worst, which—happily—was much better than the American "worst," which, I remembered, could be very bad. When I went into one of those places I screwed the pleasantness out of my face a little, and assumed an I-mean-to-take-no-nonsense air. I was usually successful, because the Swiss have a sense of fair play and would never tolerate a humiliating scene, priding themselves, as they do, in being more liberal-minded and peace-loving than the Americans.

The golden irony mischievously confused all the old perspectives in which I had formerly viewed myself and, consequently, the world. I was like a man in a room of distorted mirrors, cringing before grotesque images of myself. But once more I promised myself that I would put all such horrors behind me. I declared myself to be free—again! A benign smile disguised the grimace which I habitually wore and the bags under my eyes miraculously assumed a dimpled air. My spirits soared. I shined my shoes, changed my tie and took a bath. And then I luxuriated in my internal and external immaculateness—for a few days:

Until my shoes got dirty and my body got dirty and the tie lost its charm and the creases forsook my trousers and began to sag, and my high-blown spirits spluttered into the thin air; when, a week or a month or an hour later, on a sunny afternoon:

I Took the Tram to Wabern

BECAUSE I WAS invited to share a fondue at the home of Mr. and Mrs. C——. I was a little nervous through fear of being late. I had promised them that I would come a little early because one must eat a fondue on time, otherwise the cheese gets gummy. Mrs. C—— did not like it when that happened. The distance from the center of town to Wabern was too far to hazard the journey on foot, so I took a tram.

Now, on this particular day the electric current failed. All the trams and trolley buses were forced to stop en route and wait until auxiliary motor buses could relieve the strain on the traffic.

What a delightful thing to have happened! I thought. Something different! I had observed that Swiss institutions and public services were so tediously efficient and well controlled that I experienced a refreshing sense of pleasure when the power stopped. The other passengers felt it, too, I thought, enjoying the animate surprise which filled their faces, listening to the grumblers grumble like ducks in the rain, glad to grumble about something that could be fixed, and glad—aren't we all?—to give the government a little poke in the ribs. Indeed, we felt triumphant, heroic even!

"OH!" the ladies with puffy little dogs exclaimed, all in a flutter, clutching the little beasts to their breasts.

"I say, what—what's the matter!" cried the elderly, well-dressed gentleman, his proffered ear cupped in a megaphoned palm.

"It's the power, Papa—the power's gone!"

"What! What's that!"

The children giggled; the babies cried . . .

"Everybody out!" cried the conductor, rising dramatically to the importance of the occasion, manning his post like a sea captain on a perilous sea. "You must board the special bus at the Bahnhofplatz, in order to proceed to your destination points. Everyone will be given a transfer!"

He cut off the power just so that he might say that, I thought, as I stepped off the tram amid the general excitement. And I was delighted to find that I needed no longer to worry about the fondue getting sticky, I had the best possible excuse, one which even Madam C—— would have to accept. Besides, the day was sunny, and the Bahnhofplatz was buzzing with a bright busy confusion.

I stood in line, transfer in hand, a contented smile upon my face, waiting for the crowd to shift into the waiting buses— when suddenly I felt a soft pressure upon my head. Curiously, I turned around to see what caused it. Behind me stood an elderly man of, say, fifty-six, presentably dressed and spectacled, with a brown, freshly-cropped French poodle on a handsome yellow leash. His right arm was raised and his hand was extended to the level of my head.

Even as I watched him, paralyzed with surprise, the gentleman was stroking my hair with absorbed concentration and with a look of wonderment upon his face. Before I had time to think, I stepped back and assumed a fighting attitude, extending my left arm, at the end of which was a doubled fist, with which I was preparing to ward off the danger. But then I paused, froze in my tracks from utter embarrassment. For the gentleman, I had time to observe, was obviously helpless, too old to defend himself. Nor did he seem to be aware of the fact that it might be necessary. He continued to stroke my hair!

I was absolutely speechless. Not a word of German, French, Greek or Pali, not to mention English, came into my mind. Finally I managed to push his arm away, as gently as I could without fracturing it. The gentleman looked at me as though I were crazy, as though his curiosity were the most natural thing in the world—I must admit that it was—and that he had every right in the world to satisfy it. I looked among the crowd for a witness, in the hope of finding one sympathetic eye capable of relieving the tension within me by simply emitting a little sparkle of understanding, which would have allowed me to laugh, to make a joke of the gentleman's curious behavior. But all the expressions upon the faces which I saw were blank, indifferent.

But that cannot have been so, I tell myself even now; I must have been too blind with rage to see well.

Days later, when I related the incident to friends over the dinner table—at the house where I gave the two-hour English lesson, and where they fed me, allowed me to take baths and accepted me as practically a member of the family—the mistress of the house, my hostess, answered me with the Bernese equivalent of "How sweet!" (*Wie herzig!*) and smiled profusely. I did not understand the lady. Nor did I understand the other persons whom I told about it who failed to consider it of any importance that a man whom I had never seen in my life had walked up to me in the middle of a crowded public square on a bright sunny afternoon and examined my hair—in pretty much the same spirit of one who touches, with an extended forefinger, while looking cautiously this way and that, the surface of a freshly painted fence, in order to see if it is really wet, as the sign says! the way I have, on numerous occasions, fondled a dog.

A similar thing happened to me in Oriel College, Oxford University, shortly after the last World War. I was sitting in one of the rooms, to which I had been invited, for coffee after Hall (supper), discussing some vital topic, when one of the members of the group, a tall, blond, rather handsome young man who later became one of my closest friends, said to me, obviously embarrassed, but apparently overcome by a desire over which he had no control (he spoke with a faltering voice):

"I say, old man, may I ask you something?"

"Oh, I suppose so," I replied uneasily. The assembly grew silent.

"May I—may I—touch—your hair?"

At this, I hesitated, "taken aback," as they say, for he could not have shocked me more. Because I was ashamed of my hair, for which reason I had plastered it against my skull with a very thick, sticky pomade, which is used by many Negroes back home. It made the hair look shiny and wavy and straight, like the hair of the white folk. However, the pomade, because it was so thick, rendered the hair stiff and greasy to the touch. Not only that, when one was a little warm it melted and ran down one's forehead and down the back of one's neck.

Now, no white man had ever touched my hair, nor any part of my person before. And in "mixed" (white and black) company such delicate subjects as hair, color and physiognomy were skillfully avoided. So this young man's question raised my temperature—in an instant!—just about as high as it would go without shooting me into space like a roman candle. However, I strained to keep cool, reflecting that my companion was entirely innocent of any malice.

This is a blow to my pride which I shall have to take full in the face, with a smile! I thought, as I drew a deep breath and said, as casually as I could, "Why—yes . . ." leaning over in order to accommodate his tremulous thumb and index finger, while the other members of the group watched breathlessly. It occurred to me as I watched them that they, too, had had the same desire, but had lacked the courage to ask me. I leaned closer to him, until his fingers touched my head. He rubbed my sticky hair through the tips of his fingers. Then he looked at the greasy sheen, which glistened upon the tips, he looked at the company and finally he looked at me, blushed deeply and exclaimed:

"Amazing!"

Now that, I reflected, as I boarded the bus to Wabern, was quite different from being fingered like a freshly painted fence!

I was often distant and gloomy in the presence of my friends after that because most of them seemed to be so insensitive to my feelings—or so I imagined. I was forced to reevaluate my relationship to them, and I felt obliged to try to understand them harder than ever, since they were apparently unable—or unwilling—to try to understand me.

I flattered myself that I had succeeded in understanding them, at least partially, in bold outlines, from an anthropological or a sociological point of view, and occasionally on deep emotional levels. But personality patterns, even my own, I was forced to admit, could be astoundingly complex phenomena! Many of the minds of my friends and acquaintances appeared to me to be labyrinthine in their intricacy and perverse, beguiling in their "submarine" elusiveness; like the cavernous underworlds, of which Hugo writes, in *Toilers of the Sea*, where the sun shines through fissures eked out of rock by centuries of violent tensions to create fantastic patterns of weird, mad beauty; where precious gems lay buried amid the fossilized bones, commingled with the dust of the wary dead; where monsters whose terrible aspects surpass all imagination await the approach of the unsuspecting stranger who, fascinated, jewel in hand, marvels at the hoarded treasure of hidden sensibility which he has discovered, considering himself lucky, as he, his breath giving out now, hastens to hoist it to the safer regions of upper air where the sun shines down directly upon the sea. But the monster's tendrils reach out and grab him by a strand of hair which holds, and he dies the slow, first painful, then blissful, death of the drowned. The precious jewel drops from his grasp and he painfully expires upon the worthless, perversely flickering thing, his bones remaining, his dust remaining for other men—in time—to seek, to dare and to die.

Life for many of my friends, it seemed, was a fascinating perverse fatality, a slow strangulation of the spirit. "We are all a little mad," a well-known Bernese lady said to me, and I felt that it was true, remembering, however, the frenzied, brutal complexity of large American cities, wishing that some powerful voice might resound over the voices of the multitudes and command them to "Be still!" I reflected that often, as I had walked through the streets of those cities, I had tried to imagine such a stillness, the release from the tensions which grind us to dust.

A Parable

Two STRANGERS MET upon the highway between two cities. One of the strangers who had been running stopped to rest, panting with fatigue. He withdrew a handkerchief from his pocket, wiped his face and looked hurriedly this way and that.

"Where are you going, friend—in such a great hurry?" asked the second stranger, approaching the exhausted one in a friendly manner.

"What does it matter to you?" replied the first stranger. "Im rushing to mind my own business . . . Im going home to eat my supper; quickly, if you must know, so that I may go to the theater and see a short play, in order not to be up too late, as I have to be up bright and early in the morning, in order to attend to a bit of business by eleven because at twelve I've a very important appointment, as a result of which I may be able to get twice as much done as I'm doing now, if I don't waste the whole morning talking to you!" All this the first stranger uttered very quickly, without pause, gasping for breath.

"And then what will you do?" asked the second stranger, calmly but a little sadly.

"Grow old and die!" replied the first stranger in an exasperated tone. "Grow old and die!"

"Why do you run so fast?" asked the second stranger.

Another Parable

TWO STRANGERS MET upon a highway between two cities. One who had been walking very slowly stopped every pace or two and heaved a sigh, as though some weighty matter burdened his thoughts.

"Where are you going?" asked the second stranger, approaching the slow one in a friendly manner.

"I'm headed for that fair green hill, which lies just above that line of beech trees to the west, rising from the floor of the valley." He spoke very slowly and with great deliberation. "But the journey is long . . . I was so young when I started, and I'm not even halfway. The road is full of danger; storm and burning sun, wild beasts and dangerous men threaten the way. I must be careful, you see, and travel only in the middle of the road."

"And what lies upon that fair green hill which you seek?" asked the second stranger, calmly and a little sadly.

"My burial ground."

"Why do you walk so slowly?" asked the second stranger, resuming his own way . . .

In the city of Bern I have encountered a stillness which is as intense as the roar of the traffic of New York. There I could not hear for the noise; and here in Bern I could not hear for the silence.

—And Then, a "Parti-Valenced" Experience

. . . In the deepening twilight the meaningless words, thoughts and actions of the "past" came to me like fever to the dying, like a rasp of death in the throat. It happened this way:

A friend of mine went to work for Swiss television in Zürich as a set designer. There he learned from one of the directors with whom he worked that the company would produce a Christmas play about Jesus, about how he was born in a barn and what Joseph, his mother's husband, had said, what the others had said and all that. One of the "others" would have to be an African king named Balthazar, and since I had natural African king coloring and needed the money, he suggested me for the role. So I went to Zürich and played Balthazar in Middle High German, of which I did not understand a word. I was a raving success.

But that in itself was not so important, though rather unexpected; what was more unexpected, later, though rather natural at the time of the play, was that I had to wear a beard for the part. Everyone had said then that I looked so handsome in my beard. "Just like Othello," they agreed unanimously. I found it strange that they all thought that I looked like Othello when I was playing Balthazar! Anyway, when the play was over and I returned to Bern, one day when I was feeling low, on such a day when, were I a rich man, I might have taken a trip to Italy or Spain, I decided that some radical change in me was necessary. I remembered Balthazar, the beautiful black beard which he had worn and decided to become handsome, if I could not become successful as a writer. I began to grow a beard.

I must confess that I had no right to object to the reason suggested by David (one of my American friends, a medical student who had toyed with Freud a little in his time) as to why I was growing a beard, when he first saw me sporting the stubble on my chin. He smiled and said, "Either you don't give a damn about women, or—you're pretty sure of yourself." Perhaps I objected so strongly to his explanation because I paid more attention to the first part than to the last part; but it wasn't until I faced the violent repercussions of the town that I considered the problem seriously. For, as my beard grew longer, I discovered that there were two kinds of men in the world, those who wore beards and those who did not, and that, as a consequence, two types of women existed as well, those who liked beards and those who did not.

However, it was the women who did not like beards who drew my attention most—because they expressed their dissatisfaction in unmistakable terms; not only my friends and acquaintances, but strangers as well. Women whom I did not know and to whom I had never spoken asked me in restaurants and on street corners, while the red light held me up, "Why did you grow that ugly beard!" I was deeply impressed because they asked me this question in tones of indignation. It was only after much reflection that I was able to suggest that their violent feelings had resulted from the fact that after two and a half years, almost three, they had finally managed to get used to seeing me on the street, and that just as they were able to integrate me into their general conception of the Negro, I grew a beard! They were unprepared for such a sudden radical change. They would have to modify their previous conception, and, naturally! they did not like that.

I was almost sorry that I had done it when I finally understood, sorry that I caused so many innocent persons so much trouble. But on the other hand, growing the darned thing had caused *me* a certain amount of trouble, too. I could not just cut if off because a few—rather more than a few!—persons did not like it and had the bad taste to tell me so.

Life was strange after that. But I discovered a novel advantage which having a beard gave me. When people looked at me I could sympathize with them a little more than I formerly could because now I felt that they really had something to look at! Instead of feeling simply conspicuous, or the object of perfidious ridicule, I could feel, with some justification, but not wholeheartedly, I assure you, that they were looking merely at my little black beard!

However, this was by no means all that resulted from the drastic step I had taken. There were other very curious, humorous and finally profound effects which the people's reactions had upon me. For example, many people looked at me with wonder and decided that I was Chinese! Children greeted me on the street, in Italian! When Haile Selassie came to Bern there was a parade through the principal streets of the city and a pompous ceremony at the Bundespalace; and for two weeks after that people addressed me on the street as "*Der Negus!*" A thousand pardons to the King of Kings!

And there were also political repercussions. When the Anglo-Egyptian hostilities broke out (again) a sincere citizen approached me in a restaurant in the old town and told me that he was deeply grieved over the fate of my countrymen. He had read of the suffering of my people. He would consider it a privilege to shake my hand. Of course, I thanked the gentleman for his sympathy and tried, out of sympathy for *him*, to feel as Egyptian as possible!

Well, I withstood the storm, and after a while life became relatively normal once more. The city people who frequented the same part of town which I frequented paid less attention to me, and some even declared, that, though they had not been able to appreciate my beard at first, they now felt that I wore it quite well. But, as I have suggested, the change, which occurred within me as a result of the appearance of my beard, was quite profound. That is to say, I became more cognizant of the implications of the act which I had committed, now that I had time to abstract myself from Balthazar and from my beard—which no longer itched. I could once more reevaluate my position in the universe. Frequently now the feeling, which I had experienced on the evening of my conversation with the man who had loaned me the ten francs, came to mind and I would suddenly hear myself saying out loud, "What would *you* do?" . . . if you were me and I were you? . . .

My mind would try to fasten upon something concrete. Colors, sounds and movements, wherever I might be, at whatever time of the day or night, would become fused with the colors, and sounds and movements which I had experienced on that momentous evening, and I would be dumbfounded by a new question, which was somehow, I knew, related to the former one: *Indeed—who am I? Who might I be, when so many people in this world take me for so many different (alien!) things?* I thought not only of that particular moment, but of the *One Moment*, which appeared to be a synthesis of all the moments of my life.

Can it be, I thought, can it be that I am none of them? Not even the being whom I believe myself to be? But someone else altogether?

I was driven by a necessity far more powerful than my conscious will—I would have sworn it!—to make the following resolve: to be "myself," absolutely "myself." I was sick to distraction (again!) over the confusion as to my *real* identity. And I was mostly distressed by the fact that I who should know who I was was not sure. It's immoral! I thought. And at the same time my thoughts were harried by a grumbling undercurrent of thought or feeling, which articulated itself in the familiar but ever strange phrase, *All is illusion* . . .

One thing was clear, I could best find out who I was by first realizing that, though I was one with the human family, we were nonetheless different and that the difference was not the beard. In order to discover the nature of that difference I would try to worry less about what others thought of me and do what I did simply because I had to do it, out of the depth, the very center, of my nature. For example, I decided that I would utter no word that was not absolutely my own, think no thought that had not evolved from my own necessity to think it. And then I remembered, and not without a little embarrassment, a similar resolve which I had made almost a year previously! . . . To walk in the middle of the road, in whatever weather that blessed the skies and not to look back! . . . I marveled at the one-trackedness of my mind, and at how far, how immeasurably far, was the apparently short distance from "here" to "there," from the intuitive perception to the conscious action!

Still, I was not satisfied because once more the thought came to me that there was something more to my "sudden decision" to grow a beard than the "fact" that it symbolized, as my friend David had said, that I was ". . . pretty damned sure of myself . . ." No matter how hard I strove to be "myself" there was the disturbing "fact" that the people had proved one thing (which would have to be valid for me, whether I liked it or not): that my identity was highly arbitrary. On the other hand I felt that I had probably chosen the most direct route to the destination which I had vaguely in mind, full cognizance of Selfhood. For it was clear, even to me, that one cannot possibly be many or all things at once!

But another peculiar and contradictory thing had happened, as I pursued my lonely way: the more deeply I looked into "myself" the more I found—or thought I found—I had in common with other people. Sometimes I would look so deeply into myself and feel so deeply the experiences of others that I would be frightened by what was at once the terrible and ridiculous condition of perceiving "myself" to be just what I had—only an instant ago!—declared myself *not to be*—that is, *myself and everybody else*, at one and the same time! My senses seemed to be forever playing tricks on me. My troubled mind raced back and reviewed its little history of thought: how strangely provincial it seemed!

And then an old feeling came to me in a new way, the feeling that all of my dealings with the town, all of my painstaking analysis, was of the same genre, though not necessarily of the same quality, as the feelings which had previously made discussions with my old landlord and lady in the Kirchenfeld so painful. Time had passed, a personal history of pleasurable and painful experiences had been written upon my consciousness, and its events were commemorated by various landmarks in the town which called them to mind: that tree, that tram shelter, that apartment! Sometimes a day of celebration or of mourning could be inspired by the averted glance of a familiar eye which had once shone brilliantly on a night when there was no moon.

It was a great struggle to keep from losing "myself" in all the myriad "selves" which animated the town. I persevered, however, I insisted, I asserted myself in the face of a strong undercurrent of contrary feeling, repeating the Kirchenfeld experience over and over, but with this difference: my life was now so tied up with the life of the town, with my own personal history in the town and with the tradition which resulted therefrom, that I fought with the desperation of a lover:

"*It is all illusion, nothing but an illusion!*" cried the voice in the din of the traffic, in the ripple of the wash bubbling with the faces of all humanity, which flowed under the bridge, and in the bells which resounded from Münster tower—as our words grated against the upper levels of consciousness:

"But you *said*—such and such!" the city exclaimed.

"Yes! . . . But *that* means to me—in *English*, according to my understanding—that and that! . . ."

"That's what I meant in the *first* place!" the city would cry.

"Oh no, you didn't . . .

"Listen—you never listen to me—"

"I!—listen to *you*? . . . *You* listen to *me*! *You're* the one who never listens . . ."

. . . And so on, and on, until the "differences" melted like snow in the heat of common feelings which had necessitated them. As the wind shifted, they cooled only to emerge in another form, in other colors, which registered to our ears other sounds. Such metamorphoses often took place in less than the twinkle of an eye! And when we pointed to the forms and colors and sounds which were formerly there, over which the passionate dispute had occurred, they were always gone, had vanished! The ridiculousness of our former seriousness occurred to us in ironic ways and we had to laugh, my city and I, at all the meaningless words, at all the frenzied, hurting movements and at the din- ning, cacophonous noises—at the pile of dead bodies which we had left behind, which had looked so much like us, and yet were none of us.

"Lord," on a fit of hilarious laughter, what did the man say? "—*what fools we mortals be!*"

. . . What if there is a moon? I thought, noticing that the light had almost gone out of the sky . . . A pale thin border of blue was all that remained. What if there is a moon which casts even deeper shadows upon the landscape of my self-consciousness, and I am lured into other worlds of fantastic contradictions! . . . Anxiously I searched the sky for the moon and, finding none, sighed with meaningless relief as the darkness closed in upon me. Visibility diminished by imperceptible degrees as my body grew lighter, it seemed, as buoyant as air in an empty room. I found it difficult to imagine my feet gripping the little shelf of earth (at the highest and farthest point in space and time which my mind could conceive) which supported them. My whole being seemed to be evaporating from the very air which contained it . . .

"Not yet! Not yet!" I cried in fearful but (I knew . . .) futile alarm, fastening my vanishing eyes upon the little slither of light in the sky. Thus did the death of the thought, which was the thought of "myself," descend (by imperceptible degrees . . .) as the night descended, while words and thoughts and actions emptied memory of its content . . .

The struggle with "self" had continued, in spite of the dreamy intermittent spells of revelation, in which a deeper truth seemed to manifest itself in what would always appear to my more or less fully conscious thoughts, upon reflection, as chaos. In such intervals, however, the deep-fathomed voice would say to me:

The "self," which is Vincent, is a pompous thing! He indulges in orgies of beard-wagging and laughing out loud, of much sing- ing in the streets, satisfying himself with the excuse that the

Bernese have forgotten how to sing in the streets and how to laugh with wide-open mouths, with their heads thrown back, with tears of joy streaming down their faces, without fearing the looks of censure from their neighbors who looked censoriously only because they would sing and laugh and walk with a swinging gait, but they dare not. He walks proudly and swings his arms and bears his head high and enters public places like a rich Texan. He asserts himself with a will, in order to drown my insistent voice which roars in his ears:

Illusion . . . illusion . . . illusion!

Before My Eyes the Town Was Constantly Changing into Something Else!

FOR EXAMPLE, TAKE the attitudes of the children in my neighborhood: they used to follow me through the streets and laugh, especially the little snaggle-toothed girls. They used to run after me for blocks and giggle. The boys would walk up to me with gritted teeth and clamped lips and stuck-out chests, so that I could see that this or that one had been elected by the group, standing a little apart, to pass the courage test, which meant saying something dangerous or doing something daring, like making a fierce face or touching my hand or passing as near me as possible without touching me, as though I were the dreaded monster who threatened the peace of the realm, who had to be slain, in order to quiet the fears of the kingdom, in order to win the hand of the king's beautiful daughter, Guinivere!

With what love did I receive the taunts that slayed me—one, two, three times daily!—And yet it was quite painful for me to be the dreaded dragon, especially since I loved children so much. I was more than a little depressed because of my inability to speak well the Bernese language, which prevented me from making contact with them. So I was frustrated by two desires, to look as fierce as possible so that the brave knight's task would not be too easy and, thereby, enable him to win even greater glory, and the desire to give up my role as the monster.

In time, however, the problem was resolved for me. My novelty simply wore off. It was eventually discovered that I was not as dangerous as I looked. Even the little knights, the diapered ones and the dawdling warriors of the tricycle corps, slew me at will. I made friends with the girls first, and then I made friends with the boys. Slowly I learned their difficult language and was able to speak to them. Presently, instead of running after me and crying, "*Neger!*" they called me Mr. "Gatin," which was as close as they ever came to Carter.

Quite suddenly children became children. The whole atmosphere in the neighborhood changed. No longer did the houses look like forbidding asylums for dangerous people. I smelled the fragrance of the lilac trees when I stepped out into the morning, and sang as I proceeded up the street: "Lilacs bloom!—and all the pretty flowers!" For the first time I noticed, really noticed, the flowers in my neighbor's garden and bothered to study the sign beside his door, announcing that he was a tailor and that I, too, was welcome to commission him to make my blue serge suit. The lady druggist in the shop on the corner had a smile for me, and almost as soon as one could say, Nigger in the woodpile, after I had passed the corner, I was waving Good morning! to the street car conductor and he was waving Good morning! back to me.

Where was the old Weissenbühl which I had known? From whence came this new one, so magically sudden! Who was I now? Who would I be when I moved from the Weissenbühl to Fischermätteli, and into another, but nicer, equally small, but cheaper attic room? where I would meet new children, be slain all over again and saved once more, at last, by the redeeming fates of tradition?

And while I had busied myself with these superficial questions the voice many fathoms down in my consciousness harangued in my ears (louder now, louder than ever before, undermining the "self" which I doted upon! Winter came and went in the Pestalozzistrasse, my new street. The rent fell due and I could not pay for one, two, three months at a time. I sold less and less and finally nothing at all to the radio and had long since ceased sending my stories to America due to the prohibitive cost of postage and the frequency of rejection slips):

"Illusion . . . illusion . . . illusion!" as my friends and acquaintances came and went their various ways, shifting like mounds
of sand and settling down, in "time," as the winds ceased, to a
more or less constant few whom I saw less often. Nor did the
voice cease hounding me out of respect for my sorry condition
when money became virtually impossible to borrow, and when
the dedicated sympathies of those friends who had previously
helped me waned, as my possibilities of achieving a more or less
immediate "success" became a subject of doubt. Two years were
a long time in which to be desperate. I had to strain in order
to hear "myself" when I told "myself" that life was merely one
long desperate moment. And yet, at the same time, so raucous
was the tone of the insistent thought beneath all my thoughts
that I was constantly tickled by the rub of the ubiquitous irony.
I was compelled to laugh, whether I would or not. One part of
me could never stop laughing at the other part, even when life
seemed to be eating me down to the bone marrow!

. . . I remember once, during a hungry time, I hit upon an
interesting little scheme, by which I fancied all my problems
pertaining to subsistence could be solved. It cast my deepest
feelings into a curious perspective and brought to my mind once
more an intuitive perception, which I had experienced (I was
shocked to rediscover it, like an old Etruscan relic buried deep
in the primeval soil of my being) when I was a child, but which
I had forgotten in the process of "growing up" and assuming my
place as a not too responsible citizen of the "civilized" world. It
was not only the sense of irony, but my talk with the gentleman
who had loaned me the ten francs, as well, that prompted me to
consider suggesting this scheme to the Security Commission of
Switzerland, America, England and Russia first, because they are
probably better able to disseminate the technical skill, which is
necessary for its exploitation throughout the rest of the world.

The Scheme

WAS TO PROVIDE myself with twenty pounds of assorted vegetables, carrots, onions (many onions), tomatoes, celery, turnips, parsley, garlic (much garlic), much salt and pepper (ground, pod, red, green and yellow): and then to install myself in a properly cleaned bathtub; and after having scrubbed myself thoroughly and recleaned the tub; to refill it and set the water to boil. However, before it began to boil, when it reached—let us say—body temperature, I would insert myself and season myself with vegetables and condiments, according to taste. Then I would proceed to cook myself until I was done.

Upon this food I would feed myself freely and lavishly if I chose, partaking of all those tender delicacies which money now prevents me from enjoying in the best restaurants. I could have any cut of meat I chose, but for the cutting!

And there would be no need to complain about the prices nor the quality of the meat, since I would have it for practically nothing, and since I would know it to be my own. Nor need I ever have fears lest the supply run out, for I would regenerate myself, and grow back the consumed parts at will, using the rich residue as a "soil," in which I would plant fresh vegetables, which would be available in all seasons. I would need only the First Fire (a simple wood fire), because I would generate my own heat.

And of course I would work at it only as long as I chose, nor would I produce more of myself than I needed in order to sustain my existence. For example, I would never think of becoming a giant, or of storing up a troublesome and annoying reserve of fat, or of having six legs instead of two. Nor would I sell myself to others, nor waste myself in political pursuits, nor in social ones. No, during my spare time, and almost all of it would be spare, I would think pleasant thoughts. I would think of women and children, and having thought of them, I would choose a woman to settle down in my bathtub, which I would successfully contrive to enlarge. We would revitalize the "soup" with the fresh meat which my wife brought and with the variety of vegetables and herbs which she offered as a dowry. In due time of course, there would be children, but we would not eat them, each member of the community would be self-sufficient.

My family and I would enjoy peace and happiness. We would not have to fear theft or invasion from a foreign power; for we would possess nothing, we would have no empire, no trade, no "spheres of influence" to protect, no neutrality. As long as our bodies remained, which would be virtually forever, since with the methods I have suggested the body can be made to be absolutely and perpetually self-sustaining, the material upon which the body would sustain itself would be available. The mind would be healthy because it would occupy itself only with pleasant thoughts! There would be no need to fear Death, since your very existence would depend! upon the divine resourcefulness of that very wondrous Benefactor of mankind. Death would become, in fact, one of the principal deities in our hierarchy of deities, the most prominent of which would be, of course, the God of Meat! My family and I would personify a living testament to the wondrous fruitfulness of continual, perpetual, bountiful Change, to whom we would say prayers on the first moon of every century. And having conquered the fear of the illusion of Death, seeing Death as a Life Principle, we would Live—forever and ever more.

"What would *you* do?—if you were me . . . and I were you?"
. . . the gentleman with the ten francs had asked:

And I Gave My Thoughts to a Few
More Mundane Alternatives

BY WHICH THE Swiss nation could contrive not only to continue to survive, but to give its spirits a little more room in which to "breathe." Nor had I given up trying to expose to the conscious eye the deceiving nature of the illusoriness of experience . . .

- 1 -

Since it appeared to me that Switzerland could not expand because she lacked the physical strength necessary for military conquest, and because few of the nations with great land areas would permit an expansion of Switzerland, on its own terms, out of a spirit of altruism, the alternative which I suggested was that the Swiss people emigrate in large numbers to sizable, sparsely populated countries, such as Canada, Australia, New Zealand and Africa. The Swiss are—I have observed—magnificent when they go abroad. They build graceful bridges and bore holes through mountains. They farm the fertile lands of South American countries and help to build states like California. They poetize and romanticize as big and as free as life itself.

Now when one third of the population leaves the country, the space which is vacated can be divided among the remaining inhabitants in some equal way. This would result in a greater freedom of movement. Life, to be sure, would proceed more or less as usual, but the mere physical tensions of the citizens would be greatly relaxed. The houses would stand a little farther apart, thereby permitting one a little more privacy. There would be less fear because of the competition for employment, and so on . . .

This "solution," I admit, would not be ideal, but it would certainly help to alleviate to some small degree those tensions which tend to cramp the sensibility and atrophy the spirit of the country. The plan could be realizable within the next fifty-six years, that is, provided the world should last that long!

The remaining population might also be encouraged to inter-marry with French, Italian and German people at a greater rate because the Swiss people have inbred so long that the strain has become somewhat weakened, and their sensibilities have become degenerate.

. . . I Had Thought of Suggesting

- 2 -

THE ENCOURAGEMENT BY Swiss authorities of the immigration of huge numbers of some strong, virulent race into the country, such as the Chinese or African, but then I reflected that such an act would be dangerous, if not disastrous to the nation. For the first generation or ten would be a troublesome brood. They would kick and scratch and bite and assert themselves in myriad subversive ways with much determination. They would raise such a row that the whole system would probably be destroyed. It would go up with a bang! Many many people would have much vital fun. Much beautiful red blood would flow into the gutters and into the Aare. A magnificent autumn would descend—through eye-defying fog and mist, through chilling frost and blinding snows—upon a dying season—before spring could come, with all its capricious, vital beauty!

A Message to General Guisan:

- 3 -

ALL YOU NEED, General—Sir!—is a dozen good, fast planes, with a dozen crews from the numberless courageous pilots whom you command, loaded with atomic bombs. If "they" start anything, turn on your motors and tell the world to stand back! "Security" no longer depends upon the size of a country's military force and land area. Space and time have dwindled at a supersonic rate to microcosmic proportions. Mountains are now just little hills good for sliding down and oceans are just puffed-up rivers. Money buys uranium! and you have plenty of that. If they start trouble drop your load right on top of their belligerent heads— and run. Run down into the nation which you have built under the mountains!

I have *not* been spying. I had a dream. I dreamed that I was sliding down an Alp on a pair of skis—which was very strange, I thought, even as I dreamed because when I am awake I do not ski! Anyway, I was skiing down an Alp, and thousands of vague-looking beings were chasing me. They were about to catch me when I fell into a crevice many many fathoms deep and landed in the center of a huge place, which reminded me—strangely, I thought—of Bahnhofplatz.

There were many people stirring in the Platz, going here and there by foot, bicycle, auto and streetcar. Some stood and talked, while others sold papers and acted, in fact, as the people had

348

done in Bern. I was just about to observe that the people looked somewhat different from the people whom I had seen in Bern, that they wore strange costumes, and that their skin coloring seemed to have altered (due to submarine living, I supposed) when I was suddenly surrounded by helmeted guards dressed in gray who commanded me to follow them in a clearly understandable Bern-Deutsch! I thought my ears were deceiving me when they commanded me to follow them to the Bundeshaus!

As we made our way through the crowd that had collected (for I had landed directly in the path of the No. 9 Submarine Tram) I noticed that not only was the place into which I had fallen very much like the Bahnhofplatz of Bern, but identical in surprising detail. For example, there was a Mövenpick—just as big as life!—and busy throngs were flowing through the doors of Loeb's department store. The bank in front of the Fremo shoe store was open. Unable to believe my eyes I followed the streetcar track with a sweeping glance and saw that it led to a street, which looked exactly like the Spitalgasse, for there at its entrance stood the Evangelical Church—workmen were scraping its exterior with wire brushes! The sound made my flesh crawl, only more intensely than I remembered it to have done in Bern. It seemed to echo as though I were in a deep cave.

Presently we reached a grand, imposing building. It looked as though it were new, with a beautiful, free-moving line.

"Why this building could have been designed by Brechbühler!" I cried in wonderment. I was astounded when the guards informed me that we had arrived at the Bundeshaus.

They conducted me through spacious corridors and finally told me to wait in an outer office until the intelligence officer could talk to me. While I waited I was permitted to look out of the window. It faced a beautiful terrace, which overlooked a river that greatly resembled the river Aare. My glance swept over the river and up the pleasant valley, when suddenly my eyes were distracted by the sight which completely overwhelmed me and caused tears to flow from my eyes: it was a bridge, the Kirchenfeld bridge, or one which looked very much like it. I followed its stanchions to the Kirchenfeld and up once more toward a great hill which resembled the Gurten.

The whole scene was bathed in a strange, intense, though quite beautiful light, which I had the feeling I had seen before. In fact, it reminded me not so much of a *Föhn* sky, as a painting of one, a painting of one by Hodler! The whole atmosphere had the appearance of a Hodler painting enlarged a million times and reflected by a gigantic mirror. Which observation drew my attention to a huge light, revolving in the center of the sky like a great sun made of mirrored glass. Even in my dream I found the fantastic landscape without the window hard to believe. I was about to examine the view more closely, when suddenly the door of the inner office opened and a very worried but efficient-looking man entered the outer office. I stood up, but then he seemed to think of something, and without noticing me, returned to the office from which he had come. But this time he forgot to close the door, which remained cracked just enough to allow me to hear a loud and authoritative voice, addressing the man who had just returned. The owner of the voice seemed to be giving the man whom I had seen instructions, and he quoted figures, concerning the produce from factories and dairies and farms. He mentioned names like Brown & Bovery, Wander and Tobler. He made several references to cheese and submarine precision watch-part patents. And then the voice asked:

"Do you have the latest bulletin from Radio Bern, Submarine Division, Number 3, concerning the upper world?" But before he could answer the door was shut by someone within the office, and I heard a huge bolt being shoved home.

The noise was so startling that I awoke, only to discover that the maid was banging on my door because she wished to clean my room. Shivering with excitement, I got out of bed, dressed and headed for the Rendez-vous and a cup of coffee.

General—Sir—a dream is only a dream. However, be that as it may, you must not let the Russians and the Americans know it. Keep your secret. And when the time comes just sling those powerful slingshots, draw your atomic bows and shoot! Flood the valleys, plug up the holes and run underground until all this nonsense is over. And when it is all over—it may last a long time, but no matter—emerge victorious, and rule what is left of the world with justice and, above all, humanity!

. . . In the last glimmer of light that remained in the sky my hand was like an airy shadow before my eyes. "Just one instant more!" I cried, knowing that my every word and thought had expressed nothing; yielding to the very end to the law of denouement, which is implicit in the death of the self-consciousness; thinking vitally, vainly of an answer to the insistent question:

What would you do? if—

Nothing, I thought. Whatever happens, anywhere, to whomsoever, is all the same to me. If I stumble, then I will get up. If you stumble, then I will pick you up and continue on my way. I will walk upon the open road in the rain and in the sunshine. Nor will I walk too fast, nor too slow.

For I have seen that what I thought I saw was an illusion. When I have tried to grasp it It has disappeared. One instant it was here and the next it was there. It made me happy and it made me unhappy. Once I thought it was *I*, and then I thought it was *You*. Later I discovered that it was neither of us, but something altogether different, which was Nothing At All. I have seen that All Is Nonsense, simply because All, each and every atom embodies Sense, which makes "No Sense"? And I am beside "myself" with a sort of wild happiness, which I am at pains to control, the true nature of which I have not the slightest concrete idea, except that it, too, is illusory.

And yet "I" must declare (in the last flicker of light which illumines the instant):

It Is As Simple As One, Two, Three

MAN BEGINS WITH "I," the "One." He suffers because he imagines all, which is other than "I," the "One," to be hostile, and therefore a threat to his existence; dangerous. But the existence of "One" presupposes the existence of "Two," "You" who are other than "I." But when we investigate this entity, which is "You" and not "I," we find that it is not as un "I-like" as we imagined. The more we investigate it the more we know about it, and the more we understand about it. The more we understand it the more we love it. When love descends upon the skies of our consciousness the "one" which presupposes the existence of "two," which existence we now accept wholeheartedly, presupposes the existence of a third entity because there cannot be two without three, which contains the first and second entity. Therefore, it is only possible to have One entity if there are three. Three is the universal number, which may be said to contain all other numbers, which are reducible to the One, which cannot be reduced.

Therefore, I say, love Thyself and—

But just then "time" and "space" and all my thoughts of them were totally enveloped by the darkness, and I perceived my "parts" to be expanding, like a flame gone out, like a drop of water fallen into the sea . . .

Bern
October 25, 1957

MICHAL AJVAZ, *The Golden Age.*
The Other City.
PIERRE ALBERT-BIROT, *Grabinoulor.*
YUZ ALESHKOVSKY, *Kangaroo.*
FELIPE ALFAU, *Chromos.*
Locos.
JOE AMATO, *Samuel Taylor's Last Night.*
IVAN ÂNGELO, *The Celebration.*
The Tower of Glass.
ANTÓNIO LOBO ANTUNES, *Knowledge of Hell.*
The Splendor of Portugal.
ALAIN ARIAS-MISSON, *Theatre of Incest.*
JOHN ASHBERY & JAMES SCHUYLER, *A Nest of Ninnies.*
ROBERT ASHLEY, *Perfect Lives.*
GABRIELA AVIGUR-ROTEM, *Heatwave and Crazy Birds.*
DJUNA BARNES, *Ladies Almanack.*
Ryder.
JOHN BARTH, *Letters.*
Sabbatical.
DONALD BARTHELME, *The King.*
Paradise.
SVETISLAV BASARA, *Chinese Letter.*
MIQUEL BAUÇÀ, *The Siege in the Room.*
RENÉ BELLETTO, *Dying.*
MAREK BIENCZYK, *Transparency.*
ANDREI BITOV, *Pushkin House.*
ANDREJ BLATNIK, *You Do Understand.*
Law of Desire.
LOUIS PAUL BOON, *Chapel Road.*
My Little War.
Summer in Termuren.
ROGER BOYLAN, *Killoyle.*
IGNÁCIO DE LOYOLA BRANDÃO, *Anonymous Celebrity.*
Zero.
BONNIE BREMSER, *Troia: Mexican Memoirs.*
CHRISTINE BROOKE-ROSE, *Amalgamemnon.*
BRIGID BROPHY, *In Transit.*
The Prancing Novelist.

GERALD L. BRUNS, *Modern Poetry and the Idea of Language.*
GABRIELLE BURTON, *Heartbreak Hotel.*
MICHEL BUTOR, *Degrees.*
Mobile.
G. CABRERA INFANTE, *Infante's Inferno.*
Three Trapped Tigers.
JULIETA CAMPOS, *The Fear of Losing Eurydice.*
ANNE CARSON, *Eros the Bittersweet.*
ORLY CASTEL-BLOOM, *Dolly City.*
LOUIS-FERDINAND CÉLINE, *North.*
Conversations with Professor Y.
London Bridge.
MARIE CHAIX, *The Laurels of Lake Constance.*
HUGO CHARTERIS, *The Tide Is Right.*
ERIC CHEVILLARD, *Demolishing Nisard.*
The Author and Me.
MARC CHOLODENKO, *Mordechai Schamz.*
JOSHUA COHEN, *Witz.*
EMILY HOLMES COLEMAN, *The Shutter of Snow.*
ERIC CHEVILLARD, *The Author and Me.*
ROBERT COOVER, *A Night at the Movies.*
STANLEY CRAWFORD, *Log of the S.S. The Mrs Unguentine.*
Some Instructions to My Wife.
RENÉ CREVEL, *Putting My Foot in It.*
RALPH CUSACK, *Cadenza.*
NICHOLAS DELBANCO, *Sherbrookes.*
The Count of Concord.
NIGEL DENNIS, *Cards of Identity.*
PETER DIMOCK, *A Short Rhetoric for Leaving the Family.*
ARIEL DORFMAN, *Konfidenz.*
COLEMAN DOWELL, *Island People.*
Too Much Flesh and Jabez.
ARKADII DRAGOMOSHCHENKO, *Dust.*
RIKKI DUCORNET, *Phosphor in Dreamland.*
The Complete Butcher's Tales.

RIKKI DUCORNET (cont.), *The Jade Cabinet.*
The Fountains of Neptune.
WILLIAM EASTLAKE, *The Bamboo Bed.*
Castle Keep.
Lyric of the Circle Heart.
JEAN ECHENOZ, *Chopin's Move.*
STANLEY ELKIN, *A Bad Man.*
Criers and Kibitzers, Kibitzers and Criers.
The Dick Gibson Show.
The Franchiser.
The Living End.
Mrs. Ted Bliss.
FRANÇOIS EMMANUEL, *Invitation to a Voyage.*
PAUL EMOND, *The Dance of a Sham.*
SALVADOR ESPRIU, *Ariadne in the Grotesque Labyrinth.*
LESLIE A. FIEDLER, *Love and Death in the American Novel.*
JUAN FILLOY, *Op Oloop.*
ANDY FITCH, *Pop Poetics.*
GUSTAVE FLAUBERT, *Bouvard and Pécuchet.*
KASS FLEISHER, *Talking out of School.*
JON FOSSE, *Aliss at the Fire.*
Melancholy.
FORD MADOX FORD, *The March of Literature.*
MAX FRISCH, *I'm Not Stiller.*
Man in the Holocene.
CARLOS FUENTES, *Christopher Unborn.*
Distant Relations.
Terra Nostra.
Where the Air Is Clear.
TAKEHIKO FUKUNAGA, *Flowers of Grass.*
WILLIAM GADDIS, JR., *The Recognitions.*
JANICE GALLOWAY, *Foreign Parts.*
The Trick Is to Keep Breathing.
WILLIAM H. GASS, *Life Sentences.*
The Tunnel.
The World Within the Word.
Willie Masters' Lonesome Wife.
GÉRARD GAVARRY, *Hoppla! 1 2 3.*
ETIENNE GILSON, *The Arts of the Beautiful.*
Forms and Substances in the Arts.
C. S. GISCOMBE, *Giscome Road.*
Here.
DOUGLAS GLOVER, *Bad News of the Heart.*
WITOLD GOMBROWICZ, *A Kind of Testament.*
PAULO EMÍLIO SALES GOMES, *P's Three Women.*
GEORGI GOSPODINOV, *Natural Novel.*
JUAN GOYTISOLO, *Count Julian.*
Juan the Landless.
Makbara.
Marks of Identity.
HENRY GREEN, *Blindness.*
Concluding.
Doting.
Nothing.
JACK GREEN, *Fire the Bastards!*
JIŘÍ GRUŠA, *The Questionnaire.*
MELA HARTWIG, *Am I a Redundant Human Being?*
JOHN HAWKES, *The Passion Artist.*
Whistlejacket.
ELIZABETH HEIGHWAY, ED., *Contemporary Georgian Fiction.*
AIDAN HIGGINS, *Balcony of Europe.*
Blind Man's Bluff.
Bornholm Night-Ferry.
Langrishe, Go Down.
Scenes from a Receding Past.
KEIZO HINO, *Isle of Dreams.*
KAZUSHI HOSAKA, *Plainsong.*
ALDOUS HUXLEY, *Antic Hay.*
Point Counter Point.
Those Barren Leaves.
Time Must Have a Stop.
NAOYUKI II, *The Shadow of a Blue Cat.*
DRAGO JANČAR, *The Tree with No Name.*
MIKHEIL JAVAKHISHVILI, *Kvachi.*
GERT JONKE, *The Distant Sound.*
Homage to Czerny.
The System of Vienna.

NICHOLAS MOSLEY, *Accident*.
Assassins.
Catastrophe Practice.
A Garden of Trees.
Hopeful Monsters.
Imago Bird.
Inventing God.
Look at the Dark.
Metamorphosis.
Natalie Natalia.
Serpent.

WARREN MOTTE, *Fables of the Novel:
French Fiction since 1990*.
*Fiction Now: The French Novel in the
21st Century*.
Mirror Gazing.
Oulipo: A Primer of Potential Literature.

GERALD MURNANE, *Barley Patch*.
Inland.

YVES NAVARRE, *Our Share of Time*.
Sweet Tooth.

DOROTHY NELSON, *In Night's City*.
Tar and Feathers.

ESHKOL NEVO, *Homesick*.

WILFRIDO D. NOLLEDO, *But for
the Lovers*.

BORIS A. NOVAK, *The Master of
Insomnia*.

FLANN O'BRIEN, *At Swim-Two-Birds*.
The Best of Myles.
The Dalkey Archive.
The Hard Life.
The Poor Mouth.
The Third Policeman.

CLAUDE OLLIER, *The Mise-en-Scène*.
Wert and the Life Without End.

PATRIK OUŘEDNÍK, *Europeana*.
The Opportune Moment, 1855.

BORIS PAHOR, *Necropolis*.

FERNANDO DEL PASO, *News from
the Empire*.
Palinuro of Mexico.

ROBERT PINGET, *The Inquisitory*.
Mahu or The Material.
Trio.

MANUEL PUIG, *Betrayed by Rita
Hayworth*.

The Buenos Aires Affair.
Heartbreak Tango.

RAYMOND QUENEAU, *The Last Days*.
Odile.
Pierrot Mon Ami.
Saint Glinglin.

ANN QUIN, *Berg*.
Passages.
Three.
Tripticks.

ISHMAEL REED, *The Free-Lance
Pallbearers*.
The Last Days of Louisiana Red.
Ishmael Reed: The Plays.
Juice!
The Terrible Threes.
The Terrible Twos.
Yellow Back Radio Broke-Down.

JASIA REICHARDT, *15 Journeys Warsaw
to London*.

JOÃO UBALDO RIBEIRO, *House of the
Fortunate Buddhas*.

JEAN RICARDOU, *Place Names*.

RAINER MARIA RILKE,
The Notebooks of Malte Laurids Brigge.

JULIÁN RÍOS, *The House of Ulysses*.
Larva: A Midsummer Night's Babel.
Poundemonium.

ALAIN ROBBE-GRILLET, *Project for a
Revolution in New York*.
A Sentimental Novel.

AUGUSTO ROA BASTOS, *I the Supreme*.

DANIËL ROBBERECHTS, *Arriving in
Avignon*.

JEAN ROLIN, *The Explosion of the
Radiator Hose*.

OLIVIER ROLIN, *Hotel Crystal*.

ALIX CLEO ROUBAUD, *Alix's Journal*.

JACQUES ROUBAUD, *The Form of
a City Changes Faster, Alas, Than the
Human Heart*.
The Great Fire of London.
Hortense in Exile.
Hortense Is Abducted.
*Mathematics: The Plurality of Worlds of
Lewis*.
Some Thing Black.

RAYMOND ROUSSEL, *Impressions of Africa.*

VEDRANA RUDAN, *Night.*

PABLO M. RUIZ, *Four Cold Chapters on the Possibility of Literature.*

GERMAN SADULAEV, *The Maya Pill.*

TOMAŽ ŠALAMUN, *Soy Realidad.*

LYDIE SALVAYRE, *The Company of Ghosts.*
The Lecture.
The Power of Flies.

LUIS RAFAEL SÁNCHEZ, *Macho Camacho's Beat.*

SEVERO SARDUY, *Cobra & Maitreya.*

NATHALIE SARRAUTE, *Do You Hear Them?*
Martereau.
The Planetarium.

STIG SÆTERBAKKEN, *Siamese.*
Self-Control.
Through the Night.

ARNO SCHMIDT, *Collected Novellas.*
Collected Stories.
Nobodaddy's Children.
Two Novels.

ASAF SCHURR, *Motti.*

GAIL SCOTT, *My Paris.*

DAMION SEARLS, *What We Were Doing and Where We Were Going.*

JUNE AKERS SEESE,
Is This What Other Women Feel Too?

BERNARD SHARE, *Inish.*
Transit.

VIKTOR SHKLOVSKY, *Bowstring.*
Literature and Cinematography.
Theory of Prose.
Third Factory.
Zoo, or Letters Not about Love.

PIERRE SINIAC, *The Collaborators.*

KJERSTI A. SKOMSVOLD,
The Faster I Walk, the Smaller I Am.

JOSEF ŠKVORECKÝ, *The Engineer of Human Souls.*

GILBERT SORRENTINO, *Aberration of Starlight.*
Blue Pastoral.
Crystal Vision.

Imaginative Qualities of Actual Things.
Mulligan Stew. Red the Fiend.
Steelwork.
Under the Shadow.

MARKO SOSIČ, *Ballerina, Ballerina.*

ANDRZEJ STASIUK, *Dukla.*
Fado.

GERTRUDE STEIN, *The Making of Americans.*
A Novel of Thank You.

LARS SVENDSEN, *A Philosophy of Evil.*

PIOTR SZEWC, *Annihilation.*

GONÇALO M. TAVARES, *A Man: Klaus Klump.*
Jerusalem.
Learning to Pray in the Age of Technique.

LUCIAN DAN TEODOROVICI,
Our Circus Presents...

NIKANOR TERATOLOGEN, *Assisted Living.*

STEFAN THEMERSON, *Hobson's Island.*
The Mystery of the Sardine.
Tom Harris.

TAEKO TOMIOKA, *Building Waves.*

JOHN TOOMEY, *Sleepwalker.*

DUMITRU TSEPENEAG, *Hotel Europa.*
The Necessary Marriage.
Pigeon Post.
Vain Art of the Fugue.

ESTHER TUSQUETS, *Stranded.*

DUBRAVKA UGRESIC, *Lend Me Your Character.*
Thank You for Not Reading.

TOR ULVEN, *Replacement.*

MATI UNT, *Brecht at Night.*
Diary of a Blood Donor.
Things in the Night.

ÁLVARO URIBE & OLIVIA SEARS, EDS.,
Best of Contemporary Mexican Fiction.

ELOY URROZ, *Friction.*
The Obstacles.

LUISA VALENZUELA, *Dark Desires and the Others.*
He Who Searches.

PAUL VERHAEGHEN, *Omega Minor.*

BORIS VIAN, *Heartsnatcher.*